A Brave New World
of Knowledge

A Brave New World
of Knowledge

Shakespeare's *The Tempest*
and Early Modern Epistemology

B. J. Sokol

Madison • Teaneck
Fairleigh Dickinson University Press
London: Associated University Presses

Associated University Presses
2010 Eastpark Boulevard
Cranbury, NJ 08512

Associated University Presses
Unit 304, The Chandlery
50 Westminster Bridge Road
London SE1 7QY, England

Associated University Presses
P.O. Box 338, Port Credit
Mississauga, Ontario
Canada L5G 4L8

The paper used in this publication meets the requirements of the American National Standard for Permanence of Paper for Printed Library Materials Z39.48-1984.

Library of Congress Cataloging-in-Publication Data

Sokol, B. J.
 A brave new world of knowledge : Shakespeare's The tempest and early modern epistemology / B. J. Sokol.
  p. cm.
 Includes bibliographical references (p.) and index.
 ISBN 0-8386-3925-9 (alk. paper)
 1. Shakespeare, William, 1564–1616. Tempest. 2. Shakespeare, William, 1564–1616—Philosophy. 3. Knowledge, Theory of—History—17th century. 4. Knowledge, Theory of, in literature. I. Title.
PR2833.S63 2003
822.3'3—dc21   2003001276

for Mary

Contents

Illustrations

9

Acknowledgments

I WISH TO THANK GOLDSMITHS COLLEGE, THE UNIVERSITY OF LONDON, members of its English Department, and especially the departmental head Helen Carr for their support. At Goldsmiths I have had particular help from Ann Aldrich, Connor Carville, and Simon Reynolds. I also wish to thank the staff of the British Library; of the Public Record Office; of the British Museum; of The Royal Society Library; of the Bibliothèque Inguimbertine, Carpentras, France; and the librarians of Harvard University, Cambridge University, the Bodleian Library, The Shakespeare Institute, the Warburg Institute, the Institute of Historical Research, and The Senate House London (especially Steve Clews). Beverly Straube, Michael Lavin and the APVA project at Jamestown, and Dr. Harold Henkes and the Museum Boijmans Van Beuningen Rotterdam, have been most kind. I also wish to thank His Grace The Duke of Northumberland for permission to study microfilms of his mss.

I owe my greatest debt of gratitude to the scholarly community. My teachers, especially Ted Tayler, deserve my first thanks. I am also particularly glad to acknowledge the personal kindnesses, and the deep learning, of the late Professors David Quinn and John Shirley. Beverly Straube and Dr. Harold Henkes have helped me greatly with regard to the scientific artifacts of Virginia. I am grateful to the Durham Thomas Harriot seminar, and especially to Gordon Batho and Stephen Clucas, for allowing me to try some of my ideas on them and for providing a stream of publications, discussions, and meetings of the greatest interest. Professors Elliot Leader, Graham Rees, and Gerard Turner have also allowed me to question them about scientific and scientific–historical matters relevant to my project, and to discuss notions that may have seemed naive to them, and which they with their great courtesy and understanding may have helped put straight. Professor Inga-Stina Ewbank kindly commented on part of the manuscript in draft. All errors are mine alone.

My wife (and often my scholarly collaborator) Mary Sokol has been my mainstay in many ways during a long project.

As I have treated a wide range of materials, I have relied upon a wide range of scholarly studies. I hope I have given due credit where required and not misunderstood too many of these. My own more original contributions—such as those having to do with the implications for *The Tempest* of certain early modern discoveries in natural history, recent archaeological finds at Jamestown, or numerological patterns, or to do with the mathematical manuscripts of Thomas Harriot—are no less synthetic of others' efforts than where I have relied more completely on secondary work; no one can be original in a vacuum. My borrowings are also sometimes from my own earlier work, although these have all been reassessed and re-contextualized, and have often only been summarized. I am particularly grateful to the editors of *Annals of Science, The George Herbert Journal*, and *Notes and Queries* for allowing me to review my previous work.

Finally I want to thank both the living and the dead, those whom I have met and those who I have not, for the most fascinating of conversations.

A Brave New World
of Knowledge

Introduction

The "Scientific Revolution"?

the older conception of science would not fit the sort of knowledge the new inquiries into nature would produce . . .
—Ernan McMullan on the "Scientific Revolution"

Different methods are used in the exploration and resolution of different problems . . . The pluralism of methods has contributed to the progress of knowledge
—Richard McKeon on "Scientific Methods"

This book will treat Shakespearian literature in relation to early modern science and epistemology by exploring a range of historical and intellectual matters that are reflected in *The Tempest*. As an extended treatment of this topic is not usual, I will begin by discussing some general issues that arise from it, and some questions of approach.

Although few would deny that the early modern period in Western Europe saw a considerable increase on several fronts in what would now be called scientific activity, some of the assumptions which have accumulated behind the phrase "the scientific revolution" are now disputed. I will not need that phrase, and will not use it except when it appears in useful quotations. For the sake of brevity I will, however, use the anachronistic terms "science," "scientist," and "scientific" (although I will remark on the unformed state of a scientific profession). I will sometimes also use the term "Renaissance" to indicate a period from the Italian Renaissance and leading up to Shakespeare's time, and "early modern" to indicate a more inclusive period reaching to the time of Newton and his followers.

Terminology aside, I will be indicating that Shakespeare was surrounded by a culture developing new types, or new extensions, of rational and proto-scientific thinking, and I will argue that this affected him as a writer.

I will not be able to pin down such a contextual influence to a development of *the* unique "scientific method" generally applicable to the investigation of the world. In fact, it is questionable whether any particular methodological variation enabled the changes that I will be describing, or whether these changes were due more to new challenges to thought and resulting new emphases in outlook and attitude.

An analytic study of early modern science faces formidable obstacles beyond the scope of this book. Despite progress made since its statement, there is still much truth in Nicholas Jardine's 1988 conclusion that giving an accurate account of the epistemology of early modern European science is not possible, because "only a small part of this vast field is even touched on by recent scholarship."[1] Moreover, much valuable recent work indicates that scientific epistemology in its formative stages was extremely diverse and complex,[2] and that no single account is adequate to describe the actual practices and methods of all scientists of that time (or even of today).[3]

Yet, despite the fact that scientific method is not at all easy to describe in any unitary way, in practice scientists usually have a reasonable idea of the epistemological norms of their sub-disciplines, and of when these are exceeded.[4] At least, nearly all scientists are able to discuss such issues, and despite challenges to their outlooks which have emerged, to date most have subscribed in time to evolving new views of the acceptability of various types of arguments. In hopes of contributing to something of a similar sort for my own discipline, in this Introduction, and later, I will raise some methodological points which may be pertinent to a current widespread questioning of literary-critical methods and motives.

A FEW REMARKS ON "TWO CULTURES"

Before turning to questions about critical method, and to more specific textual and historical matters, I want briefly to remark on a few aspects of the broad cultural context of *The Tempest* concerning the relations of "art" with "science."

A simple statement would be that there was no early modern division between "two cultures." One might note that Kepler sought musical harmonies in nature;[5] that Galileo's father, an important influence on him, was an eminent musical theorist;[6] that Galileo was a literary scholar;[7] that Girolomo Fracastro (called by Panofsky "one of the real geniuses in medicine"), Kepler, and Thomas Harriot wrote poetry;[8] or that Kepler and Newton each gave much attention to philological questions.[9]

Other instances of similar conjunctions bring in more complex issues. An overlap may be seen in the fact that Leon Battista Alberti (originally a lawyer), Leonardo da Vinci, and Albrecht Dürer, among others, were formidable mathematicians and proto-scientists as well as visual artists. The well-known importance of abstract mathematical speculation for early modern science will be illustrated in chapter 2, below. But the examples of such theoretical work shown in that chapter will not provide evidence in support of Edwin Burtt's arresting but debatable thesis that the mathematization of Renaissance science grew out of Neoplatonism.[10] A potential application of such ideas as Burtt's would arise here if the Neoplatonic ideas of, say, a Giodorno Bruno were to be seen as significant for *The Tempest*. But, *pace* Frances Yates and her school,[11] finding distinct traces of Pythagorean, Neoplatonic, or Hermetic influences in Shakespeare's work (other than in sly parodies) seems mainly impossible.[12] And anyway Johannes Kepler's mathematical Platonism, to take a crucial instance contemporary with Shakespeare, included astonishing degrees of dedication to numerical precision and to observed facts; these Kepler allowed to overthrow his most-treasured prior assumptions and most-laboriously-won conjectures.[13] Such subordination of speculation to the precisely observable, and humility in relation to self-effort, were not, to say the least, the norm for Renaissance Neoplatonic enthusiasts.

The issues of accuracy and faithfulness to empirical observations link with questions of Renaissance art and science in a second way. There is much disagreement as to the extent, if any, to which a new facility in the Renaissance visual arts for fresh vision and avidly communicative depiction of what is seen may have corresponded with, or even inspired, the growth of the natural sciences. Such avid communication in the visual arts was more than a matter of literal accuracy about closely observed details.[14] The great practitioners, who included da Vinci, Dürer, and the scientific illustrators Weiditz and Gesner, also used tactics new to Renaissance art (including chiaroscuro modeling, false perspective, and sectional or cutaway or partly enlarged or rotated or transparent or "exploded" views),[15] and other even more subtle means, to allow their depictions to communicate significant spatial arrangements, and moreover to convey qualities which various critics have called "vital," "lifelike," "dynamic," or conveying a "creative knowledge

of reality."[16] Some scholars argue that the development of sophisticated and subtle techniques by the visual arts and the rise of science were synergetic and non-coincidental.[17] Others express
doubts that Renaissance visual art enhanced scientific understanding, or even claim that the distractions caused by, or the lack of
abstraction in, the beautiful work of Renaissance illustrators actually detracted from the scientific enterprise.[18]

These debates have a special bearing here because the argument
in chapter 2 will maintain that something akin to the dedication
and exactitude of Kepler's mathematical physics can be found in
the work of a visual artist contemporary with Shakespeare. This artist so accurately recorded remarkable impressions that these may
have helped a mathematical scientist to derive radically new ideas
about demographics, culture, and ecology.

More generally, it will be argued that the development of scientific thinking did not depend on the aesthetics of surprise so much
as on the aesthetics of truthfulness and order (or of seeking order
among confusing and multifarious experiences).[19] It will also be argued that, despite its obvious incorporation of wonder-provoking
moments, *The Tempest* shares a similar aesthetic. It will especially
be urged that truthfulness is a major topic of *The Tempest*.

A Brief Discourse on [Interdisciplinary] Method, or
Treating "Con-texts" Without Conning Oneself

A key theme of this book will be how an impetus to accept grand
schemes, or other forms of self-deception, can overrule clear perceptions and clear thinking in many areas. Many examples of this
process will be analyzed in *The Tempest* and in its contexts. Here
the way in which wishful thinking can encumber insight will be
considered in relation to some current trends in critical approaches
to the play. In examining my own and others' approaches I will
touch on matters with some general applicability.

The current book will closely consider a variety of contexts of *The
Tempest*,[20] and to do so it will often consider concrete instances. In
doing this I will try to avoid following a method of argument-by-
anecdote where the examples selected are often quite remote from
the play, yet are nonetheless alluring to today's readers because
they are resonant with favored concerns of our own time.[21] Nevertheless, some of my specific instances will point toward broad

themes pertinent to Shakespeare's world: these will include the themes of new knowledge which overturns conventional wisdom; new knowledge which is hard to absorb or acknowledge; new knowledge based on approximations or otherwise known to be partial; and new knowledge based on the recognition and refutation of paradoxes. My purposes do not include philosophical discussion of such topics concerning knowledge, but rather an assessment of their impact on Shakespeare and his environment at the time of the writing or first performances of *The Tempest*. This is just as well, as I am not equipped with the tools of a philosopher.

The task I have set myself is daunting enough. It is evident that in any attempt to "read the mind" of a past age the encountering of more or less severe uncertainty and incompleteness will challenge the recovery and interpretation of appropriate historical information. Nevertheless, such an attempt does have the advantage of raising proposals that can be offered for correction or amendment, and not pronouncements seeking converts. My frequent reference to other critics' work, and comparison of my views with alternative ones, will, I hope, embed my endeavors in a virtual conversation where disagreements need not be conducted in terms of caricaturing reductions or fervid denunciations of heresy.

It may be very difficult to find a satisfactory answer if one asks oneself "What did Shakespeare or his audiences know of such-and-such novel ideas or puzzling occurrences in 1610–11?," or, worse still, "How did they react to possessing knowledge, or to possessing ignorance, or to the intellectual and ethical challenges presented by currently accelerating knowledge acquisition?" But facing such difficulty is in fact a relief when compared with the melancholy circumstances described long ago by Henry James, who commented on the many critics of *The Tempest* who sought transcendent meanings. James wrote that in *The Tempest*, what he called "the Questions":[22]

> hover before us in their most tormenting form . . . [while] the large body of commentary and criticism of which this play alone has been the theme abounds much rather in affirmed conclusions, complacencies of conviction, full apprehensions of the meaning and triumphant pointings of the moral. The Questions, in the light of all this wisdom convert themselves with comparatively small difficulty, into smooth and definite answers . . . Everything has thus been attributed to the piece before us, and every attribution so made has been in turn brushed away; merely to glance at such a monument to the interest inspired is to recognise a battleground of opposed factions, not a little enveloped in sound and smoke.

Thankfully, the aim of this present study does not include considering any such great "Questions." It is rather to examine, in relation to the play, certain fine-grained historical specifics which, while not only of antiquarian interest, yet are still empirically led.

An inevitable limitation of my project arises because excavating the origins of Shakespeare's creative thinking is a doomed and impossible task. Shakespeare worked not "from" but rather "off of" many texts and other influences, some no doubt now untraceable. Moreover, even his "known" sources of language or plot, his recognized influences from philosophy or received ideas, and his evident uses of known genres, tropes, or conventions, were all transmogrified by his imagination. For these reasons, among others, any fresh starts that may be found here are only for "getting on with."

Like science, literary-historical research may be at its best when tackling specifically delimited questions, and also like science it will never be able to settle on the nature of things with finality.[23] Therefore no claim will be made here that the *whole* original import or impact of *The Tempest* is even approached. There will not even be a claim that the present study gives a fully balanced account of the play. My excuse is that *The Tempest* is too complex and multitudinous in its themes, modes, and references to allow more than an increment of understanding to any single book or point of view.

The question of complexity raises a further issue. Two decades ago Marco Mincoff calmly expressed a view that "the very multiplicity of themes [in *The Tempest*] speaks rather strongly against the possibility of granting absolute prominence to any one of them."[24] By now it may invite a hot response to suggest that *The Tempest* relies on and presents no single "master-discourse."[25] Yet that is what I propose.

To illustrate the dangers of seeking a "master-discourse" for the play I will not cite any easy target, but rather an astute and valuable essay on *The Tempest* by Jonathan Bate which I generally much admire. This essay centrally contends that the "field of texts within which the individual text makes—perhaps has to compete for—its meaning" is dominantly in the case of *The Tempest* the "master-discourse" of humanism.[26] Bate first emphasizes the greater importance of intertextuality than of direct sources for Shakespeare's thinking, thus arguing that Shakespeare knew his humanism well, and yet need not have been "widely or deeply read in Erasmus," for instance, to have absorbed from the "intellectual and social air" of his time ideas that were originally or most clearly expressed by Erasmus a century earlier.[27] However, Bate very sensibly does not accept intertextuality as wholly free-floating. He also stresses the particular importance of some textual affiliations over others by adopting the hyphenated orthography of "con-text," in order, he says, to "get away from the pushing to the background that is implied by 'context.'"[28]

After such theoretical preliminaries, a great many aspects of *The Tempest* are fascinatingly linked by Bate to particular precepts of humanism, and especially to Northern European humanistic ideas about education. Nevertheless, such valuable perceptions do not prove Bate's proposal, made near the outset, "that humanism is a master-discourse, containing all the others [relevant to *The Tempest*]."[29] Neither do they make clear what motivates such a proposal. The motivation is, however, revealed when Bate contradicts the claim that colonialism is the "dominant discursive con-text" of the play, as famously made by Barker and Hulme.[30] Bate seeks to overturn the totalizing views of such critics (who would label all who disagree with them as complicit with colonialism) by alleging an alternative dominant "con-text" of humanism for *The Tempest*. But this (perhaps rhetorical) attempt leads to some odd distortions of focus and losses of rigor in Bate's mainly lucid and erudite essay. An analysis of one of these distortions will illustrate this point, and will also serve later discussions in the present book.

Bate claims that "Erasmus wrote that the Christian prince should abhor slavery, yet Prospero does not hesitate to call both Ariel and Caliban his slaves."[31] This remark is made in the service of a larger and generally well-supported argument that Prospero fails, in the terms of Northern humanism, both as an educator and as a prince. However, on his particular point about slavery Bate is simply and revealingly wrong. Misled by a search for a "master-discourse," he ignores the subtle text of the play. It is true enough that "Thou poisonous slave," "Thou most lying slave," and (three times) plain "slave" are among the many ugly epithets applied by the angry and intemperate Prospero to Caliban, while the First Folio's "Names of the Actors" identifies Caliban as "a saluage and deformed slave." Even Miranda refers to Caliban as an "Abhorred slave."[32] But, in fact, Prospero never "calls" Ariel his "slave," nor addresses him, nor refers to him, nor even thinks of him as a slave.[33]

What an extremely exasperated Prospero does say, in the single passage of the play in which he names slavery in conjunction with Ariel, has precisely the opposite implication. In the lead-up to the passage in question, Prospero is obliged to "recount" once again the history of Ariel's thralldom to Sycorax. While testily complain-

ing that he must repeat the same weary schooling "Once a month,"
Prospero says:

> This blue-eyed hag was hither brought with child,
> And here was left by th' sailors. Thou, my slave,
> As thou report'st thyself, was then her servant;
> And for thou wast a spirit too delicate
> To act her earthy and abhorred commands,
> Refusing her grand hests, she did confine thee
> By help of her more potent ministers,
> And in her most unmitigable rage,
> Into a cloven pine; within which rift
> Imprisoned thou didst painfully remain
> A dozen years, within which space she died
> And left thee there, where thou didst vent thy groans
> As fast as mill-wheels strike.
>
> (1.2.270–82)

The emphasis on the extreme cruelty of Sycorax, and the clear
notes of irritation in Prospero's wearyingly repeated narration, contribute along with the syntax of the passage to produce the sense
that Prospero insists here that only Sycorax, and by contrast not
himself, has abused and enslaved Ariel. So the ambiguous second
and third lines, which might seem to say the opposite, must be read
as poetically enjambed, and as conveying a sarcastic contrafactual
(here emphasized by my added "scare" quotes and italics):

> Thou, my "slave,"
> As *thou* report'st thyself, was then her "servant"
>
> (1.2.271–72)

In this reading, an irritable remark which Ariel has formerly made
concerning himself being (used as? treated as?) Prospero's "slave"
provokes the latter's outraged reply. This reply bears unmistakable
tones of sarcasm and reproach. By means of such verbal gestures,
Prospero in fact insists that he has *not* enslaved Ariel, and that in
contrast Sycorax has done so.[34]

Piqued by the injustice of Ariel's claim of having being enslaved
not by Sycorax but by himself, and further incensed by his own reflections on the "Dull thing" Caliban,[35] Prospero goes on to
threaten to outdo Sycorax in cruelty to Ariel. He does not actually
carry out these threats against his servant spirit, but the fact that he
makes them, transferring his anger at a different ingratitude and a
different rebellion to a present interaction, is redolent of a weak-

ness in Prospero's self-knowledge and self-restraint that will be discussed at length in the final chapter of this study.

A prologue for understanding Prospero's poor self-control lies in the realization, overlooked by Bate, that "slave" is nearly always a term of disparagement and abuse in Shakespearian contexts.[36] Thus, in fact, Shakespeare generally maintains the humanist perspective on slavery; here he uses this perspective (probably derived from Bate's sort of intertextual Erasmian discourse) not to indicate Prospero's deviation from humanism, but on the contrary to signal dramatically an irrational anger that is set off because as a humanist Prospero finds it infuriating to have been identified by Ariel as a slavemaster.

So Prospero in effect differentiates Ariel's servitude from Caliban's (a matter crucial for the play), and is infuriated when implications are made that these were treated by himself as equivalent. Bate's essay elides this important point on account of its impetus to identify a "master-discourse" of humanist ideas.[37]

IN THE SCIENTIFIC RENAISSANCE, THE SKY WAS NOT THE LIMIT

There will be no claim in the present study to "pluck out the heart of [the play's] mystery." Only the lesser claim will be made that themes such as the power conferred by knowledge, and the limits of such power, bear on *The Tempest* with an emphasis more specific and more subtle than formerly has been analyzed. Put in another way, the attempt here will be to show that pursuing certain little-studied epistemological themes of the play will add valuable insights to be placed alongside perceptions relying on other approaches, including those recognizing the affiliations of the play with biblical, classical, Romance, and other traditions.

To date, when scientific or epistemological aspects of *The Tempest* have been confronted, these have usually received tangential attention in discussions focusing on other matters.[38] For instance, Frances Yates's study of Shakespeare's late plays commented that all of these reflected a "late period of Renaissance magic," and that *The Tempest* "would be one of the supreme expressions of that vitally important phase in the history of the European mind, the phase which borders on, and presages, the so-called scientific revolution of the seventeenth century." This promising start, however, is followed by the bald assertion that Prospero is "clearly the magus as scientist, able to operate scientifically within his world view, which includes areas of operation not recognised by science proper," and then Yates leaps past the play's text to pursue Christian Rosencreutz and his followers. There is no consideration at all of why (or even the fact that) Shakespeare portrayed Prospero as repudiating what is stated to be his scientific/magical way to "operate."[39]

Similarly, critics of Shakespeare with interests primarily focused on agendas concerned with "religion versus science," for instance, or on early modern "discourses of colonialism," have often elided crucial details of *The Tempest* and its contexts. The claims made by some in pursuit of "discourses of colonialism" in *The Tempest* will be addressed at length in chapters 2 and 3 herein. Here, with the aid of excellent recent studies of early modern intellectual developments, I will comment briefly on the views of some critics of *The Tempest* who have accepted that the story of early modern science consists of a single pattern exemplified in the woes of Galileo.

It has become a gesture typical of some critics to illustrate a part of their standpoint by recounting personal anecdotes. In the hope that employing such a gesture may help to focus discussion, I will tell a story. Recently my wife and I made a pilgrimage to Isaac Newton's childhood home. The tourist guide there gave visitors a lengthy account of Newton's brave fight against the authority of the pope of Rome, to which was attributed the long delay in this scientist's publication of his "proof" (!) of the beleaguered Copernican heliocentric model of the world. This guide's historically shaky performance, and its unquestioning (or polite?) reception by the visitors, suggest that the hoary legend of scientific martyrs locked in battle with religious dogmatism is as alive today as it was when my kindergarten class was forced to dance out the trajectories of the "true" heliocentric system on the asphalt of a 1948 New York school playground. The legend of that "truth" (which ignores Einstein's long-well-established early-twentieth-century principle of relativity) was and still is endlessly parroted, although Newton's neurotic postponement of publication of his monumental contributions to celestial mechanics had nothing to do with Galileo's troubles with the Church.

Recent historical work has also dethroned the myth that the heroic struggles against obscurantist religious forces of a new astronomy, leading toward a mechanistic celestial and terrestrial kinematics, constituted the sole essence of seventeenth-century science. Such an account in its usual outline neither is accurate (for instance, it ignores Jesuit appreciation of the new astronomy),[40] nor does it by any means give a balanced account of early modern scientific enterprise (which had many classical, medieval, and non-European roots, and many branches other than physics and astronomy).

Nor did the Copernican revolution, or the aftershocks of Galileo's 1610 *Sidereus nuncius*, comprise the whole body of the scientific epistemological challenges of Shakespeare's time. In fact, as will be mentioned here once and for all, Shakespeare did once show a possibly substantial awareness of Copernicanism;[41] this is in *Troilus and Cressida* 1.3.85–94.[42] This instance is not accompanied, however, by the sense of intellectual or spiritual stress that may be felt in John Donne's responses to the new astronomy in *Ignatius his Conclave* (written 1610),[43] and his two *Anniversary* poems (1611 and 1612).[44] Rather, the Ptolemaic, Copernican, and possibly even the Tyconian models of the universe are either quite blandly, or perhaps quite cynically, imaged side by side in *Troilus and Cressida*.

This occurs in a context, as well as in a play, inclined to induce doubt about every possible point of view (especially about every kind of idea of permanently valid human values). In one part of his now notorious[45] speech on "degree," Ulysses seems a supporter of heliocentricity:

> And therefore is the glorious planet Sol
> In noble eminence enthroned and sphered
> Amidst the other, whose med'cinable eye
> Corrects the ill aspects of planets evil
> And posts like the commandment of a king,
> Sans check, to good and bad.
>
> (1.3.89–94)

However, in the lines just preceding these, Ulysses also alludes to a geocentric solar system: "The heavens themselves, the planets, and this centre / Observe degree, priority, and place, / Infixture, course, proportion, season, form, / Office and custom, in all line of order." It may be wondered if, at least for the pragmatic Ulysses, earth as "this centre,"[46] and Sol (which is "enthroned . . . Amidst the other"), are capable of exchanging positions of centrality with a lability implying relativity according to perspective.

Although a worrying moral relativism may be surmisable from this play's presentation of multiple viewpoints on Cressida, there is no parallel anxiety implicit in its presentation of Ulysses' possibly relativistic cosmic perspective. Ulysses seems indifferent as to whether a monarchial "sol," or humanity/earth, is central, so long as there is an hierarchical order of some sort, so as to allow "high designs" or "enterprise" (1.3.102–3). His sole concern is praxis, not ontology or metaphysics.

Likewise in *The Tempest* the Copernican challenge is elided in Caliban's affecting description of his former education given by Prospero, which featured astronomy. There is no detectable sense of anxious cosmological doubts over the center of the universe in his recollection of how formerly:

> Thou strok'st me and made much of me, wouldst give me
> Water with berries in 't, and teach me how
> To name the bigger light, and how the less,
> That burn by day and night; and then I loved thee . . .
>
> (1.2.335–38)

Here it may be noted that Captain John Smith's first published account of Virginia, *A True Relation* of 1608, includes an incident of December 1607:[47] "I presented [Opechancanough, the Pamunkey "king"] with a compass diall . . . he suffered me to proceed in a discourse of the wonders of the earth, the cause of the sun, moone, starres and planets." This "discourse" on cosmology (illustrated by the demonstration of a scientific instrument) indeed fascinated the Native American "king" in a way that ties into some important background issues for *The Tempest* which will be explored in chapters 2, 4, and 6 (while Smith's "compass diall" will be thoroughly discussed in chapter 5). Here it can be noted initially that John Smith sharing such knowledge in Virginia may not seem very remote from Caliban's "teach me how / To name the bigger light, and how the less, / That burn by day and night." But Caliban's lament over his lost former relations with Prospero also had a far deeper contemporary connection with problems of knowledge than any concerned with the teaching of astronomy (a part of the classical quadrivium), as shall be seen in chapter 3.

Still, several critics have alleged that Shakespeare, in *The Tempest* or other plays, directly responded to a Copernican or even a Galilean challenge. These critics have drawn widely differing conclusions, ranging from seeing *The Tempest* as championing a Copernican revolution, to seeing it as promoting Ptolemaic orthodoxy.

The most vehement among the critics who have alleged Shakespeare was a Copernican was William Empson.[48] Indeed Empson speculated that not only advanced, but actually prophetic, astrophysical thinking had a direct bearing on Shakespeare's treatment of the fairies in *A Midsummer Night's Dream*: in particular, that those fairies are depicted as entering a satellite's orbit around the earth.[49] However, these notions do not really depend on the Copernican hypothesis, as Empson thought they did. They depend instead on Empson's separate conjecture that by the 1590s Thomas Harriot had derived a good part of the future gravitational physics of Galileo and Newton, and had privately conveyed these results to Shakespeare.[50] This last is no more substantial a speculation than a parallel one also made by Empson that Harriot had written a second book, on Copernicanism, after his *Briefe and True Report*, but that it had been suppressed by "still invisible" English censorship.[51] Such conjectures advance a myth that early modern science was pitted against a Church and state apparatus of reactionary repression, except for which it would have easily and swiftly advanced to its present highly progressive level. Ironically, in the name of anti-authoritarianism and anti-clericism, these imaginings characterize scientific advances as improbably easy to arrive at, detracting from the enormous boldness, novelty, difficulty, and achievements of early modern science.

In contrast with Empson, the three literary critics claiming a Copernican influence on *The Tempest* I have been able to locate all have religious questions at the center of their interests. Very recently Grace Hall has claimed that *The Tempest* "uses" a Ptolemaic system in the organization of its characters and episodes in order to convey a mystery play–like Christian agenda.[52] Twenty years earlier R. Chris Hassel Jr. concluded a book on Shakespeare's comedies with a remark on the "last plays":[53]

> As these last plays return to the comic-Christian sense of human life as an insubstantial pagent with a benevolent, forgiving auditor, so they urge upon their Renaissance audience a comforting old response to the new scientific rationalism that may be threatening their composure. Remember the ethical and epistemological humility preached by St. Paul and Erasmus; "set yourself free from contemporary philosophic despair."

It would seem that such despair is assumed to arise from the "rationalism" of the Copernican revolution—such is the argument of Hassel's earlier article on "Donne's *Ignatius His Conclave* and the New Astronomy."[54] In his article and his book alike, Hassel praises a faith that challenges and ultimately dismisses "reason or consciousness."

By contrast, in the 1930s Emma Brockway Wagner saw *The Tem-*

pest as an allegory in which Prospero as well as Miranda symbolize
"the intelligent and spiritual Christianity which automatically went
out of the Church when ecclesiasticism—a credal faith—came
in."[55] Prospero is seen as representing the understanding mind,
reason, and the logical faculty, and his books represent science.
Prospero's dukedom represents the Church, which Prospero abandons because he "says": "better knowledge without the Church
than the Church without knowledge." Further equivalents are
made of the island with the mind, and of Sycorax with superstition.
An assumed view is of "the history of the ecclesiastical Church
whose every effort was to stifle all knowledge not strictly in accord
with its cherished dogmas."[56] Therefore, for Wagner *The Tempest*
allegorizes the same heroic struggle of science against the Church
as Newton's career exemplified, according to our house guide. So,
although Wagner's avowed aim is to praise "true" religiosity, she
reiterates a myth of the march of ever-increasing scientific virtue
and truth overcoming forces of religious darkness and ignorance.

The Benefit: The Charms of Epistemology

Avoidance of this or other similarly monocular historical myths
opens the way for consideration of the impact on *The Tempest* of
much more complex and ramified early modern scientific and epistemological themes. Yet such themes need not be abstruse or rebar-
bative. Instead, it will be seen, they have contributed to the
extraordinary charm and lasting appeal of *The Tempest*. Part of that
appeal results from the play's peculiar ability to carry off lightly an
unsurpassed intricacy of conceptual allusion while maintaining a
clean steadiness in dramatic unfolding. This results in a sense of a
great simplicity of outline enclosing powerful intensity and depth;
the impact of such simplicity is equivalent to that of the rarest pu-
rity of line in graphic arts.

A peculiar paradox lies in the fact that *The Tempest* has long conveyed to many a feeling of integrity and compactness vastly differing from the concocted or pastiched, and yet (as has been
mentioned) this play draws on widely varied biblical, classical, Romance, and Renaissance traditions. Moreover, it will be argued, it
reflects a wide range of the intellectual concerns of its own time. In
a further paradox, despite the great importance of contemporary
references and resonances in *The Tempest*, a four-hundred-year

history of adaptations, appropriations, and widely varied performances suggest something mythic or classic about this play.

An explanation of these paradoxes, and of the strong and lasting
appeal of the play, may partly emerge from the present study. This
will propose that new ways of confronting or searching for truth developing in his age were taken up by Shakespeare's adsorbent
mind, and that his reactions to these were especially reflected in
The Tempest. Although clearly topical, the play's epistemological
concerns may also have been perennial. For, just as splendid line
drawings appear among the earliest traces of humanity, so epistemological interests and dilemmas may always have been of deep interest. If this is so, its inclusion of epistemological themes may help
explain why *The Tempest*—despite being wholly unique in construction, style, and fable—still feels mythic and elemental, conveying a sense of having "always been there."

The proper study of mankind may well be epistemology, and
never more so than right now. In recent times all foundations for
human knowledge have been challenged, and that has entailed
challenges to the very notion of humanity. This present study will
not contribute directly to the heroic efforts of the likes of Saul
Kripke, Hillary Putnam, Richard Miller, or Nicholas Jardine, who
have recently attempted to recuperate Truth, Reason, Science, or
History. However, if it succeeds in its more limited aims, it will help
make it possible to believe that increments of sober insight, astute
clarity, and indeed intellectual honesty have been seen in history,
and especially at the time when Shakespeare wrote and presented
The Tempest.

1

The Natural History of Pearls and the Pearls in Ariel's Second Song

Full fathom five thy father lies.
Of his bones are coral made;
Those are pearls that were his eyes;
Nothing of him that doth fade
But doth suffer a sea-change
Into something rich and strange.
Sea-nymphs hourly ring his knell:
　　　　　Ding dong.
Hark, now I hear them. Ding-dong bell.

CHAPTER PROSPECTUS

THE BRIEF LYRIC ABOVE HAS BEEN DESCRIBED AS "ONE OF THE MOST beautiful songs in the world."[1] This song from *The Tempest* will be here newly related to a scientific discovery of the later Renaissance, and through that in turn to a major theme of the play. A secondary aim of the present chapter will be to explain how this particular scientific discovery was exemplary of new ways of thinking about the world that had a greater general cultural impact in Shakespeare's time than is often realized.

This chapter will hinge on a single minor event in the advancement of scientific understanding. This was an increment in knowledge of something which was often treasured or even revered, but also sometimes seen as trivial, vain, or gaudy: that something was the pearl in an oyster. On one hand I will consider the changes in life sciences at the time of *The Tempest*. On the other hand I will survey how the poets and dramatists of Shakespeare's milieu used images of pearls; this will reveal a greater variety and sometimes greater seriousness in this usage than might be expected. That seriousness will then be connected to the image of pearls in Ariel's sec-

30

ond song quoted above, and thence to a reading of the song showing it to be an extraordinarily paradoxical creation.

It will be seen that the song is at once both limpid and complex; it has exceptional charm and grace, yet the image within it of eyes-become-pearls is dark, discordant, painful, and only superficially consolatory. The song will be seen to convey a powerful ethical content, yet be in no way moralizing. It is simultaneously succinct, graceful, artistically integral, and yet thematically elaborate.

These paradoxes arise in part due to the song partaking of a contemporary suspended contradiction between an "exotic glamor and/or magical perfection" connotation, and a "painful disease" connotation, of pearls. To establish the how and why of this, a detailed investigation is in order.

The Status of Life Sciences in Shakespeare's Age

Renaissance advances in the study of animals and plants have been linked to momentous changes in Western modes of seeking knowledge. One authority has claimed that "in the sixteenth and seventeenth centuries it is obvious that the scientific revolution owed more to the botanists and zoologists and to the doctors and explorers than to the astronomers."[2] But this has not been obvious to all, and instead, more usually, the astronomers and physicists (and some of the physician-anatomists) are the ones given star billing in histories of early modern science. Indeed, David Hoeniger has felt the need to warn historians not to ignore:[3]

> The sixteenth-century students of plants and animals . . . If we therefore ignore or only depreciate them, our understanding of the development of science in the Renaissance will be incomplete, perhaps even mistaken. For what these men did was remarkably new, very much in the late Renaissance spirit, and essential to scientific progress.

This warning is apt, because depreciating botanists and zoologists has been a common outcome of the great appreciation of the theoretical (and especially the mathematical-theoretical) successes of early modern astronomy and physics. As another recent scholar puts it: "natural history occupies a shallow niche in most accounts of the Scientific Revolution."[4]

Nonetheless, as shall be seen in chapter 2, there are examples available in which the same kind of mathematical theorizing as that which advanced physical science also had an impact on life and human sciences in Shakespeare's time.[5]

It is still undoubtedly true that terrestrial and celestial kinematics made more spectacular breakthroughs within the early years of the seventeenth century than did, for instance, chemistry, zoology, ecology, ethnology, or anthropology. But this does not mean that these other sciences did not make excellent progress also, by the measure that science progresses in proportion to the degree to which it replaces old irrational pseudo-explanations with perplexing new questions susceptible of better explanations.

One particular development of a better explanation in natural history may have had an unexpected reflection in *The Tempest*. This development, of an explanation of pearl formation, did not conform with the great advances of mathematical or physical-theoretical sciences in its age, yet it still evidenced a profound epistemological change. The behavior of one of the several actors in this story helps illustrate the nature of that change. This was Dr. Guillaume Rondelet, who was Professor of Medicine and from 1556 the Chancellor of the University of Montpellier (and, incidentally, a friend of Rabelais).[6] Rondelet undertook a wide-ranging study of marine animals from about 1550, bringing to this project humanism's respect for antiquity.[7] Yet Rondelet, in common with other pioneers of a new natural history, became dubious about the reliability of classical authorities on natural history, such as Pliny.[8] In the place of authority, Rondelet turned to the testimony of experienced fishermen, and, where possible, to the collection and observation of living marine specimens themselves.[9] In consequence, he (among others) found a wholly radical explanation for the formation of pearls.

CLASSICAL IDEAS OF PEARL FORMATION
AND RENAISSANCE REVISIONS

The early modern European discovery of a better explanation for pearl formation was a specific advance in natural history which typified a shift from magical and analogical thinking toward more rational modes of pursuing knowledge.[10] Yet this advance in knowledge did not result from a sudden or zealous revolution in scientific thought. It will be seen, in fact, that its hesitant proponents were often quite apologetic. This accords with David Hoeniger's observation that "The sixteenth-century students of plants and animals regarded themselves as reformers, not revolutionaries."[11]

The facts of a gradual discovery make incomplete the recent claim that "Not until Renaissance times was the theory advanced that pearls were merely an oyster's way of dealing with irritants."[12] This claim is true, but not sufficiently historically nuanced: it elides the important facts that a new understanding of pearl formation was not once and for all "discovered," nor rapidly disseminated, nor all at once accepted or acclaimed.[13] Rather, this understanding emerged in a piecemeal fashion, was repeatedly rediscovered, and took over a century to become generally known. By 1610 its main revisionary idea was multiply available in print, but was not seen as a scientific "fact," dogma, or new paradigm. There developed instead a range of inchoate or tentative understandings of the matter.

A good starting point for tracing this development is the widely noted view of pearl formation found in Pliny's *Natural History*. Pliny's Latin text, dedicated in A.D. 77, was largely a compendium of earlier classical knowledge. Philemon Holland's 1601 English translation of chapter 35 of the Ninth Book of Pliny's *Natural History*, entitled "of Pearles," provides a comely account of a classic fantasy:[14]

This shell-fish which is the mother of Pearle, differeth not much in the manner of breeding and generation, from the oysters: for when the season of the yeere requireth that they should engender, they seeme to yawne and gape, and so doe open wide; and then (by report) they conceive a certaine moist dew as seed, wherewith they swell and grow bigge; and when time commeth, labour to be delivered hereof: and the fruit of these shellfishes are the pearles, better or worse, great or small, according to the qualitie and quantitie of the dew which they received. For if the dew were pure and cleare which went into them, then are the pearles white, faire, and orient: if grosse and troubled, the pearles likewise are dimme, foule, and duskish; pale (I say) they are, if the weather were close, darke, and threatening raine in the time of their conception. Whereby no doubt it is apparent and plaine, that they participate more of the aire and skie, than of the water and the sea; for according as the morning is faire, so are they cleere: otherwise, if it were mistie and cloudie, they also will be thicke and muddie in colour. If they may have their full time and season to feed, the pearles also will thrive and grow bigge, but if in the time it chaunce to lighten, then they close their shells togither, and for want of nourishment are kept hungrie and fasting, and so the pearles keepe at a stay and prosper not accordingly.

The main impetus of this passage and of its moralizing context was to censure the vanity of valuing gems. Yet the fanciful notions presented were likely also to have charmed or amused readers.

Nonetheless, some notice of natural realities creeps into the continuation of the same passage. This suggests that dew-conceived, yet vanity-serving, pearls possess in actuality some peculiar characteristics challenging to a ruling analogy:[15]

> Certes, I cannot chuse but wonder how they [pearls] should so greatly be affected with the aire, and joy so much therein: for with the same they wax red, and loose their native whitenesse and beautie, even as the bodie of a man or woman that is caught and burnt with the sunne. And therefore those shells that keepe in the maine sea, and lie deeper than the sun-beames can pierce unto them, keepe the finest and most delicate pearles. And yet they, as orient as they be, waxe yellow with age, become riveled, and looke dead without any lively vigor: so as that commendable orient lustre (so much sought for our great lords and costly dames) continueth but in their youth, and decaieth with yeeres. When they be old, they will proove thick and grosse in the very shells, and sticke fast unto their sides, so as they cannot be parted from them, unlesse they be filed asunder.

In the last sentence Pliny alludes to what are now called *chicot* or blister pearls, which are ill-formed, non-spherical pearls found fused onto the inside of damaged bivalve shells.[16] Pliny associates these and other imperfections of pearls with youth's decay into "yeeres," making an analogy with the fall of human vanity, even of great lords and costly dames, into yellowed and "riveled" old age. Just before this he refers to two other actual facts about pearls, again giving these meanings by analogy with human frailty. These facts are that in time fine pearls are inevitably degraded through aging and exposure to environmental contaminants (this frailty is unique among valuable gems),[17] and that larger pearls are typically found in deeper waters. The destruction of pearls due to their exposure to "aire" is simply linked with anthropomorphic sunburn. But still, despite the tendency to closure of an analogical mode of thought, a logical contradiction arises: the fact that "the finest and most delicate pearles" lie in deep waters is hard to square with a belief that all pearls "participate more of the aire and skie, than of the water." The problems here seem indeed signaled in Holland's opening phrase: "Certes, I cannot chuse but wonder how . . ."

Antonia McLean claims Pliny was "certainly one of the most widely used and widely read authors in the sixteenth century," adding that the *Natural History* "was never lost" to Western scholars, and that "Pliny must rank as one of the most formative influences on scientific thought in the West."[18] The *Natural History* was a school text in Shakespeare's youth, and a note by T. W. Baldwin claims that Shakespeare probably remembered the Latin and did not always use Holland's translation when he echoed Pliny in his plays.[19] It is widely accepted that in *Othello* and elsewhere Shakespeare relied upon Pliny for matter, and echoed Holland's translation verbally.[20] Yet, except once indirectly,[21] Shakespeare does not allude to the famous story, found in Pliny's chapter on pearls, of Cleopatra drinking down a dissolved pearl of enormous value.[22] However, he does employ the same fable in the business of Gertrude drinking from a cup containing a poisoned "union,"[23] this being a pearl of vast cost (*Hamlet* 5.2.220–21).

Before the time of *The Tempest* a number of European pioneers of empiricism and rational skepticism challenged Pliny regarding the origins of pearls. Their ideas are often recorded in contexts concerned with world exploration and expanding European economic horizons. Such ideas might have been particularly noted in London at the time of the tumultuous establishment of the second Virginia colony (1606–10),[24] and so may have come to Shakespeare's attention when he was writing *The Tempest*, a play reflecting New World settlement attempts and allied economic themes.[25]

Several among the first English explorers and settlers of Virginia remarked on the quantity and often good quality of pearls possessed by native Algonkians. These remarks, often found in promotional materials for the Virginia Company,[26] allude to an enviable Spanish precedent. In the sixteenth century the best pearls were still described as "orient," and many poets automatically associated pearls with the East. But in fact from the early sixteenth century onward pearls came in great quantity to Europe not from Arabia or India, but from Spanish-dominated regions of South and Central America.[27]

In accord with the arrival of fabled quantities of pearls from America in Spanish treasure ships, perhaps enough to ballast them, Shakespeare's sole use of the word "America" arises in connection with the shipping of gems. This appears in Dromio of Syracuse's impudent description of Nell the kitchen wench's "spherical" form, "like a globe"; on her, as on a living map, "America, the Indies" are found "upon her nose, all o'er embellished with rubies, carbuncles, sapphires, declining their rich aspect to the hot breath of Spain, who sent whole armadas of carracks to be ballast at her nose."[28]

The Spanish South American pearl fisheries are described in one of the first published European accounts of the New World and its wonders, Peter Martyr of Anglerie's 1517 *De Orbe Novo*. It is generally agreed that Richard Eden's translation of this book was known to Shakespeare when he wrote *The Tempest*.[29] In the third Decade of this volume, just before an account of "the Caribes or Canibales,"[30] Martyr marvels at the size and quantity of pearls found on the New World's coastal islands. Martyr then intends to "speake somewhat" of pearl formation. He begins "Aristiotell and Plinie his folower were of dyvers opinions as concernynge the generation of perles,"[31] thus indicating that unsettled questions merit further discussion. Martyr notes that experienced Native American pearl fishers discount the theory of dew-engendering, but adds that "the perfecte knowledge hereof is not to bee looked for at the handes of these unlearned men whiche handell the matter but grossely, and enquire no further then occasyon serveth." However, he immediately gives further voice to these men, who daily handle pearls, who say of these gems that:[32]

> the smaulest differ from the byggest in a certayne swellynge or impostumation whiche the Spaniardes caule a tympane. For they denye that to be a pearle which in oulde muscles cleaveth fast in the shel: But that it is a warte, which beynge rased from the shell with a fyle, is rounde and bryght but only of one syde, and not precious, beynge rather of the nature of the fyshe it selfe, then of a perle.

Here again *chicot* pearls which are fused with a damaged or "old" shell are noted, and it is suggested that the substance of a *chicot* pearl and of the shell of the "fyshe it selfe" might after all be the same. Yet Martyr concludes his discussion with apologies for having contradicted "the afore named famous autours," adding: "For their opinion herein is not utterly to be rejected, forasmuche as they were learned men and travayled longe in the searchynge of these thynges."[33]

The knowledge that an intrusion of a foreign body into a mollusk's shell will stimulate pearl formation was applied practically in China from medieval times.[34] The beginnings of a similar insight is adumbrated in Martyr's description of a "swellynge or impostumation," although a fully scientific testing in the West of the theory that pearls are responses to an irritant was still some two centuries away.

During Shakespeare's lifetime a number of writers came close to establishing the true connection. A 1908 compendium of pearl lore by Kunz and Stevenson is a good guide to these,[35] but its readings of early texts are typically jauntily facetious or reductive, and so require rereading. Among the authors Kunz and Stevenson cite is Pedro Teixeira, who was an inquisitive yet cautiously controversial

Portuguese linguist and traveler. Seemingly merely for the sake of the experience, Teixeira voyaged to dangerous remote places, and also circled the world. In 1610 he published an account of his journeying across Near Eastern deserts, and with this included a history of Persia and a "Short Narrative of the Origin of the Kingdom of Harmuz." The Harmuz history contains a politely iconoclastic digression on the generation of pearls:[36]

> with due respect to all writers on the subject, I must say that it seems to me unreasonable to assert that pearls are engendered of dewdrops. To this there are a thousand objections; for instance, that the oyster itself, which is heavy and clumsy, cannot come to the surface to receive the dewdrop; still less can it reach him pure at the bottom through so much salt water. Moreover, we know by experience that the deeper the water where the oyster is obtained, the more and finer are the pearls and seed-pearls, and those of the shallows less, in number and in size.
>
> Now it would not be thus if they came of the dewdrops, for those oysters nearest the surface would get most and purest dew, and would be most influenced by the sun, acting more strongly on what is nearest him than on more distant objects. But the contrary is the case. And my opinion is favoured by what I have often seen and tried . . . That is, that we took out of the oyster-shells, with tools made for that purpose, pearls and seed-pearls produced by the shells themselves . . . These . . . yet remained united to the oyster-shell, of whose substance they were formed. But when they had been detached, polished, and set in order, they looked as if they had been born apart like the perfect pearls, and fetched very good prices.
>
> Wherefore I hold it for certain that pearls are born and formed of the very matter of the shell, and of nothing else; since this is very likely and the objections to the other opinion so great. And this is supported by the great resemblance of the pearl and the oyster-shell in substance and colour. Further, it is a thing observed and well vouched for, that whatever oyster contains pearls has the flesh unsound and almost rotten in those parts where the greater and less pearls are produced, in proportion to their quantity. And those oysters that have no pearls, or so few and small as not to be worth reckoning, are sound and clean-fleshed. And this is no weak argument in favour of my opinion, subject always to correction of better judgement.

Here a logic that defeats Pliny, observations of the shell-like substance of pearls, and notice of the inflammation of the mollusk flesh surrounding pearls all suggest new ideas about pearl creation, although in a deliberately unchallenging way.[37]

Quite similar observations are made by an English sea adventurer in *The Observations of Sir Richard Hawkins Knight, in his Voyage into the South Sea. Anno Domini 1593*:[38]

> And here let me crave pardon if I erre, seeing I disclaime from being a naturalist, by delivering my opinion touching the breeding of these Pearles [of Mussels], which I think be of a farre different nature and qualitie to those found in the East and West *Indies*, which are found in Oysters; growing in the shell, under the ruff of the Oyster, some say of the dewe, which I hold to be some old Philosophers conceit, for that it cannot bee made probable, how the dew should come into the Oyster; and if this were true, then, questionlesse, wee should haue them in our Oysters, as in those of the East and West *India's*; but those Oysters, were, by the Creator, made to bring foorth this rare fruite, all their shels, being (to looke to) pearle it selfe.

Here again Pliny's absurdity is noted (again with an apology), as is the identical substance of shells and pearls. It is, however, open to doubt if Shakespeare could have seen this, as it was first published in 1622.[39]

But in 1579, decades before the composition of *The Tempest*, there was published in French a "widely and eagerly read"[40] translation of a 1565 Italian traveler's tale, Girolamo Benzoni's *Histoire Nouvelle du Nouveau Monde*.[41] This edition, as "Extracted from the Italian" and significantly "enriched with many discourses . . . by Urbain Chauveton," again offers an account of the origins of pearls rejecting the authority of Pliny and others:[42]

> as for [the arguments of Pliny], & Albert the Great, & other writers on the generation of Pearls, who said, that Oysters conceive them by means of the Dew which they sip: & according to whether the Dew is clear or obscure, the Pearls are also fair or dim: because they partake more of the Air than of the water: in such wise that if the weather is fine & serene when the dew falls, the Oysters which then gape & half open their shells, conceive beautiful Pearls: on the contrary if the sky is gloomy and cloudy, the Pearls which are then engendered are of their own accord straw coloured, wan, brown, or of an indifferent colour & rusty. That is a little troublesome to believe. For, on the other hand experience shows today that all the Pearls that are found in one and the same Shell (as often many may be found there) are not of the same quality, nor of the same roundness, nor of the same perfection in colour, nor of the same size, as they would be, or wellnigh must be, if they had been conceived by the Dew, all at one time.

Benzoni continues that the supposed action of morning dew and the fifth essence of the air are hard to reconcile with pearl formation deep under water, and he offers instead a theory of pearls growing organically like eggs inside hens.

Other, more professionally scientific experts of Shakespeare's time completely overturned the traditional understanding of pearl formation, although the transmission of such learning to Shakespeare and his English milieu requires considerable effort to trace.[43] These experts found that pearls are composed of thin layers of the same material as the shells of the enclosing mollusks, and that they arise from morbid concretions deposited in order to isolate unexpelled irritants. Two such savants were medical doctors familiar with protective pathologies. One was Anselmus de Boodt, a physician in the service of the gem-loving Emperor Rudolf II (a patron and collector to be met again in this study). Boodt's 1609 *Gemmarum et Lapidum Historia* explicitly discredits Pliny on pearl formation, offering an alternative theory based on good observational evidence and appropriate medical models (Boodt likens pearls to gall stones and bladder stones, and to the "bezoar" [*OED* 2.a] stones found in Indian goats).[44] Even earlier, in 1555, in the second part of his *Libri de Piscibus Marinis*, the above-mentioned Guillaume Rondelet arrived at parallel conclusions; he found the origin of pearls to be disease, and likened them to "grando" (*OED* q.v.) in swine or urinary stones in bladders or kidneys.[45]

PEARLS AND RENAISSANCE POETS

Next I want to explore how the English poets of Shakespeare's time represented pearls. An examination of over two thousand poetic and dramatic instances reveals that pearls often imaged beauty or perfection, but they also—more rarely—imaged imperfection or worse.[46]

In translations of the Bible and in devotional poetry a pearl was often used as a symbol of perfection. In contexts like the medieval poem *Pearl* notice was never taken of the frequent irregularity and universal impermanence of actual pearls; rather, the gem's spherical form symbolized either beauty, truth, salvation, or the ultimately estimable.

Despite a contrary claim once rashly made that Shakespeare absorbed no such influences,[47] the parables of a merchant's pearl of supreme value in Matt. 13:45–46, and of pearls cast before swine in Matt. 7:6,[48] are clearly reflected in several Shakespearian uses. So Troilus says of Helen of Troy "Why, she is a pearl / Whose price hath launched above a thousand ships / And turned crowned kings to merchants,"[49] oddly merging Saint Matthew with Marlowe. Likewise, Othello sees himself "Like the base Indian, threw a pearl away / Richer than all his tribe,"[50] and Holofernes says "pearl enough for a swine."[51]

Otherwise, poets regularly described perfect female teeth or fingernails as pearl-like, or spoke of lovely pearls of frost or dew, or associated pearls with high status or sumptuous opulence. Shakespeare often followed these and other typical conventions, such as of likening pearls to tears, or even drops of sweat.[52] In one particularly interesting context, in Sonnet 34, Shakespeare likened pearls (as rich gems) to human tears:

> Ah, but those tears are pearl which thy love sheds,
> And they are rich, and ransom all ill deeds.

This sonnet concerns tears of penitence, which will be seen to approach the main theme here; it also begins with an image of atmospheric disturbance, which is a central image in Pliny's lore of pearl formation (and in *The Tempest*).

Although the new natural history offered an alternative to Pliny's theory of the dew-engendering of pearls, until the late seventeenth century both poets and scholars regularly associated dew with pearls.[53] For instance, a submerged image of orient pearls informs the opening of Marvell's exquisite "On a Drop of Dew":[54]

> See how the Orient Dew,
> Shed from the Bosom of the Morn . . .

In a similar vein, the opalescence of pearls is imitated verbally in Shakespeare's Lysander's beautiful image: "Tomorrow night, when Phoebe doth behold / Her silver visage in the wat'ry glass, / Decking with liquid pearl the bladed grass."[55]

Despite these conventions of idealization, sometimes poets of Shakespeare's time noted that pearls could be irregular and could (or would) decay. For instance, in 1614 John Norden offered a theory that "The perfect pearle, is precious permanent; / The counterfeit, decayes incontinent."[56] Others, working athwart associations of beauty and perfection, defied the conventions of extolling pearl-like forms. This was sometimes done lightheartedly, as when Pan in John Lyly's play *Midas* sings of "Dairie girles, / With faces smug, and round as Pearles,"[57] or when in Dekker's *Satiro-mastix* a bald skull is mock-praised as an "Orient pearle."[58]

Sometimes, however, deliberate inversions of traditional pearl imagery bore a sharp or satiric edge. In a particularly interesting example of this, an English epigrammist mocked the marveling at

New World gems that often featured in contemporary propaganda for investment and settlement in America. Such propaganda (some of it conveyed in dramatic literature) typically alleged that grateful Native Americans would gladly donate masses of gems in return for the benefits of access to Europe's civility and its gospel.[59] For instance, a 1610 Virginia Company promotional pamphlet claimed that the best method of conversion of native Americans "belongs to us [English], who by way of marchandizing and trade, doe buy of them the pearles of earth, and sell to them the pearles of heauen."[60] A wholly subversive view of the same exchange is presented in Thomas Bastard's Epigram 13:[61]

> *Indie* newe found the Christian faith doth holde,
> Rejoycing in our heauenly merchandize.
> Which we haue chang'd for pretious stones & gold
> And pearle and feathers, and for Popingyes.
> Now they are louing, meeke and vertuous,
> Contented, sweetly with poore godlinesse.
> Nowe are we saluage, fierce and barbarous,
> Rich with the fuell of all wickednesse.
> So did *Elishaes* seruant *Gehazye*,
> With *Naamans* goolde, buy *Naamans* leprosye.

This comment, published in 1598 when the second Virginia settlement was in the planning stage, had an even earlier parallel concerning cultural difference in a poem by George Gascoigne, published in 1576, which answers "well" to its own question: "How live the Mores, which spurne at glistering perle . . . ?"[62]

There was also a misogynistic school of verse which imaged the sheen of pearls in contexts of physical disgust, travestying notions of pearly beauty. Several Elizabethan epigrams had an exactly similar thrust,[63] but these are surpassed in verbal energy by Sir John Suckling's sardonic "The deformed Mistress":[64]

> Her Nose I'de have a foot long, not above,
> With pimples embrooder'd, for those I love:
> And at the end a comely Pearl of Snot.
> Considering whether it should fall or not.

Even more harshly condemning women, John Davies of Hereford was repeatedly censorious when imaging pearls, and in a 1609 poem wished upon "(The skumme of Nicenesse) *London* Mistresses" pearl-like boils of fatal disease: "Their skins imbroder with plagues orient Pearls."[65]

Joshua Sylvester's translation of Du Bartas is also moralistic when imaging pearls, punningly condemning: "These parasites are euen the Pearls and Rings / (Pearls, said I? Perils) in the eares of Kings."[66]

Sometimes pearls themselves retained positive value for poets, but their origins did not. For instance, John Lyly in "This Song of the Fisherman" echoes a proverb concerning disproportion: "rich pearles are found in hard and homely shels."[67] A theory of pearls arising from a diseased shellfish may even be adumbrated in Shakespeare's "Rich honesty dwells like a miser, sir, in a poor house, as your pearl in your foul oyster" (Touchstone in *As You Like It* 5.4.59–61). Phineas Fletcher's *The Purple Island* notes the fact that malformed shells often contain pearls, "So richest pearls ly clos'd in vilest shells,"[68] thus alluding to some of the factual evidence alleged for a disease theory of pearl formation.[69]

In addition to such poetic contexts, there was also in Shakespeare's time a second meaning of "pearl" that would have had a bearing on the juxtaposing of eyes and pearls in Ariel's song. A lexical doubleness of that time paradoxically combined a connection of the eye's translucence with pearls (*OED* II.4.a) and a connection of pearls with cataracts that spoil the same translucence (*OED* II.4.b). Some contemporary poetic uses reflected the negative ocular association. For instance, in common with Shakespeare's Dromio's description of the nose of globular Nell, two later plays of the period associate gems with feminine noses, and add imagery of pearls in eyes, meaning visible defects of the eye:

> No pearl in eye, nor ruby in her nose
> No burn nor cut, but what the Catalogue shows
> (Thomas Middleton, *Women Beware Women*)[70]

> Her eyes, though dimme, do seem cleere,
> And they of Rheume can well dispose,
> The one doth blinke, the other blear
> In Pearl-drops striving with her nose
> (Thomas Heywood, *Loves Maistresse*)[71]

More distinctly still, King James VI of Scotland's "The Furies" has: "The Pearl upon the eie, / That dimmes the shine, and Cataract, / That dark and cloudie bee."[72] Likewise, John Davies of Hereford's 1609 "Picture of the Plague" holds "damn'd disguis'd, man-pleasing Sanctitie" and "Simony" to be "Pearles that quite put out the eies / Of Piety in Christian Common-wealths." And again, Barnabe

Googe's 1570 "englishing" of Thomas Naogeorgus's "The Popish Kingdome" has "as may the eye / Forbear the webbe and painefull pearle?" (lines 171–74).

Significantly, although biblical translations always refer to perfect pearls, a marginal comment of the Geneva Bible often used by Shakespeare annotates "bleare eyed" in Lev. 21:20 with: "Or that hath a web, or pearle."[73] And indeed, for Shakespeare himself pearls can be destructive to eyes. So dark complexioned ("black" faced) Thurio of *Two Gentlemen of Verona* is reassured by Proteus in terms of an "old saying" that " 'Black men are pearls in beauteous ladies' eyes,' " but Julia, perverting the proverb and deriding Thurio, adds aside, " 'Tis true, such pearls as put out ladies' eyes.' "[74]

ARIEL'S SECOND SONG AND FERDINAND'S SWEET AIR
"ALLAYING BOTH [THE WATERS'] FURY AND MY PASSION"

What good can all the preceding literary, cultural, and scientific contextualizing do? None, I would say, if its implications collide with the law that a genuine poetic utterance may trump any precedents or circumstances external to the verbal gesture, or tone, of that utterance. This law seems to me indisputable, for if poems were deterministically controlled in their communication by precedents how could they achieve their capacities for disruptive (or sportive) paradox, and more crucially their powers to convey that which is wholly unprecedented and yet totally recognizable?[75]

Therefore, if Ariel's lovely songs in *The Tempest* promote only consolation, or lyrical release into pure delight, it would be folly to attempt to align the dark and gritty contexts discovered above with Ariel's image of eyes-become-pearls. Of course it is impossible to say that nothing dark pertains to Ariel's later song beginning "While you here do snoring lie, / Open-eyed conspiracy / His time doth take" (2.1.305–7). More will be said later in this book about a "time" fit for conspiracy, and also about Ariel's verbal earthiness.[76] But when it comes to Ariel's second song, many critics sense only charm and consolation.

For instance, the sensitive critic James Torrens, writing on the development of T. S. Eliot's views of Shakespeare, pointed out an allusion to "Full fathom five" contained within Eliot's opinion that Shakespeare was "occupied with the struggle—which alone constitutes life for a poet—to transmute his personal and private agonies into something rich and strange." This sentence from Eliot's

"Shakespeare and the Stoicism of Seneca" is quoted by Torrens in support of a conclusion that for Eliot:[77]

> in the years after *The Waste Land* Ariel's music, suffusing all the late romances of Shakespeare, came as a more and more acceptable counterpoint to contemporary discords . . . During his long sojourn on Leman, T. S. Eliot was both humbled and encouraged by the exquisite music from Shakespeare that crept by him upon the waters.

For this critic, then, Ariel's exquisite music serves as a balm for the modern man spiritually beset, which Eliot, at length, could accept.

But Eliot himself goes beyond such a notion of a "counterpoint to contemporary discords." The words that immediately follow his allusion to Ariel's song in his essay emphasize Shakespeare's "gigantic attempt . . . to metamorphose private failures and disappointments," and add a clear implication that Shakespeare's private "general cynicism and disillusionment" was in fact not altogether private: "The great poet, in writing himself, writes his time."[78] Not consolation but exemplary moral suffering is emphasized, and the metamorphic act of writing cannot forget that suffering. Thus, in a context that alludes to Ariel's second song, Eliot finds an ethical dimension in personal suffering. I will investigate the song itself following a similar notion.

In fact, if intended only to soothe grief, Ariel's musical offering to Prince Ferdinand would convey a very odd sort of consolation. For, by it, Ferdinand is tricked into believing falsely that his father is dead.[79] In fact, Ferdinand says only of the song's melody or "air,"[80] and not of its words or "ditty," that: "Sitting on a bank, / Weeping again the King my father's wreck, / This music crept by me upon the waters, / Allaying both their fury and my passion / With its sweet air" (1.2.394–96). Thus he speaks while the song's prelude is being played, and only after the song's (misleading) words are heard does he add "The ditty does remember my drowned father" (1.2.408).

While enchantment, or consolations, arise from the tuneful waters, we as an audience may take closer note of the song's words.

ARIEL'S SECOND SONG AND PEARLS

Ariel's image of living eyes becoming pearls does not concern a metamorphosis from mortality to natural living beauty (as of the dead Adonis to a flower in Ovid or in Shakespeare's *Venus and Ad-*

onis). For, as Shakespeare knew, pearls in marine animals (and pearls in human eyes) are not living things like flowers, but rather symptoms of disease. But what is King Alonso's disease?

Of course it is impossible that Alonso's eyes could have become hardened or mineralized only minutes after his supposed drowning, but realistic time is not a factor in Ariel's song. Past and present are rather short-circuited in some parts of *The Tempest* (in a manner to be discussed below, in chapter 5). As soon as Alonso is seen after the storm he is depressed, brusque, and uncommunicative. It is proposed by the Neapolitan courtiers that he is inward and grieving on account of his loss of a son and daughter. But his abiding misery, and his certainty that Prince Ferdinand is lost, are seen to be not of the present and not rational. Their true basis is revealed to be instead his guilt over something that happened long ago. Alonso is obsessed with the memory of what he feelingly calls "my trespass," his twelve-year previous countenancing of Prospero's removal, and to this he attributes, in terms of "Therfor," the present loss of his son (3.3.95–102).

Reading backward (or allowing foreshadowing), the implication of this is that King Alonso's disease, the cause of the mineral transformation of his eyes, is his longstanding disease of "disowning knowledge" (to borrow Stanley Cavell's phrase). This is the knowledge of his old complicity in the usurpation of Prospero.

Ariel's image of eyes-becoming-pearls therefore links to moral blindedness and consequent affliction. Hence I would hold that Ariel's second song is ethically profound, because it is concerned with sin and suffering. Yet Ariel's song clearly contains no kind of moral imperative, is not homiletic in tone.

Like the "Allaying" air or tune heard by Ferdinand, its "ditty" which "does remember my drowned father" at first seems absolutely pellucid. In fact it remains so: when the lyric is discovered to be pregnant with moral meaning, the limpidity of its diction does not disappear or seem to have been illusory. Almost miraculously, the song's absolute simplicity not only remains unencumbered but even seems enhanced.

Yet it may be seen that the lustrous diction of Ariel's song also encloses a kind of intrusive grit. The more elaborate mixed-tense syntax of "Those are pearls that were his eyes" contrasts with that of the simpler preceding line "Of his bones are coral made." The juxtaposing of past against present in "Those are pearls that were . . ." presents for contemplation a process in which tender and sensitive eyes have become hard and obdurate pearls. This can work in either or both of two ways. In one an implication arises that a vision-dimming or vision-destroying pearliness has overtaken Alonso's perceptual inlets; this aligns with the scientific meaning of "a pearl in the eye" for Shakespeare's age, which was a cataract. But Shakespeare's age also knew the scientific theory that pearls (as gems) are formed in the sensitive living tissue of oysters or mussels to make bearable an intrusion, often of rough irritating grit. This would align with a notion that Alonso was not altogether insensitized to his guilt, but had covered it over with a protective shield that had hardened within him.

To see how brilliantly Ariel's image of pearls works in relation to that second scientific theory it is useful to consider an almost as brilliant use of pearl imagery in another English play, first performed circa 1613. In this, when she is forced to view capering madmen, her own coffin, her executioners, and her destined garrote, John Webster's tortured Duchess of Malfi wittily depreciates rich pearls. Refusing to be terrified, she asks "What would it pleasure me, to have my throate cut / With diamonds? / . . . or to be shot to death, with pearles?."[81] Thus scorning Bosola's attempts to unnerve her, she derides pearls as symbols of her high status (the very status that inspires his cruelty). Instead she identifies hard round pearls as mere matter, no more or less fit for fired missiles than are lead musket balls, and equally with them paltry compared with the human life that they may grossly subdue.

The Duchess's mockery of pearls as mere spherical lumps of matter is very clever, but Shakespeare's subversion of the typical poetic connotations of pearls is even subtler. Ariel's lyric debases not pearls as matter inimical to flesh, but rather (following the affliction/disease theory of pearl formation) identifies pearls as flesh degraded to inorganic matter.

That is to say, implicit in Ariel's eyes-become-pearls image lies the possibility that a living human eye can become either filmed over or hardened, made nacreous or mineral-callous, by habitual mental evasions and hypocrisies. In disowning knowledge, especially self-knowledge, humans may be blinded by calcifications that are caused by, and only partly alleviate, intrusions of moral "beams in the eye."

As in a shellfish physically, so in a human spirit morally, irritants (or painful truths) may be coated over by anodyne smooth secretions which harden around them. Such hardening or affective encasing is, in spirits, emotionally deadening. But in the late Shakespeare plays some who are so afflicted achieve a renewal of their deadened selves or numbed moral senses through undergoing a "sea-change."

Conveying more or less minor echoes of this kind of change, all of Shakespeare's Romances contain images of perceptual reawakening or recovery. A recovery from hearing loss, for instance, is imaged in *The Tempest* in Miranda's "Your tale, sir, would cure deafness" (1.2.106). More poignantly, the resolution of *Pericles* requires an unconscious woman to be brought to her senses and a catatonic man to recover all of his. Something even more akin to the reversal of Alonso's moral blindness is seen in *Cymbeline*, which ends with the recovery of the true sensibilities of a king erstwhile besotted in "eyes" and "ears" (5.6.62–64) by his wicked queen. King Cymbeline became not only morally obtuse under her influence, but was probably actually drugged by his wife (1.5.62–63); his eventual recovery has a premonitory echo in the recovery of Imogen from drugs "Murd'rous to th' senses" which, however, only "stupefy and dull the sense a while" (4.2.328 and 1.5.37).

Perhaps the most powerful Shakespearian representation of petrified human being becoming flesh again occurs in *The Winter's Tale* when (because Leontes realizes he is "more stone than it") a "dear stone" is transformed to warm softness and sensibility, so that it can live and "Be stone no more."[82]

In Alonso's case, as in most of these parallels, suffering must precede the recovery of his sense and his true senses. As Alonso recovers his long-dimmed moral sight he is seen to pay the price of an anguished "beating mind" (5.1.249). So he becomes "frantic" (5.1.57), undergoes "madness" (5.1.118), or, in Prospero's words, has "brains, / Now useless, boiled within thy skull" (5.1.59–60). Then, finally, fully repenting the harms that he had committed against Prospero and Miranda, and craving their forgiveness (5.1.120–21 and 5.1.201), Alonso regains undimmed vision.

Ariel's marvelous second song foreshadows these changes, mixing the tenses and senses of words as if they had already happened. So, in the song, temporal, semantic, and dramatic order is disrupted, but to a greater end. Although (and indeed, because) Ariel's second song deceives by offering false consolation for a nonexistent death, and deceives also by describing an impossible metamorphosis, it faithfully portrays "a sea-change / Into something rich and strange." That "something" is brilliantly represented by an image of half-organic, half-mineral pearls.

2

Scientific Theory: The Example of Thomas Harriot and Virginia

FROM EMPIRICISM TO SCIENTIFIC THEORY

As HAS JUST BEEN SEEN, THE RENAISSANCE ADVANCE IN THE UNDER-standing of pearl formation arose from factual observation and clear reasoning which replaced reliance on ancient authority. In these respects the method of that advance accorded with Francis Bacon's promotion of empiricism and rationality in his 1605 *Of The Advancement of Learning*. However, in other ways it failed to correspond with Bacon's ideas, and particularly his proposals for a wide-ranging research program that would systematize which questions should be answered, and that would organize cooperative investigations and a sharing of the results by a scientific community.

Also as has been mentioned, historians and sociologists of science have shown that in their practices early modern scientists (and later scientists) seem to resist conformity not only with Bacon's ideas of method, but also with any tidy formulations of a single means to scientific achievement or of a specific "scientific method." Rather, in Shakespeare's age proto-science gradually accumulated a heritage of methods and structures of thought that had an ability to alter or build upon themselves, and which could therefore evolve and adapt to meet new informational and conceptual challenges.[1] In an important particular instance analyzed by Alistair Crombie, "Galileo's normal method was to deal with problems piecemeal, and he often used different arguments tactically which cannot each be generalized into a total point of view."[2]

No Baconian collaborative research program or other "total point of view" was involved in the Renaissance advance concerning pearl formation, and neither was the contribution of any single individual uniquely important to that discovery. Instead, at around the same time, a number of writers (and probably others also who did not publish their discoveries) independently and often tentatively arrived at similar results. The repetitive rediscovery of the new theory about pearls indicates poor scientific communication, but also that there was beginning to be a widespread mindset that was capable of (and interested in) reassessing traditional beliefs by empirical and rational means.

Why did an increment of knowledge about pearls occur when it did? There was no new evidence available as such (although more pearls had arrived from America); the new theory could have arisen much earlier, for instance, from knowledge which had long been available of *chicot* pearls. Neither did this theory require the new mathematics, or new instrumentation, or new physical concepts of the late Renaissance. Indeed the experiments that would at long last (well after Shakespeare's time) confirm the theory for Europeans had been done many centuries before, in a practical context, in China.

Neither was the new European theory of pearl formation the product of a newly rising profession: only a minority of its discoverers could in any sense be called proto-scientists. What all the independent discoverers mentioned in chapter 1 shared, rather than a vocation or profession, was the desire to better understand a natural process, and a temper of mind which confronted the world more empirically, more logically, and less analogically than was previously typical. In this way this modest advance in knowledge may model a significant epistemological shift.

This is a model, however, quite contrary to that posited in some recent theories of scientific progress. These modern theories hold that during revolutionary or at least dramatic periods of intellectual ferment Kuhnian "paradigm shifts" or successive incommensurable "epistemes" have produced many of the great changes in human knowledge.[3] Oddly, such modern proposals of intellectual change partly resemble notions of the great epochs of human knowledge found in certain ancient systems of belief. These systems of belief began a long, slow, and still incomplete decline in the late Renaissance.

According to the studies of Nicholas Jardine and Anthony Grafton, Johannes Kepler was a leading early figure in the weakening of the hold of epochal historical thinking.[4] Kepler, the Imperial mathematician and astrologer to the Holy Roman Emperor Rudolf II and Rudolf's successor Mathias, was one of Shakespeare's most fascinating contemporaries. Astrology, as it was used by him (when he was not forced to prognosticate against his will),[5] was not predictive but served rather as a framework for sophisticated historio-

graphic and psychological speculations.[6] For instance, he wrote
concerning his own scientific achievements in relation to his birth
horoscope that: "My heavenly bodies were not the rising Mercury
in the angle of the seventh house in quadrature to Mars, but Copernicus and Tycho Brahe . . . The only thing which the birth constel-
lation has effected is that it blew the little flame of aptitude and
discernment, spurred the mind on to tireless work and increased
the thirst for knowledge."[7] He continued that an inclination or
temperament could be astrologically influenced, but that many
other factors (including gender, appearance, education, the support of patrons, and family or political circumstances) are crucial
for finding wisdom, fortune, or creativity.[8]

Uses of astrology also suggested to Kepler the understanding,
which he then backed up with considerable historical research,
that human progress (or decline) is usually developmental and ac-
cumulative rather than the product of "sudden seismic shifts en-
gendered from on high";[9] it is not struck on the anvil of fate by
blows of fortune, but usually follows the trends of the time. Nevertheless, some developments in early modern science did have a
dramatic impact. Most famous are Galileo's telescopic discoveries,
which burst on the world following the 1610 publication of his *Sidereus nuncius*. But even these discoveries had some unpublished
precedents made by Thomas Harriot and others,[10] they certainly
depended on a long development of optical lenses by anonymous
craftsmen,[11] and moreover the sudden widespread fame of *Sidereus nuncius* was due in part to an engineered campaign for publicity.[12] More often, even following very important early modern
scientific advances, full comprehension and reception typically followed a gradual path.[13] Kepler's own great discoveries (as they must
be retrospectively seen) of his three laws of planetary motion were
buried in digressive, abstruse, and mystical contexts,[14] and did not
have a great immediate impact (they were hardly noticed by Galileo, for instance). They only became world-shaking after nearly a
century had passed, when they were seen to support Newton's synthesis of celestial and terrestrial mechanics.

Nor was it true that martyrdom for truth and heroic resistance
were the inevitable hallmarks of the accelerating scientific achievements of Shakespeare's age. Aside from his colossal mathematical
labors, perhaps Kepler's greatest personal struggle in a life lived
amidst religious wars and turmoil was in a futile quest to obtain his
much-needed back pay from the emperor (indeed this killed
him).[15] Nevertheless it did take great courage for Kepler to depart
from his own favored presumptions. This he did especially on one

occasion,[16] leading to his most revolutionary scientific contribution (his planetary laws, paving the way for Newton). He did this despite the fact that it forced him to discard the seemingly graspable and replace it with the highly perplexing. This cost him Herculean mathematical efforts; it was part of Kepler's greatness that he was able to overcome his own natural dismay at departures from his earlier assurance. What in particular gave him the courage to venture forth from his own hard-won former views, with no safe haven in prospect, was a very small numerical discrepancy between his own theory's predictions of the motions of Mars and the excellent observational data he had misappropriated from the estate of Tycho Brahe.

Noting Kepler's way of dealing with an eventually hugely fruitful disruption brings into focus a source of early modern advances in scientific knowledge that is possibly even more significant than an increasing empiricism or skepticism. This source was the inspiration and direction supplied by speculative hypotheses, often accompanied by mathematical theory.

As more sophisticated methods of mathematical analysis were devised during the early modern period, scientific thinkers like Thomas Harriot and Kepler increasingly sought the true outlines of the world in correspondences between observation and mathematical-theoretical patterns. The emergence of scientific "laws" (that is, invariances or patterns) from the chaos of empirical data then would increasingly depend on a two-way traffic between the abstract (mathematical) and the concrete (physical) thinking of scientists.

Before undertaking the examination of an actual example of early modern scientific theoretical speculation, it is worth wondering why the importance of such work has been so frequently overlooked by scholars with literary interests, who often, in consequence, adopt reductive views of science.[17] This was not the case for the mid-seventeenth-century English poet Margaret Cavendish, who showed a clear understanding of the crucial importance for science of speculative theory. This was partly because she was kept unusually well informed about the progress of speculative science and mathematics by her savant brother-in-law, Sir Charles Cavendish, to whom her first book, *Poems and Fancies* (1653), was dedicated.[18] Thus *Poems and Fancies* contains a number of poems based on abstruse mathematical topics undoubtedly derived from the work of the great English mathematician and Kepler's correspondent, Thomas Harriot.[19]

Cavendish's scientific interests, expressed in verse and prose, have often been either unnecessarily excused,[20] or else dismissed and derided,[21] although some scholars have had better insight.[22] The usual reason for the misappreciation of Cavendish's scientific interests throughout the twentieth century was a repeated misconception that seventeenth-century science in England used only a purely experimental method,[23] or that it followed a "prevailing Baconian paradigm" of pure empiricism,[24] or even that it had only "utilitarian aims."[25] Quite to the contrary, Cavendish wrote "that Experimental and Mechanical Philosophy cannot be above the Speculative part, by reason most Experiments have their rise from the Speculative."[26]

Next I will illustrate what a *real* speculative mathematical theory of the Elizabethan period looked like.

A Real Theory

An example of a scientific theory using a hypothetical-mathematical-deductive method, and one that can still be easily outlined here, may be taken from the unpublished manuscript papers of Thomas Harriot (1560–1621). These are the same writings that inspired some of the poetry of Margaret Cavendish. Although the subject of this particular theory is not directly reflected by Shakespeare in *The Tempest*,[27] there are some links that bind its concerns with important aspects of the play.

The theory chosen derives from Harriot's computations of potential human population growth over time. These sums depend on the combinational mathematics of whole numbers (although some of the theory's conclusions move toward the mathematics of continua and limits); such mathematics is much less abstruse than the pre-calculus that paved the way for Newton's mechanics, for instance, and which was developed in Shakespeare's time by Cavaleri, Kepler, and others.[28]

It is not known why Harriot undertook the laborious calculations required to investigate the hypotheses of his theory, nor why he chose the particular simplifying hypotheses that he used.[29] He may have been simply following a mathematician's propensity to seek the pattern governing anything that is calculable, or he may have been asked to do this work by an interested patron, for instance Sir Walter Raleigh when the latter was working on his *History of the World*. It is at least certain that the hypotheses Harriot used cannot lead to an underestimate of the growth potential of human populations, so he may have chosen—or been asked—to estimate worst case demographic scenarios. In any case, implicit in his results are conclusions of general interest beyond the resolution of any particular questions he may have been addressing, whether of biblical or world chronology,[30] or of England's potential for overpopulation.

Harriot began by calculating the land area of England ("including rivers and all wastes") using "Saxton's great map" (published 1583, the sole surviving copy is in the British Library), and the surface area of the earth based on a spherical radius of 3437.747 miles (see figure 1).[31] He then placed these figures into a proportion together with the population of England (assumed to be five million), using as an additional assumption that half of the surface of the globe is "terra" rather than ocean. He thus derived the figure of just over seven billion, or actually "7,081,758,800 persons on the earth." Harriot probably knew that the earth is not on average as agriculturally fertile as England, so the number he arrived at for the world's population would be a bounding figure, a likely maximum. This population, Harriot worked out, is equivalent to there being about 250,000 square feet, or $5^8/_{11}$ acres, per person. Next Harriot calculated an ultimate upper bound on the population of the earth on the assumption that "six men may stand in one pace square" (Harriot's pace is $^1/_{1000}$ of a mile). Then the "number of persons yt may stand on the earth" works out at 42,490,552,800,000. That would be the number independent of all factors of the earth's fertility or the need for food.

Harriot's further calculations, which are very laborious, use combinational mathematics to determine how long a single pair of parents and their offspring would take to fill up the earth (see figure 2).[32] Assuming an unrealistic (or Old Testament?) level of human fertility and longevity, he proved "That in 400 yeares upon the former suppositions there would be more men then can stand on the face of the whole earth." The proof of this proposition contains an insight much more powerful than the raw calculations that lie behind it. Harriot made calculations for all the periods of years increasing by decades from 10 to 340 years, and as the intervals increase in size these sums become more lengthy and laborious. Then, after 340 years, he stopped calculating and applied the law of progression that emerged: "I find that in 340 yeares they will make a number of 14 places . . . Therefore in 400 yeares they will make a number of 16 places which is more than can stand on the face of the earth." Thus Harriot understood that unchecked population totals could grow at a rate of tenfold per three decades; that is to say, he saw that the increase was in a geometrical progression.

Such a "Malthusian" mathematical insight was once believed to

Figure 1. Mathematical manuscript of Thomas Harriot, British Library *Add.* 6782, fol. 31 recto. This folio recto and verso summarizes Harriot's work on population growth. By permission of the British Library.

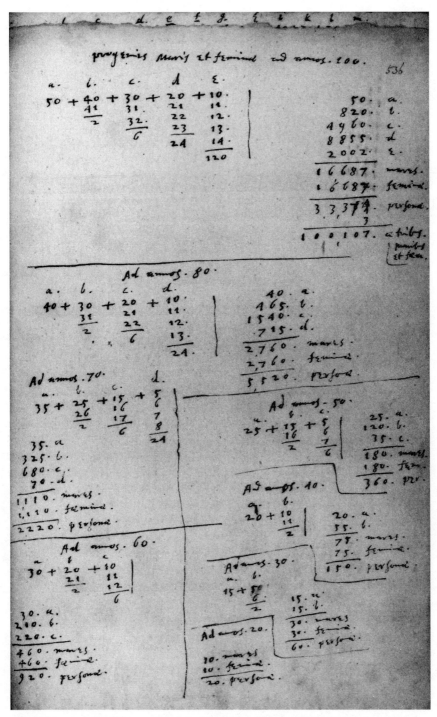

Figure 2. British Library *Add.* 6788, fol. 536r, in which Harriot computes human population growth after 20, 30, 40, 50, 60, 70, 80, and 100 years. By permission of the British Library.

have been nonexistent before Linnaeus in 1740, and Sir Walter Raleigh's understanding of population pressures in his *History of the World* was seen as a guess at best.[33] Harriot in fact went further in his Malthusianism. On an apparent assumption that the earth's area and mean fertility would limit its human population to about seven billion, he calculated that within six thousand years (an assumed age of the earth) as many people had lived as would occupy standing an area "3 times greater than England." There is no knowing if he was calculating the real estate needed for Heaven and Hell, or just pursuing mathematical curiosity, but his assumption of a fixed maximum population, that "there was always one time with an other the same number," suggests his model takes into account a limitation on populations imposed by the limits of food and other resources.

Harriot's unpublished and highly disordered mathematical papers cannot be dated, so it is not known if his theoretical work on demographics predated the composition of his famous 1588 treatise on "Virginia" (to be discussed next). However, questions of Algonkian food production and native populations in Virginia are highly significant in this treatise, as shall be seen presently. Likewise questions of population pressure were prominent in the English debates at the time of *The Tempest* over the planting of a large colony in Virginia, as will be seen in chapter 3.

Generally, the present and the next chapter will investigate some now-little-considered issues concerning the physical and human ecology of the New World that were very challenging to conventional European outlooks at the time of the writing of *The Tempest*. In his pioneering work Harriot brought to these issues important theoretical and speculative perspectives. To introduce the issues, and to clear away obstructions to seeing them clearly, the remainder of this chapter will confront recent attacks on Harriot's reputation, and will show how greatly his work on the New World differed from presently widespread views of it.

Thomas Harriot's *Report* and its Vicissitudes

In 1588 Harriot brought out in a small quarto volume the only portion of his work that was published in his lifetime, *A briefe and true report of the new found land of Virginia*. This was based on his explorations of parts of the North Carolina and Virginia coastal regions between April 1585 and June 1586.[34] The first edition of this scientific classic is now extremely rare; it was soon followed by a number of reprints, and it was translated into several languages.

Today Harriot's *A briefe and true report* has become notorious because of the focus on it in Stephen Greenblatt's often-republished essay "Invisible Bullets: Renaissance Authority and its Subversion, *Henry IV* and *Henry V*."[35] It will be argued that this widely influential essay misunderstands Harriot's text, and does Harriot's achievement scant justice.[36]

Thomas Harriot was a brilliant and prolific mathematician and scientist, but he was very secretive about his researches. His contemporary fame was mainly due to his friendships with powerful figures who were his patrons. He was best known as Sir Walter Raleigh's invaluable "friend-companion-advisor."[37] Harriot remained close to his friend throughout the latter's prosperity and ignominy, keeping faith with Raleigh after the disgraceful kangaroo trial of 1603 and during Raleigh's long imprisonment in the Tower of London. Finally Harriot privately recorded the details of Raleigh's brave behavior at his execution for treason in 1618.[38]

In the 1590s Harriot also obtained the patronage of Henry Percy, the so-called "Wizard Earl" of Northumberland, and more than patronage according to John W. Shirley, who claims that "Harriot's role in the Northumberland household was . . . more that of a friend than of a subordinate."[39] Northumberland gave Harriot a very generous pension, a house at Isleworth alongside his own Syon House, and the freedom to pursue whatever studies he chose.[40] These benefits continued after 1605 when Northumberland too became a prisoner in the Tower, having been implicated in the Gunpowder Plot.[41]

Opponents to the members of the Northumberland circle, who included King James, named Harriot as this circle's tutor in atheism.[42] Harriot thereby acquired an ill-reputation as an occult magus, some sort of "devil or doctor."[43] This may be because much of his scientific work was so advanced as to be incomprehensible to many, but perplexity and speculation about Harriot's work was also no doubt due to its lack of publication.

It is particularly sad that a "large discourse" on Virginia's "naturall inhabitants, their natures and maners," promised in *A briefe and true report* to appear at some "time more conuenient hereafter,"[44] never appeared during the remaining thirty-three years of Harriot's life. There is scant evidence of it among his numerous surviving papers.[45] Perhaps his failure to deliver on his promise of this "large discourse" resulted from frustration rather than from Harriot's habitual reticence; many of the valuable materials for his ethnographic studies were jettisoned when Sir Francis Drake rapidly evacuated the Roanoke settlement by sea in 1586.[46]

The full title of *A briefe and true report* is of interest:

A briefe and true report of the new found land of Virginia: of the commodities there found and to be raysed, as well marchantable, as others for victuall, building and other necessarie vses for those that are and shalbe the planters there; and of the nature and manners of the naturall inhabitants: Discouered by the English Colony there seated by Sir Richard Greinuile Knight in the yeere 1585, which remained vnder the gouernment of Rafe Lane Esquier, one of her Maiesties Equieres, during the space of twelue monethes: at the speciall charge and direction of the Honourable Sir Walter Raleigh Knight, Lord Warden of the stanneries; who therein hath beene fauored and authorised by her Maiestie and her letters patents: Directed to the Aduenturers, Fauourers, and Welwillers of the action, for the inhabiting and planting there: By Thomas Hariot; seruant to the abouenamed Sir Walter, a member of the Colony, and there imployed in discouering.

This clearly indicates a commercial and political motivation for publication, and at its outset the tract unequivocally states that its purpose is to correct "diuers and variable reportes, with some slaunderous and shamefull speeches bruited abroad" by detractors and calumniators of Raleigh's project "for the inhabiting and planting in Virginia" (320). Compared with the flamboyant diatribes in the Virginian pamphlet and pulpit war of the next decade (the decade of *The Tempest*),[47] Harriot's tract fulfilled its brief to defend Raleigh's Virginian "enterprise" in a very sedate manner. He merely proposed to present, and then did present, more accurate information to counter certain false or malicious rumors.

In fact Harriot did not restrict himself to this narrow purpose. He even revealed serious misdeeds of members of the expedition he accompanied, and, more importantly, presented an account of Virginia having considerable scientific value. Thus his report presents much information for the sake of its intrinsic interest as well as for commercial promotional reasons, and it contains much implicit analysis, showing that Harriot's official employment in "discouering" at Virginia had provoked and challenged his remarkable intellect.

It is useful to review several assessments of that intellect. In a close study of Harriot's pioneering astronomical work, which included his telescopic discovery of sunspots independently of Galileo, John Roche remarked:[48]

Harriot's thinking was characterized by concentrated and extensive study, clarity and depth of thought, independence of mind, originality, and an economy of style . . . He stubbornly pursued problems until he solved them . . . Characteristic of him also is the accuracy and honesty with which he records his data, whether it be favourable or unfavourable. In doubtful cases he called in other observers to check his results.

Similarly, in the judgment of Jean Jacquot, "Harriot's papers bear witness that close-knit reasoning and careful experimentation were the chief activities of his mind."[49] For D. G. James such intellectual qualities also suggest moral ones; while applying Harriot's *A briefe and true report* to an interpretation of *The Tempest* James characterized Harriot as "a man of rare quality and integrity."[50] The rigor and rectitude of Harriot's intellect is borne out also by my own researches in his manuscript writings, such as those on population.

Such attractive characterizations of Harriot as a seeker of truth are very far from the counterimage of him argued in Stephen Greenblatt's essay. In this, with cognizance taken of only a few parts of only one of Harriot's numerous texts, Harriot is portrayed as a representative European intellectual of his period in being destructive, bigoted, and fraudulent, and in particular in being inevitably bound to undermine and ruin the culture and the livelihood of the peoples he observed and studied.

For instance, Greenblatt presents Harriot's pioneering linguistic efforts to learn and record the difficult and formerly unknown Algonkian language as acts of unwarranted colonial appropriation, inevitably destructive and oppressive. Amusingly, in an earlier essay (entitled "Learning to Curse" with an echo of Caliban's complaint against Prospero), reprinted after "Invisible Bullets,"[51] Greenblatt conversely characterizes other Europeans' reluctance to learn or appreciate newly discovered languages as just as destructively colonialist.

In fact, prior to his 1585 voyage of exploration to Virginia Harriot learned as much as he could of the difficult North Carolinian language by conversing with Manteo and Wanchese, two Algonkians who sailed back to England with Raleigh's first expedition of 1584.[52] *A briefe and true report* shows that in the course of "discouering" Harriot became expert enough to be able to comment on dialectical variants between differing Virginian "gouernment[s]" or tribal groups. Armed with this ability, Harriot traveled widely in 1585–1586, in company with the visual artist John White, and collected a great deal of data about Algonkian culture.

A key to understanding Harriot's and White's abilities to make accurate observations may be found if a comparison is made between the surviving watercolor drawings made by John White in Virginia, and the later illustrations based on White's drawings that were made for the sumptuous third edition of *A briefe and true report*. This illustrated third edition, entitled *America, pt. i*, was published simultaneously in German, French, Latin, and English by Theodore de Bry in 1590.[53] Harriot provided Latin captions for the engraved illustrations, and these were translated into English by Richard Hakluyt and/or Theodore de Bry himself for the English-language version of this multilingual edition.

The 1590 English de Bry edition reprinted the text of *A briefe and true report*, and followed it with a table of illustrations, an elaborate full-page allegorical frontispiece, an Epistle to the reader, and finally the numbered engravings that were made or commissioned by de Bry. First seen is the frontispiece engraving (see figure 3), which is neither listed nor numbered with the illustrations based on John White's drawings, and is certainly not one of White's designs. In its central foreground it depicts a wretched Adam and Eve at the moment of the Fall. Two additional background scenes show a woman on the left holding a child under a crude shelter, and well separated from her on the right a man working a hummock of earth with what appears to be a rough tree branch. The living conditions of this fallen and sundered pair are in many ways much worse than those of the Native American peoples described by Harriot and depicted by White. In strong contrast with the barren hillock and primitive tool of the fallen man are the fertile maize fields and ingenious Algonkian pre-metallurgical implements described by Harriot. Likewise the frontispiece image of the fallen woman's rough shelter and even her uncomfortable posture in holding her child contrast with the comfortable Native American lodgings and the convenient Algonkian mode of child conveyance reported on in the text of the edition, and pictorially illustrated there. Perhaps most striking is the contrast between the miserable separation of the fallen couple in the frontispiece and the images of Native American men and women shown by White (and commented on by Harriot) companionably eating and consorting together.

These contrasts between de Bry's image of Mankind's Fall and the bounteous American realities delineated by Harriot and White strongly suggest stereotyped Renaissance notions in which newly discovered Native American peoples were seen as somehow pre- or extra-lapsarian, or still of the mythic Golden Age. These stereotypes are also reflected in the contrast of de Bry's frontispiece illustration with his own preface printed on the facing page:[54]

Figure 3. Frontispiece to the section of engravings in Theodore de Bry, *America, Part i* (Frankfort, 1590). British Library G.6837. By permission of the British Library.

Although (frendlye Reader) man by his disobedience, weare depriued of those good Giftes wher with he was indued in his creation . . . although [this sauage nations] haue not true knoledge of God nor of his holye worde and are destituted of all lerninge, Yet they passe vs in many thinges, as in Sober feedinge and Dexterite of witte, in makinge without any instrument of mettall thinges so neate and so fine, as a man would scarclye beleue the same.

Although some of these remarks are drawn from the accurate observations of Harriot and White, the juxtaposition of de Bry's text with his facing illustration suggests stereotypes that were typically sentimental and self-contradictory; aspirations derived from the same stereotypes are satirized in the passage of *The Tempest* 2.1 concerning Gonzalo's utopian commonwealth project.

Similar stereotypes of Native Americans living in a golden age permeate an early account of American exploration which Harriot most probably studied before his own journey. This is the *Discourse* of Captain Arthur Barlowe, one of the two ship masters of Raleigh's Virginian reconnaissance of 1584.[55] The frequently repeated key words of Barlowe's account are "sweete," "delicate," "goodly," "plentie," "fat," "aboundance," "fruitfull," "wholesome," and especially "the best of the world."[56] Barlowe also extolled Virginia's "very handsome, and goodly people" who proved themselves to be "mannerely," "ciuill," hospitable, sensitive, fair-dealing, and showing "smiling . . . all loue, and familiaritie" toward the English.[57] However, as D. B. Quinn has demonstrated, Barlowe not only overstated the material riches of Virginia, but also his account of the Virginians was "the most precise example in Renaissance English of the myth of the gentle savage."[58] Still, Barlowe's *Discourse* includes some valuable observation, although it is not always even self-consistent. Thus at one point Barlowe reports that recent "cruell, and bloodie" wars caused "the people [to be] maruelously wasted, and in some places, the Countrey left desolate," and tells of a particularly treacherous massacre at a feast,[59] yet he states elsewhere that "Wee found the people most gentle, loueing, and faithfull, void of all guile, and treason, and such as liued after the manner of the golden age."[60]

This confusion contrasts with Harriot's far more diligent comments on the peoples of Virginia. For instance, Harriot's captions for two illustrations in the de Bry edition of 1590 praise Algonkian technology without romantic exaggeration, yet with a particular pointedness they acknowledge that the English in Virginia were not as "cunninge" in feeding or outfitting themselves as were the Virginians:[61]

They also make weares, with settinge opp reedes or twigges in the water, whiche they soe plant one within a nother, that they growe still narrower, and narrower, as appeareth by this figure. Ther was neuer seene amonge vs soe cunninge a way to take fish withall.

Their woemen know how to make earthen vessells with special Cunninge and that so large and fine, that our potters with [their] wheles can make no better.

Harriot's considered opinion of the good behavior and virtue of the Virginians is suggested in two more of his captions to de Bry's 1590 engravings, and again he sees their superiority to Europeans:[62]

they are verye sober in their eatinge, and drinkinge, and consequentlye verye longe liued because they do not oppress nature;

Yet they are moderate in their eatinge wher by they auoide sicknes. I would to god we would followe their example.

Unlike Barlowe's, Harriot's own claims of the superiority of the Algonkians over Europeans have a precise basis in observation. This can be proved by a consideration of a three-way relation between Harriot's above caption on moderation, the corresponding plate in de Bry's—*America, Part i* (figure 4), and a related John White watercolor drawing (figure 5).[63] The John White drawing shows a man and woman seated on mats sharing corn in a dish placed between them. It is not only the knowledge that its subject was met at first hand that prompts a belief that White's image more closely resembles an actual American scene than does de Bry's derived engraving. For White's drawing, entitled "Theire sitting at meate,"[64] contains inherent clues to a remarkable accuracy of observation. These include its splendid depiction of Native American faces; by contrast (and as always) the faces are Europeanized in de Bry's corresponding engraving. Likewise, the man and woman in White's drawing are shown sitting with their legs tightly folded under them in a way uncongenial to Europeans, while in the de Bry version they sit in attitudes more familiar to and more conventionally graceful for Europeans. In fact, it has been claimed with regard to these particular drawings that "many of the postures shown by White lack prototypes in European Art, yet do occur in recent ethnographic photographs from other parts of the world," and also "White's pictures provide one of the very few reasonably reliable sources of postural data . . . prior to the use of photography."[65]

Figure 4. Plate 16 in de Bry, 1590. By permission of the British Library.

For the present purpose the verisimilitude in White's drawing "Theire sitting at meate," and its unusual freshness of vision, are important in indicating an unusual accuracy and truthfulness. The portrayal of the food dish in White's drawing as compared to de Bry's corresponding engraving is of particular interest. Thanks to the differing placement of the Native American couple's legs in White's drawing compared to that in de Bry's Europeanized version, White is able to foreground an extremely large quantity of food being shared, while de Bry does not. Thus White is seen to record the very impression that may have produced Harriot's caption, for he shows a slender couple sharing a superabundance of food. That is, the visual truthfulness of the drawing explains the first word "yet" in Harriot's: "Yet they are moderate in their eatinge wher by they auoide sicknes. I would to god we would followe their example."

Some of White's other drawings go even further toward explaining the basis of Harriot's judgment that the Virginians were very well supplied with food, although temperate in appetite. Note the impression given, more clearly in White's drawing (figure 6) than in the corresponding de Bry engraving (figure 7), of the economy of the unenclosed village Secotan. The labels on the three corn

Figure 5. Watercolor drawing by John White, British Museum P. & D. 1906-5-9-1 (20). © Copyright British Museum.

fields are very prominent in White's drawing, and are far less so in de Bry's version.[66] The large labels on White's drawing clearly indicate in adjacent plots: "Corne newly sprong. Their greene corne. Their rype corne." These adjacencies are *not* necessarily a synchronic representation of stages of growth in different seasons of the year (which would parallel the spatially schematic presentation of simultaneous front and rear views of the same woman and child in de Bry's plate 10, showing the Algonkian mode of holding a child),[67] for the text of *A briefe and true report* describes the use in Virginia of three varieties of maize which ripen at different times.[68] Harriot also stresses that the soil and climate make it easily practicable (but superfluous) for the Virginians to double-crop maize "if neede require, but that there is ground enough."[69] Thus Harriot

Figure 6. Watercolor drawing by John White, British Museum P. & D. 1906-5-9-1 (7). © Copyright British Museum.

Figure 7. Plate 20 in de Bry, 1590. By permission of the British Library.

emphasizes that the Virginians enjoy abundance but have moderate appetites.

The unusual possibilities of maize culture described by Harriot pointed toward some startling economic conclusions, which in some ways resemble, yet basically differ from, typical "Golden Age" myths about the New World. In brief, maize is described by Harriot as so fertile that there need never be scarcity and very small effort is needed to obtain subsistence. Recall that Harriot used the ratio of 5,000,000 persons in England to 50,000 square miles of land to estimate the earth's mean fertility (although whether he did this before or after writing *A briefe and true report* cannot be said). Of course Harriot did not have the equivalent of Saxton's accurate "great map" of England for North America, nor could he have assessed, as modern scholars do, a late-sixteenth-century North American population of fewer than one million persons.[70] But it is notable that in his applied mathematical work on population, as in his theoretical mathematical work, Harriot was especially advanced and sophisticated in working out bounding cases.[71] *A briefe and true report* notes the fewness and small size of the towns near Roanoke, and the superfluity of land around them.[72] Thus by extrapolating on a mathematical basis he would have judged the territory capable of supporting a vastly increased population.[73] This suggests that settlement was possible without (if Giovanni Botero's and Raleigh's understandings of the demographic causes of war were correct) any necessary territorial war or conflict.[74]

In addition Harriot calculated that the effort required to support an enlarged American population would be minimal. The human cost would be less than Thomas More's *Millennium* proposed, which suggested that if every person worked only six hours every day in the fields the entire Utopian population could be fed.[75] Harriot reported the fecundity of maize to be so great that the ratio of increase from seed grains to crop grains may reach two thousand, so that each acre of unmanured ground gave two and a half times the yield of the best English acre.[76] Thus:[77]

> the increase is so much that small labour and paines is needful in respect that must be vsed for ours. For this I can assure you that according to the rate we haue made proofe of, one man may prepare and husband so much grounde (hauing once borne corne before) with lesse then foure and twentie houres labour, as shall yeeld him victuall in a large proportion for a tweluemoneth, if hee haue nothing else, but which the same ground will yeelde, and of that kinde onelie which I haue before spoken of: the saide ground being also but fiue and twentie yards square.

These ratios show Virginia's fields to have been over forty times as fertile as the average English land of the time,[78] mathematically proving an easy abundance. Harriot then proceeds to the comment already noted on the ease of double-cropping maize "if neede require," proving that the Native Americans of Virginia were not greedy.

Harriot's ratios show that the Algonkian agricultural economy was better than that of Europeans. They also implicitly cast doubt on the universality of the curse in Gen. 3:19: "In the sweat of thy face shalt thou eat bread"; Adam's sin had no apparent impact on the Algonkians. But Harriot did not draw heterodox conclusions in his *Report*. The costs of expressing heretical speculations were too well known to him: Giodorno Bruno (whom Harriot almost surely knew) was burned at the stake in 1600 and Galileo was condemned by the Holy Office for his *On the Sun Spots* in 1616. Harriot himself was often suspected of atheism, and with Raleigh was officially questioned about this. *A briefe and true report* gave plenty to think about, but Harriot let readers draw their own conclusions.

Nonetheless Harriot's sophisticated mathematical analyses gave a basis for doubt that went beyond the loose connections made by Thomas Nashe, Robert Greene, Giodorno Bruno, and others between misgivings about the literal truth of Genesis and the recent "discovery" of Native Americans.[79] This point opens up the important question of scientific reasons for heterodoxy, which in Harriot's case had mainly to do with his beliefs concerning atoms.

It is better to defer a close consideration of Harriot's atomism for a short while (for its details will inform a later argument); here it is interesting to consider its general import and temper.[80] Jean Jacquot has described this by noting that, although "sincerely religious," Harriot at the same time held:[81]

> philosophical opinions that were at variance with the letter of the Scripture or the dogmas of the Church. Atomism could not easily be dissociated from other aspects of Democritean philosophy, and postulating the indestructibility of matter inevitably led to denying that the world had been created. According to one Mr. Hagar who was a mathematician and well acquainted with Harriot, he could not believe in the story of Genesis.

Such doubts regarding the Creation credited to Harriot cannot be categorized as seemingly-subversive-yet-unconsciously-contained-by-authority, as all heterodox views are proposed to be in "Invisible Bullets." Rather, as will be seen, Harriot's atomism had a firm basis in his understanding of particular physical evidence. In a parallel way, if Harriot suspected that the Algonkians of North America did not suffer the consequences of Man's Fall, the basis of this would have been his untrammeled use of numerical methods, not his susceptibility to the cultural containment of his thought.

Indeed, "Invisible Bullets" contains a broadside attack on Harriot. It first uses a portion of his *A briefe and true report* to exemplify a supposed Renaissance "hypothesis" that the "primary function" of religion is "not salvation but the achievement of civic discipline," a position claimed to be also implicit in the works of Machiavelli and Christopher Marlowe.[82] This position is said to have been absorbed into *A briefe and true report* whether Harriot knew it or not: "Harriot's text is committed to record what I have called his confirmation of the Machiavellian hypothesis, and hence too the potential subversiveness of this confirmation is invisible not only to those on whom the religion is supposedly impressed but also to most readers and quite possibly to Harriot himself."[83]

Greenblatt is careful to recall that "charges of atheism leveled at Harriot or anyone else in this period are difficult to assess."[84] Nevertheless, the ill-reputation Harriot obtained as an agent of the devil in his time has an equivalent in ours: "the colonial power produced the subversiveness in its own interest."[85]

The one passage of *A briefe and true report* crucial for "Invisible Bullets" concerns Harriot's display of the products of Europe's advanced mechanical, chemical, and optical technologies to some Algonkians.[86] Greenblatt's essay holds that Harriot's motive in doing this must be understood in the light of Machiavelli's conjectures that the miracles of Moses were juggling tricks intended to bamboozle the Hebrew masses, joining "fraud" with "force" in the foundation of "princely power"; that is, that Harriot scornfully deceived credulous "natives" in order to control them. Although in Harriot's own account of this episode he does seem pleased that the Virginians were impressed by his devices, and does acknowledge a potential advantage in that fact, quite other reasons for his pleasure are likely aside from satisfaction in a manipulative motive. After all, when their gadgets or marvels are appreciated technologists are naturally pleased; when warmed by appreciation they are far more likely to consider their audiences astute than to scorn them as inferior beings.[87] Despite this Greenblatt uses his allegation of a "Machiavellian hypothesis" to "conjure up" an image of Harriot showing his toys to the Algonkians as a cynical magician/trickster, exploitative and contemptuous of his audience. The image is offered in the words of an unnamed "colleague" who suggests it would "be just like"[88]

> an establishment intellectual, or simply a well-placed Elizabethan bour-
> geois, to accept that his superior "powers"—moral, technological, cul-
> tural—were indeed signs of divine favor and that therefore the
> superstitious natives were quite right in their perception of the need to
> submit to their benevolent conquerors.

Now the demonizing categories "establishment intellectual" and "well-placed Elizabethan bourgeois," as easily applied now as "devil or doctor" were in Harriot's witch-fearing age, need more than the word of a "colleague" to be proved. In fact, although Harriot clearly thought well of the technologies that he demonstrated, he thought even better of Algonkian technologies in the Virginian economic sphere, as has been seen. There is also much evidence in his *Report* of Harriot's admiration for the moral character, fine handicrafts, and religious sentiments of the Algonkian people.

Harriot was moreover an unlikely candidate for the part of a su-borned lackey of monological Elizabethan state power. Rather than an "establishment intellectual," Harriot was, if anything, clearly (to counter one anachronism with another) a "counter-cultural" fig-ure. And he was certainly not a bourgeois; documents such as Ra-leigh's will and Northumberland's household accounts show he lived from early in life to the end of his days on terms of near-equal-ity with his eccentric aristocratic patrons.

But this name-calling is trivial, and comes nowhere near the seri-ousness in the claims made in "Invisible Bullets" concerning what Harriot was and did. In fact Harriot and even Shakespeare are set up in this essay as straw men. The purpose appears to be to show that if even the greatest of Elizabethan scientists and poets were unconsciously agents of state power, then *a fortiori* no one was free. In the later versions of the essay Shakespeare becomes more the main target; Harriot's supposedly colonialist activities are in-creasingly used to provide a model for Shakespeare's validations of the oppressive "monological" state in his English history plays.

Thus the true target of "Invisible Bullets" is neither Harriot nor Shakespeare, but instead any notion that untrammeled thinking was in any degree possible in early modern England. Due to uncon-scious constraints, "virtually" no one could have had any true inde-pendence of thought. As a result, a Renaissance "intellectual" engaged in "discouering" must inevitably have assisted the "rapac-ity and aggression" of the powers he served.

Two of the earlier published versions of "Invisible Bullets" begin with a grotesque anecdote: a semiliterate late-sixteenth-century Friulian miller innocently conceived highly heretical ideas, entirely original to himself, for which he was burned alive.[89] This story at first seemingly contradicts the notions that all subversion was contained, and that seriously heterodox thinking was invisibly controlled. However, according to Greenblatt this episode truly shows that, on the contrary, any Renaissance individual's "challenge to the principles upon which authority was based . . . was virtually impossible," because exceptions like the ridiculous miller could only be "extravagant" and "zany." The removal of this anecdote from later published versions of "Invisible Bullets" does not alter in them the centrality of the meaning alleged for it in the first versions: in all but "zany" cases, universal internalization of monological power ensured full containment in early modern Europe of any challenging independence of thought or outlook.

A full refutation of the proposition that all early modern independence of thought was thus excluded can be provided by a single instance of a genuinely challenging idea pursued at that time by a not-at-all-zany mind. Harriot's interest in atomic theory provides a good example of just such an instance.

ATOMISM AND THE ALGONKIAN THEORY OF "INVISIBLE BULLETS"

For Harriot, the theory that the world is made up of imperceptibly minute particles that move and interact in a vacuum according to mathematically comprehensible dynamic laws did not arise from any eccentric inspiration (such as the Friulian miller's brainstorm that the universe is a wormy cheese), but from a context of other theories and observations, coupled with bold logical analysis.

The earliest evidence that Harriot was at least on the track of atomic ideas arises from dated marginalia that prove he was concerned with the optical phenomenon of refraction of light in 1584, the year before his American sojourn.[90] These marginalia, containing notations of refraction angles, were written by Harriot in his personal copy of Risner's edition of Vitelo's *Optics*.[91] This edition, published 1572, was of a thirteenth-century work that transmitted and extended the classic work on optics by the tenth-century Islamic physicist Ibn al-Haitham, known in Europe as Alhazan.[92] Harriot subsequently speculated on why light rays incident on a transparent medium are partly reflected outward and partly admitted and refracted, and conveyed his thinking to Kepler in a letter dated 2 December 1606. In this letter Harriot wrote that since un-like effects must have unlike causes,[93]

> A dense diaphanous body, therefore, which to the sense appears to be continuous in all parts, is not actually continuous. But it has corporeal parts which resist the rays, and incorporeal parts [vacua] which the rays penetrate.

This analysis of partial reflection clearly supports a theory that material substances consist of small particles and large intervals of empty space or vacuum. But such an atomic theory was very dangerous to hold in an age when it was still associated with the atheism of Lucretius and Epicurus.[94] So Kepler, in his reply, sent after a thoughtfully long interval on 2 August 1607, refused to follow Harriot into the theologically dangerous realms of "atomos et vacua." On 13 July 1608 Harriot again wrote Kepler, admitting that "my doctrine is founded upon the doctrine of a vacuum . . . But things are such that I cannot as yet freely philosophize."[95]

Although Harriot's caution concerning too-free speculation is evident here, so is a non-zany yet highly heterodox theory which would in time gather adherents and grow in importance. To suggest that at that time independent thinking was impossible, or that all thinkers were unconsciously "constrained" to serve an hegemony, requires one to overlook or perhaps not comprehend the boldness, application, care, subtlety and finesse, repeatedly shown in the seventeenth century in speculative processes directing scientific inquiries, in the gathering of experiential data, and in the construction of new theories.

A further attack on Harriot in "Invisible Bullets" concerns his acquisition of the Algonkian language. This essay claims that an identical pattern involving "glorified usurpation and theft" governs both the language studies of Harriot and of Shakespeare's slumming Prince Hal in *King Henry IV Part I*; the "bourgeois" Elizabethan scientist and the inquisitive fictional prince were equally constrained in their "recording" of "alien voices," whether Algonkian or Eastcheap, to hold these others in contempt in order to master them. But why must attempts to communicate with culturally different persons automatically entail contempt and oppression? According to "Invisible Bullets," in addition to overbearing Machiavellian fraud, "subversion and its containment in Harriot's account" had a "second mode . . . the *recording* of alien voices, or more precisely, of alien interpretations."[96] This concept, making all attempts to appreciate "alien interpretations" destructive to the possessors of the alien voices, brings Greenblatt's essay to its discussion of the actual matters of the "invisible bullets" which were spoken of by the Algonkians and recorded by Harriot; to these matters I will follow it.

At issue were the terrible epidemics of fatal disease unwittingly brought to America by Europeans. Harriot records concerning these that some Algonkians prophesied of the English:[97]

> there were more of our generation yet to come, to kill theirs and take their places, as some thought the purpose was by that which was already done.

> Those that were immediatly to come after vs they imagined to be in the aire, yet inuisible & without bodies, & that they by our intreaty & and for the loue of vs did make the people to die in that sort as they did by shooting inuisible bullets into them.

It might seem possible to take Harriot's recording of this remarkable theory as a sign of his disparagement of superstitious credulity, especially as he next writes about the chicanery of certain Algonkian medicine men concerning these "inuisible bullets." Greenblatt certainly claims that Harriot saw the Algonkians as "backward." But the truth may have been quite otherwise.

As noted above, Harriot stressed in two of his captions to de Bry's engravings that the Virginians were "verye sober in their eatinge, and drinkinge, and consequentlye verye longe liued because they do not oppress nature" and "moderate in their eatinge wher by they auoide sicknes." Intemperance and ill-climate were understood in Harriot's time to be the two chief causes of early death. *A briefe and true report* describes the climate of Virginia as especially "holsome," and so notes that "there were but foure of our whole [English] company (being one hundreth and eight) that died all the yeere . . . For all foure especially three were feeble, weake, and sickly persons before euer they came thither."[98] Yet Harriot also records that whole Algonkian villages were taken sick after being visited by the English. Given these conflicting observations, and given Harriot's tenaciously inquiring mind, it is inevitable that he would have searched for an understanding of the anomaly.

Therefore, fascinating possibilities arise. As has been noted, Harriot was an early atomist. In fact Robert Kargon argues that Harriot's atomism was universal, accounting for all phenomena (especially the "occult" in a technical sense) in terms of the interactions of invisible particles.[99] It is thus possible that the Algonkian theory of invisible bullets might have been part of the inspiration for Harriot's universal atomism, for if all powers and all substances are composed of atoms why not the vectors of a mysterious disease? Or, more extraordinarily still, Harriot's atomism and the Algonkian hypothesis of invisible bullets taken together might have suggested the existence of imperceptibly small particles of disease, actual invisible bullets. So, it is possible that Harriot and the Algonkians collaboratively created a theory that microbes cause infections.[100] Although conjectural, this gives quite a different picture from that of contemptuous early modern Europeans holding the trump cards of knowledge, and despising simple native peoples.

In Balance . . .

Whether such a conjecture is tenable or not, Harriot certainly did not look with superior scorn and blinkered incomprehension upon the Algonkians whom he met and studied. Quite to the contrary, he greatly admired them and sincerely strove to understand them. According to Myra Jehlen he may even have found genuine friends among them.[101]

Moreover Harriot and early modern scientific Europe generally certainly did not take a racist-superior view of all "alien interpretations." It is well known that instead they respected and built upon the lucid understanding of, for instance, Ibn al-Haitham, and of others from outside their culture who had preserved and enhanced classical science, mathematics, and philosophy. Thus, in important ways Harriot and his age were not ideologically constrained from extending the boundaries of knowledge, and could look beyond the bounds of strictly European culture.

Of course Harriot did carry to Virginia numerous preconceptions, some lying hidden in his language and cultural assumptions. Except where mathematics was his method he was forced to translate the language of another culture through his own language and tacit schemes of valuation. Thus he showed sympathetic interest in, and real admiration for, Algonkian religious ideas, but nevertheless still attempted to make Christian converts among the Native Americans. He also admonished "some of our companie [who] towards the ende of the yeare, shewed themselues too fierce, in slaying some of the people, in some towns, vpon causes that on our part, might easily enough haue bene borne withall,"[102] yet he believed that the Algonkians should have submitted to the English in order to obtain the benefits of education, civilization, and Christianity.[103] So Harriot did not practice a fully objective sort of anthropology, if such is ever possible. But this does not undercut the importance of his devoted attempts to see the unfamiliar avidly and freshly, and to seek truth to his best ability.

Even in his own time Harriot's perspicacity received recognition alongside more typical jibes. "The Preface to the Reader" of George Chapman's translation of *The Iliad* acknowledges no other assistance except in "some one or two places I have shewed to my worthy and most learned friend, M. Harriots, for his censure how much mine owne weighed: whose judgement and knowledge in all kinds I know to be incomparable and bottomlesse—yea, to be admired as much as his most blameles life."[104] Chapman praises Harriot even further in the long dedicatory poem of his complete translation of Homer, "To my Admired and Sovle-loued Friend Master of All Essential and True Knowledge, M. Harriots."[105] One couplet of this poem states why the authentic products of intellect cannot be eclipsed indefinitely by superstitious fears or passing fashions—it is because these products possess inherent good sense:

> True learning hath a body absolute,
> That in apparent sense it selfe can suite.
>
> (ll. 63–64)

3

The Tempest and New World Cultural Encounter

we are taught to acknowledge every man, that beares the Impression of Gods stampe, to be not only our neighbour, but to be
our brother, howe far distinguished and removed by Seas or
lands soever from vs

a manuscript of William Strachey, c. 1609–12

OVERVIEW: ETHNOLOGY AND *THE TEMPEST*

THAT, AS HAS JUST BEEN SEEN, AN ELIZABETHAN SCIENTIST (TEAMED
with an Elizabethan visual artist) found Algonkian culture to be
highly admirable and even in some ways worthy of emulation by
Europeans may well be considered surprising. In this chapter it will
be further argued that certain elements in *The Tempest* required
audiences of the play to respond to images of exotic Others using
a culturally relative outlook somewhat similar to that of a Thomas
Harriot or John White. Early modern speculative freedom, I will
suggest, was not restricted to scientific or artistic professionals.

The argument here will propose that the first audiences of *The
Tempest* would have sensed in the play a condemnation of European mores and behavior, as compared with the mores and behavior of non-Europeans. This argument will uncover a repetition of
links between the advent of new knowledge and the themes of
shame and remorse in *The Tempest*, a linkage also encountered in
the connection discussed earlier between Ariel's lyrical image of
pearls and a specific Renaissance scientific advance. Here, however, the linkage connects a far larger scientific context with a
wider poetic structure of *The Tempest*.

The wider poetic structure to be considered here comprises the
dramatic construction of Prospero's servants, and the linked larger
scientific context is the contemporary growth of knowledge and of
challenges to existing knowledge arising from exploration, settle-

ment, and cultural encounter in the New World. This is not an un-usual area for study, but there will be a new take on the familiar material.

Indeed, ethnology is the only scientific discipline that has re-ceived any widespread detailed attention from students of *The Tem-pest*.[1] Yet it is necessary to re-examine early English cultural encounters in North America in connection with the composition of *The Tempest*, because, for some time now, typical readings of the play have related it solely to a "dominant discursive con-text" [*sic*] or "master-discourse" of English colonialism.[2] Some recent read-ings of *The Tempest* have been so insistent on their theorized no-tions as to condemn any "critical practices" that might disagree with these notions as "complicit, whether consciously or not, with a colonialist mentality."[3] Although sometimes less prescriptive (and, as one critic says, less immune to any "practical counterevi-dence"[4]), many other readings of the play still suppose that Shake-speare's portrayal of *The Tempest*'s island sojourners must echo attitudes congruent with those of an eventually triumphant and tri-umphalist British imperialism.[5] Yet this is not historically support-able; of late even some critics who are broadly in sympathy with colonialist discourse readings of *The Tempest* have demurred that these "sometimes yield interpretations that elide the complexities embedded in the text's response to specific currents and interests emerging and taking form in its day."[6]

A few years ago my wife and I published a detailed study of the legal aspects of the English project to settle in Virginia. We showed that before 1610, and contemporary with *The Tempest*, an exten-sive political, constitutional, and jurisprudential controversy ad-dressed the possibilities of justification for that project.[7] This controversy was expressed in English and offshore pamphlets, ser-mons, plays, court masques, and the law courts. Our study puts to rest claims that *The Tempest* blandly mirrors or is contained by pro-colonialist ideologies, and particularly the assertion that Prospero's response to Caliban's complaint that the island "mine, by Sycorax my mother," is:[8]

> performative of the discourse of colonialism, since this particular retic-
> ulation of the denial of dispossession with retrospective justification for
> it, is the characteristic trope by which European colonial regimes artic-
> ulated their authority over land to which they could have no conceiv-
> able legal claim.

Such an assertion lacks historical awareness of the numerous historical and legal discussions of "conceivable legal claims" that fully recognized that the taking of native lands might be unjust.[9] Our article also shows why this style of reading *The Tempest* is strikingly unresponsive to the historical reasons for Shakespeare's caution when alluding to issues concerning the ill-treatment and ill-governance in the English New World. Some poets or playwrights who were not cautiously oblique found themselves imprisoned; others, as we show, used indirect means to call for the application of justice in colonial dealings. In general we demonstrate that *The Tempest* and its historical context offer no evidence of a limitation on thought that "exiles the unthinkable" in order to sustain a belief in "the impossibility of any transgression on the part of the colonial power";[10] on the contrary, claims of just such transgressions were hotly contested in Shakespeare's time.

It is very important to differentiate artistic re-writings or renditions from scholarly and critical interpretations. There is nothing wrong—and quite a lot that is interesting—in the many post-colonial appropriations of *The Tempest* that have re-written the play to reach conclusions dictated by latter-day "moral and sociopolitical agendas";[11] however, logical difficulties arise when such agendas direct literary scholarship which lays claim to an historical grasp. The trouble is not that moral outrage anachronistically mis-targets supposed offenders or cultural productions; this kind of condemnation can be answered on the basis of historical evidence, or even sometimes internal evidence, as when John Jowett points out that *The Tempest* ends with a return to Europe, so that it "can be absolved from the guilt of a world it at most merely foreshadows. To future colonial projects it is practically blind."[12] The greater problem is that an emphasis on anachronistic concerns (or the need to retort to this emphasis) interferes with needed analysis of the subtle interactions of literary and historical matters. A number of historically focused scholars have been attempting recuperation from this; in such a spirit the question of the bearing on *The Tempest* of problems and outlooks coming from the New World can, and should, be reconsidered.

In brief, it will be shown here that at the time when Shakespeare wrote *The Tempest* England's newly established North American settlement was actually in great trouble, and English colonialist triumphalism was far in the future. At exactly 1610–1611 the conditions in the first English settlement that would survive in America were indeed dire, and entirely unlike those that may have inspired colonialist jingoism in 1810–1811 or 1910–1911. The contemporary troubles of Jamestown were highly relevant to *The Tempest*, because in an oblique way the play reproduced the effects of the disturbing news coming to England from Virginia that by 1610 could not be suppressed. This news conveyed the nearly indigestible facts, the scandalous facts, that English settlers at Jamestown, and on their way there, were shamefully beleaguered by their own vices, and that if their deficiencies were contrasted with the conduct and abilities of antagonistic native Virginians these contrasts would produce effectively a living rebuke to the Europeans.[13] Thus Shakespeare's play reflected how new knowledge of a previously unknown culture produced a very troubling insight into the known culture.

THE IMPACT OF JAMESTOWN AT THE TIME OF *THE TEMPEST*

I will argue that the contemporary problems of actual English settlement infused *The Tempest* with its New World theme. Thus I will not join the very few who have denied that Shakespeare intended any topical allusions to the New World in *The Tempest*.[14]

Yet, it is still possible to note that Shakespearian source-hunters have been unable to make very tight cases for many of the links alleged to exist between *The Tempest* and specific New World documents. According to Kenneth Muir, for instance, there is "little doubt" about connections between *The Tempest* and the events of the 1609–1610 *Sea-Adventure* shipwreck and salvation en route for Virginia, but Muir adds that when considering alleged "Bermuda pamphlet" sources of the play "the extent of the verbal echoes . . . has, I think, been exaggerated."[15] Geoffrey Bullough further suggests that some of the writings imputed as verbal sources of *The Tempest* may instead be more "useful in showing what must have been common talk [about America in Shakespeare's] time." Bullough adds that "One must guard against ascribing to literary influences features which Shakespeare could well have got from talking with returned [Virginia] voyagers."[16] It is indeed important to note that Shakespeare may have obtained news of Virginia through his many likely personal contacts with members of the Virginia Company Council.[17] This is especially so since the matters to be considered here are of a sort that were likely to be suppressed in publications yet would have been inviting for personal communication.

The limited adverse public comment on the 1606–1607 Virginia settlement that did appear in controversial pamphlets (mainly of offshore production), or in mocking stage plays, was sternly opposed by the Virginia settlement's powerful promoters.[18] Among the more vehement replies were a 1608 sermon by William Crashawe, given at Paul's Cross, a venue which has since been described as the "Broadcasting House of its age." In a further 1609 sermon, Crashawe opposed various "discouragements" and attacked especially "Plaiers" who "abused Virginea";[19] this is probably an allusion to the scandalous play *Eastward Ho!* (produced and three times printed in 1605), which satirized both the wilder promises of Virginia's promoters and the low motives and personal ethics of would-be settlers.

Negative publicity also very likely arose in relation to the story of the 1609 wreck of the ship *Sea-Adventure*, even though the salvation of its crew and passengers was a near-miracle that was the talk of London in 1610. This vessel, carrying the leaders of an expedition conveying hundreds of male and female settlers to Virginia, was driven apart from the rest of the flotilla by a hurricane. Sad news of the believed loss of all on board reached London in 1609. Just so, Ariel reports that following the storm in *The Tempest*:

> for the rest o' th' fleet,
> Which I dispersed, they all have met again,
> And are upon the Mediterranean float
> Bound sadly home for Naples,
> Supposing that they saw the King's ship wrecked,
> And his great person perish.
>
> (1.2.233–38)

The *Sea-Adventure* was frantically pumped out by all on board including the expedition's leaders, Sir Thomas Gates and Sir George Summers, which makes a contrast with Shakespeare's idle courtiers aboard the foundering ship in *The Tempest*. Then the Gates and Summers ship beached amazingly on an island, as did the fictional one, without loss of life. Following a year-long island sojourn, almost all of the Gates and Summers party escaped from the Bermudas to continue onward to Virginia. From there news of their arrival, and Gates himself, reached London by 1610.

This adventure, usually taken as a seed for the shipwreck plot of *The Tempest*, has a sorrier continuation which I think is crucial to the play.[20] Together with the news of the safety of those thought dead came very worrying intelligence of the Virginia colony. Surviving documents, and doubtless returning voyagers, reported appallingly undisciplined behavior in the Bermudas and at the Jamestown settlement.

The best extant source of this information, a long eyewitness letter from William Strachey to an unknown lady, was published only
after Shakespeare's death, and then in a probably toned-down version, but for verbal reasons it is still judged to be a source for *The
Tempest*.[21] Like other accounts of the wreck, Strachey's letter lauds
the Bermudas as fertile and secure, unpeopled, even by the "Devils
and wicked Spirits" reputed to live there.[22] Here Strachey repeats
the common legend partly inspiring the creation of Prospero's
haunted island. But even in such a paradise some of the marooned
settlers mutinied. The escape to Jamestown was no improvement.
There a "blessedly holp hither" Gates and Summers party arrived
to find Jamestown on the point of defeat because of a well-orga-
nized Algonkian trade boycott. This successful stratagem, amount-
ing to warfare by sanctions, was greatly aided by the settlers' own
depravity. Its results were starvation, disease, and insurrection. By
the time that the Gates and Summers party arrived from the Bermudas the English settlement of five hundred had been reduced to
about sixty starving wretches; although it was agreed that all of
these should depart for England, the survivors had to be restrained
from burning down the fort to prevent any possible forced return.[23]

Such news substantiated rumors which had been circulating in
England for several years about insubordination, laziness, and disorder at Jamestown.[24] By 1610 even an *official* Virginia Council report confirmed that certain English renegades had "created the
Indians our implacable enemies by some violence they had offered," while detailing as "an incredible example of [the settlers']
idleness" that "some of them eat their fish raw, rather than they
would go a stones cast to fetch wood and dress it."[25]

The news also matched contemporary anti-English jibes in pamphlet literature emanating from Catholic Europe that many dra-
gooned Virginia settlers were unfit and unwilling rogues.[26] The
atrocious horrors of the colony during the "starving times" in
1609–1610, including renegading, mutiny with stealing of food,
drinking the blood of the wounded, disinterring and eating of
human corpses, wife-murder with (unborn) infanticide for purposes of cannibalism, hoarding at outposts while many starved at
the main fort, and a popularly demanded massacre of Algonkian
women and children, were later recounted in detail in a manuscript by the then-president and governor, George Percy (who will
be met again in chapter 4).[27] It is not conceivable that such out-
rages were entirely unknown in contemporary England; the news
of them would have made any contrasts lauding English over Al-

gonkian civility wholly threadbare. For even if Percy's manuscript was not generally known before the writing of *The Tempest*, Strachey's letter and other published accounts do not hide an implicit contrast between the wretched undisciplined settlers and the flourishing, well-focused, and united Algonkians.

UTOPIAN AND DYSTOPIAN NEW WORLD SETTLEMENTS: STARVATION AND MORAL EDUCATION

This situation is highly relevant to *The Tempest*. At the play's outset, as in Virginia in 1610, sojourning Europeans almost entirely depended upon the services of native inhabitants for material survival, and especially for food. The Algonkians were able to thrive in their environment, but as an irate John Smith wrote to the Virginia Council in 1608, "Though there be fish in the Sea, foules in the ayre, and Beasts in the woods, their bounds are so large, they are so wilde, and we are so weake and ignorant, we cannot much trouble them."[28] Therefore, in reality, as in the play, the practical services of native inhabitants were found to be absolutely necessary; as Prospero says of despised Caliban, "We cannot miss him" (1.2.313). In both the play and Virginia these services had at first been voluntarily offered, then they were purchased or extorted, and finally there was refusal, resistance, and rebellion.[29]

But the exact historical reality was not portrayed in Shakespeare's always prudent and magic theater. Not only concerns for his safety or his friendship with Virginia promoters caused him to envelop the contemporary situation with fantasy. Among the many advantages of his fabulation of a unique playworld was that, in being a parable rather than a parallel, *The Tempest* gained in the depth of its representation of a most puzzling cultural encounter.

In its very strangeness, by means of an Aristotelian dramatic positing of the probable impossible, Shakespeare's fabulation in *The Tempest* represented an experience of epistemological overload, of genuine bewilderment. So Gonzalo cries out: "All torment, trouble, wonder, and amazement / Inhabits here. Some heavenly power guide us / Out of this fearful country!" (5.1.106–8). Such dramatized perplexity accorded with the emotional impact of contemporary fact. Many Europeans could not candidly *see* America, and the island of *The Tempest* is only ambiguously situated westward near the "still-vexed Bermudas" (1.2.230) of the play.[30] Likewise many Europeans could not imagine Native Americans as fully human, and so Shakespeare's island's inhabitants are morally and often actually invisible to the interlopers. Thus *The Tempest* includes a complex allegory of the imperfect perceptions underlying New World cultural encounters of that time.

The play shows that the magician Prospero's "forgetting" (4.1.139) through despising of the indigenous Other was not a real option; Caliban's demeanor and actions were strongly felt, and demanded response (this point will be much expanded upon in chapter 7). Likewise in the actual New World of Virginia any tendency to the magical rendering invisible, through dismissive despising, of Algonkians had proved untenable. Thus Edward Bond argues in a fascinating study of the Jamestown settlement from the point of view of religion: "the natives presented less a military than a cultural threat . . . Virginia's native peoples presented such a tremendous cultural threat because they simply were not alien enough . . . As a culture the natives were alien; as men and women they were not."[31]

Perhaps very much as in Virginia, in addition to material threats made against Prospero's symbolic settler's household by active resistance, the facts of propinquity, neediness, and wonder also conspired to undermine dismissiveness of the Other. So I maintain, despite recent so-called "theory," that Shakespeare's representation of cultural encounter does not center on power relations alone, divorced from wider human possibilities, including terror, ferocity, curiosity, tenderness, and even love.

This may not seem borne out in Strachey's letter, which resembles all the officially sanctioned Virginia tracts in characterizing native Virginians as impediments to Europe's expansion. Thus Strachey labels Powhattan's politic refusal to supply food *gratis*, or sell it to Jamestown, as "subtile" treachery, and applauds the salvation of the fort by a last-minute consignment of food from England.[32] Correspondingly, it might seem, Caliban rebels against serving Prospero, although he reinstates his formerly voluntary offers to provide food when he meets the renegades Stephano and Trinculo.

But also, and very crucially, in *The Tempest* quite another sort of denial of sustenance to hungry Europeans is enacted by Ariel. His assistants first offer the Neapolitan nobles a much-needed banquet, taking native inhabitant shapes that Gonzalo finds benign if inhuman:

> For certes, these are people of the island,
> Who, though they are of monstrous shape, yet note,
> Their manners are more gentle-kind than of

Our human generation you shall find
Many, nay, almost any.

(3.3.30–34)

But then Ariel descends "Like a Harpy" to terrorize the guilty-minded rapacious Europeans, removing their food and calling their leaders "men of sin." Here, in a point I would much emphasize, a native islander shows an ability to reveal and rebuke Europeans' sins. This of course could have recalled how the Virginia Algonkians effectively shamed contemporary English settlers.

In presenting the image of an exotic islander reproaching Europeans, *The Tempest* implicitly conformed with some other exceptional Renaissance texts. In these, encounters with New World peoples stimulated a skeptical sort of "curiosity about contemporary life."[33] Classic among them is Michel de Montaigne's essay "Of the Cannibals," which marvels at native Brazilian practices, and questions presumptions of superiority in European mores.

As is well known, this essay is actually quoted in *The Tempest* almost exactly as translated by John Florio.[34] But Shakespeare, it might seem, sidestepped Montaigne's subversive stance. For the play uses the essay only when dithering Gonzalo fantasizes on an ideal "plantation" for Europeans, intended "T' excel the Golden Age" (2.1.174). Contrary to the spirit of Montaigne's essay, Gonzalo is wholly unconscious of non-Europeans, wishfully imagining Prospero's isle to be "desert" as well as fertile. Gonzalo also seemingly fancies himself as an original thinker, while plagiarizing for the innovations of his plantation Montaigne's reportage on the existing Brazilian polity. In several ways, indeed, Gonzalo's dream of eliminating all scarcity, conflict, and work is framed as farcical. His relentless and boastful optimism, although inverse to Jaques's boastful melancholy in *As You Like It*, attracts similar derision from shrewder, more worldly members of a castaway court, who rightly convict him of self-contradiction.

Borrowing Florio's exact language, Gonzalo describes a commonwealth dispensing with "name of magistrate; / Letters . . . riches, poverty, / . . . contract, secession, . . . use of metal, corn, or wine" (2.1.155–59). But, as would-be King, he skips Montaigne's "no name of . . . politike superioritie"; and then he trips, when he adds to Montaigne's list of things the Cannibals eschew: "No sovereignty." The contradiction prompts Sebastian's and Antonio's:

Seb.   Yet he would be king on 't.
Ant.   The latter end of his commonwealth forgets the
          beginning.

(2.1.162–63)

Behind this valid *reductio ad absurdum* lies the dilemma of any version of right-mindedness that feels a need to impose itself forcefully, and yet claims to serve only liberty; this dilemma was called by Harry Levin "Gonzalo's paradox."[35] Gonzalo overlooks this problem because his style of enthusiasm is oblivious to logic, and because he hears in its expression merely another of Sebastian's sneers. Without pausing, Gonzalo relentlessly elaborates on his utopian scheme until King Alonso caps repetitions of "Prithee, peace" with the groan "Prithee, no more. Thou dost talk nothing to me" (2.1.176).

The formerly power-grabbing Alonso lacks interest in visionary dreams because he believes he has deservedly lost his son and daughter. In contrast, the unrepentant Antonio and Sebastian find Gonzalo's day-dreams not "nothing," but an irritant. They jeer when Gonzalo distorts Montaigne's claim that cannibals have "no occupation but idleness." Montaigne clarifies, by describing their daylong dancing, hunting, drinking, and exhorting one another to the virtues of valor and of *"lovingnesse unto their wives."* Gonzalo insists rather on torpid ease: "all men idle, all; / And women too— but innocent and pure / . . . All things in common nature should produce / Without sweat or endeavour" (2.1.160–66). Goaded by Gonzalo's mawkishness, the courtiers speculate:

> *Seb.*   No marrying 'mong his subjects?
> *Ant.*   None, man, all idle: whores and knaves.
>
> (2.1.171–72)

This cynical remark closely matches allegations of idleness and marriage irregularities made against many of those conscripted for the Virginia settlement.[36]

In fact the fleering courtiers make telling points only where Gonzalo diverges from Montaigne's text,[37] and especially where he advances overblown promises of unlimited "foison" absent in Montaigne but common in many New World promotional writings.[38] Therefore, in fact, Antonio's and Sebastian's critique does not actually challenge Montaigne's radical cultural relativism, reflecting Shakespeare's own dubiety over it, as has sometimes been claimed.[39] Similarly, their sarcasms express only their own beliefs that all men are grasping and selfish, not Shakespeare's beliefs nor the consensus in his society. For, despite contrary claims, evidence is lacking in *The Tempest* or elsewhere that Shakespeare's age shared certain reductive,

> contemporary ideas about human nature. Relationships between people were seen as always potentially involving conflict and treachery. Keeping your guard up was universally necessary.

These ideas have been alleged to have been the common outlook of the settlers of the first failed English colony in Virginia, at Roanoke,[40] but in *The Tempest*, certainly, they are shared only by dramatic characters specifically created by Shakespeare to be seen as unpleasant.

Indeed, ironically, the would-be-sophisticated materialistic court scoffers of *The Tempest* actually misconstrue sovereignty more egregiously than had weakly-reasoning Gonzalo. The practiced usurper Antonio inveigles Sebastian into an assassination attempt on King Alonso, ignoring the fact that they are marooned on an island far from coveted Naples. Compared with such folly, Caliban's, Stephano's, and Trinculo's mutiny is rational, aiming at kingship of the island and sexual possession of Miranda.

CONTEMPORARY PERCEPTIONS OF VIRGINIA AND VIRGINIANS AND THEIR COUNTERPARTS IN *THE TEMPEST*

So, in the fictive wilds of *The Tempest*, high and low alike attempt to wrest precedence but then have strange confrontations with native inhabitants, much as did the pioneers of the Jamestown settlement. A pattern was set by depressingly frequent instances of miserable turmoil among the leadership of the ill-governed Virginia settlement—as was obviously known to the Virginia Council, and thus to Shakespeare and many others.[41] Lord Gonzalo, in a seeming exception to the pattern, does not strive for actual dominion, but he does fantasize grandiose sovereignty: "I would with such perfection govern, sir, / T' excel the Golden Age" (2.1.173–74). Like Francis Bacon in his prudential essay "Of Plantations" (1625), Gonzalo would avoid any interactions with native inhabitants. Then, on seeing some "people of the island," Gonzalo supposes them "more gentle-kind than of / Our human generation" (3.3.30–33). But lastly he flees in terror from a manifestation which their native-born leader presents of moral judgement.

The contradictions of Gonzalo's "Golden Age" fantasies about the island and its people are deeper, but just as weakly reasoned, as are the parallel fantasies about Virginia of Raleigh's Captain Arthur Barlowe. Barlowe's *Discourse* of his 1584 voyage, previously discussed, found the Virginians stereotypically "gentle, loueing, and faithfull, void of all guile, and treason, and such as liued after the manner of the golden age," and yet also perpetrators of pointless warfare and treacherous massacres.[42] For promotional reasons, Barlowe may even have hushed up killings of his own men.

Barlowe's kind of glossing over of the dangers of Virginia was by 1610 fit for derision (by implication, and on stage, so are Gonzalo's plans). As has been seen, by then the English Jamestown settlement was well known to be challenged by very "un-loving" Algonkians. There was also widespread understanding that the actual colony had been undermined by the deportment of both high- and low-born settlers, closely resembling the violent usurping younger brother Antonio and the loutish rebellious Stephano respectively.

In fact arrogance and folly among some New World prospectors was not altogether news. Between 1581 and 1583 Raleigh's half-brother Humphrey Gilbert, fancying himself a great feudal land-owner in North America, fraudulently "sold millions of acres . . . which he had never seen, to anyone who would give him money for it and agree to hold it under his lordship."[43] Following this lead, the haughty attitudes of younger sons of good family, or would-be aristocrats, beleaguered successive Virginian administrations.[44] Early on, despite repeated calls for a Virginia colony based on (in the words of Jeffrey Knapp) "georgic labor" as opposed to "gentlemanly idleness,"[45] a 1608 letter of John Smith to the Virginia Council indicated a great shortage of practical abilities among the first settlers: "When you send againe I intreat you rather send but thirty Carpenters, husbandmen, gardiners, fisher men, blacksmiths, masons, and diggers vp of tree roots, well provided; then a thousand of such as we haue."[46]

Moreover, Shakespeare had no lack of models for the crassness of Sebastian and Antonio, who remark, probably thinking of a commercial freak-show exhibition of Caliban: "Will money buy 'em?" (5.1.268). Many Englishmen apparently had similarly flippantly curious/dismissive attitudes toward Native Americans,[47] although Shakespeare clearly satirizes that in *The Tempest* when Trinculo remarks on England:

> There would this monster make a man. Any strange beast there
> makes a man. When they will not give a doit to relieve a
> lame beggar, they will lay out ten to see a dead Indian.
>
> (2.2.30–33)

However, quite different views of Native Americans were also recorded in Shakespeare's age. Thomas Harriot's *A briefe and true report of the new found land of Virginia*, which has been considered at length in chapter 2, showed a particularly open attitude: in this treatise Harriot opposed the oppressive actions of the 1585–1586 Virginian expedition which he accompanied,[48] and reported with great admiration elements of Algonkian technology, mores, and beliefs. Harriot's sympathy and concern was not entirely anomalous. The laws officially promulgated for the Roanoke colony and those promulgated later for Jamestown severely penalized oppression of native inhabitants and especially theft from them.[49] These laws suggest at once a need to restrain possible European misdeeds, and a belief that Algonkians would reciprocate decency.

Yet, in the context of propaganda for a commercial enterprise, quite different attitudes are revealed in two 1610 publications of the Virginia Company. Both of these pamphlets are included by Geoffrey Bullough with "probable sources" for *The Tempest*.[50] One of them states as being among the *"Maine Ends"* of the Virginia plantation:[51]

> to preach, & baptize into *Christian Religion*, and by propagation of that *Gospell*, to recouer out of the armes of the Diuell, a number of poore and miserable soules, wrapt vpp vnto death, in almost *inuincible ignorance*.
>
> Secondly, to prouide and build vp for the publike *Honour* and *safety* of our *gratious King* and his *Estates* . . . some small Rampier of our owne [against Spain], in this opportune and generall Summer of peace, by trans-planting the rancknesse and multitude of increase in our people; of which there is no vent, but age; and euident danger that the number and infinitenesse of them, will out-grow the matter, whereon to worke for their life, and sustentation, and shall one infest and become a burthen to another . . . *Lastly*, the apparance of assurance of *Priuate commodity* to the *particular undertakers*, by recouring and possessing to them-selues a fruitfull land.

The conjunction here of saving "poore and miserable soules" with "trans-planting the rancknesse and multitude of [English] increase" into their territory is repeated in the other Virginia Company tract of 1610. This second tract begins with praise for English motives as compared to Spanish ones with regard to the inhabitants of the New World:[52]

> . . . to preach the Gospell to a nation conquered, and to set their soules at liberty, when we haue brought their bodies to slauerie; It may be a matter sacred in the Preachers, but I know not how iustifiable in the rulers. Who for their meere ambition, doe set vpon it, the glosse of religion. Let the diuines of *Salamanca*, discusse that question, how the possessor of the west Indies, first destroied, and then instructed.
>
> The [best method of conversion], belongs to vs, who by way of marchandizing and trade, doe buy of them the pearles of earth, and sell to them the pearles of heauen . . . it is not unlawfull, that wee possess part

of their land and dwell with them, and defend our selues from them. Partlie because ther is no other, moderate, and mixt course, to bring them to conuersion, but by dailie conversation, where they may see the life, and learn the language each of other.

Partlie because ther is no trust to the fidelitie of humane beasts, except a man will make a league, with Lions, Beares, and Crocodiles.

However, it too repeats Elizabethan ideas of North American settlement of surplus English populations:[53]

He is ouer blinde that doth not see what an inundation of people doth ouerflow this little Iland: Shall we vent this deluge, by indirect and vnchristian policies? shal we imitate the bloody and heathenish cousell of the Romanes, to leaue a Carthage standing, that may exhaust our people by forraine warre? . . . If all these be diabolicall and hellish proiects, what other meanes remaines to vs, but by setling so excellent a Plantation, to disimbarke some millions of people vpon a land that floweth with all manner of plenty?

Plans for the settlement of millions on the basis of saving the souls of "Lions, Beares, and Crocodiles" may suggest, as demonstrated in *The Tempest* of Gonzalo's settlement plans, that "the latter end of [the] commonwealth forgets the beginning."

Contradictions underpinning English relations with Native Virginians went deeper than sanctimonious excuses for mercantile or colonial gains. Harriot was exceptional among English writers in expressing strongly reasoned personal admiration for the Algonkians, but even the 1610 propagandist tracts cited above suggest benefits from "dailie" contact between nations who "see the life, and learn the language each of other." Other observers such as Strachey could not help indicating in scattered and evasive ways the finesse of the Algonkians' well-adapted culture. So Strachey's letter, probably seen by Shakespeare when he wrote *The Tempest*, admires "a delicate wrought fine kinde of Mat the Indians make, with which (as they can be trucked for or snatched up) our people do dresse their chambers . . . which make their houses so much the more handsome."[54] Thus, even while parenthetically condoning theft,[55] Strachey reveals his admiration of the splendid abilities of generally despised savage weavers.[56]

Some English observers found reason to admire the Algonkians even in the moral sphere. Such praise, other than that of Thomas Harriot, tends to be found in asides or sideways notices, as in William Strachey's comment in a manuscript on the conduct of the Algonkians' skillful game of football: "they never strike vp one an-

others heeles as we doe, not accompting that praise worthy to purchase a goale by such an advantage."[57] The critic Charles Sanders
notes that this pictures Algonkians showing "more sportsmanship
than the British," and adds "It may be remembered that Kent in
King Lear expresses no high opinion of English football players."[58]

Despite such patchy admiration, many of Shakespeare's contemporaries seemingly lacked the will or capacity to think about or
imagine the unfamiliar cultural forces binding the humanity of the
denizens of a New World. Rather, they typically characterized one
and the same people as "savage" and "noble" according to perceptions of their "grosser" or "finer" characteristics.[59] Such bifurca-
tions find a fabulous representation in *The Tempest*, partly through
the division of the personages Caliban and Ariel. Yet these two dramatic creations are not simply figures in an allegory or double
moral vision of the "savage" and "noble." Rather, each separate
figure in itself serves as a mirror of living mental confusion. So
there is Caliban's famous refinement in poetic diction, and his artistic responsiveness to "sweet airs, that give delight and hurt
not."[60] And although Ariel is "delicate" and "dainty," yet he is also
awkwardly sulky, "quaint," and "tricksy." Ariel's attendants "are of
monstrous shape" in the Harpy scene, yet present "a most majestic
vision" in the masque.

Nevertheless, as has been said, despite schizophrenic English
perceptions of the New World peoples, the supposedly inhuman
native inhabitant Ariel judges the conscience of noble Europeans,
and in some instances stimulates it. This fact underlies the claim
at the heart of this chapter: that the image of Ariel rebuking Europeans corresponded with at least a shadowy experience of ethical
self-condemnation on the part of Shakespeare's contemporaries
when they were confronted with knowledge from the New World.

That is to say, the play emotionally mirrored the shameful fact
that well-adapted, well-governed, and personally self-controlled native Americans were bettering roguish and anarchic European interlopers in Virginia; shocking ethical and epistemological
implications of news from Jamestown were reflected in Shakespeare's play, although the exact details of events in Virginia were
not.

REPRESENTATIONS OF VIRGINIANS AND OF PROSPERO'S ISLANDERS

To pursue this further it is useful to distinguish between two
types of early modern European writings on the peoples of the New

World. In the first type native Americans are seen as exotic, and often savagely so. Thus, in a brief report of the voyages of Magellan, Peter Martyr Anglerie's *De Orbe Novo* depicts exotic Patagonian "giants." Shakespeare apparently knew this report through a translation of the book by Richard Eden;[61] it includes two mentions of a native Patagonian god "Setebos," the name also of Sycorax's god invoked by Caliban in *The Tempest* 1.2.375 and 5.1.264. The god is named in Anglerie 1555 at leaf 219v in the often-cited "they rored lyke bulles and cryed uppon theyr greate deuyll *Setebos* to helpe them," and again at leaf 220v, which describes a Patagonian's reaction to seeing a crucifix: "On a tyme, as one made a crosse before him, and kissed it, shewyng it unto hym, he suddenly cryed *Setebos* [fearing] Setebos would enter into his bodie and make him brut." This second instance, in which Martyr depicts a cultural encounter producing superstitious fears of punishment, based on savage terror and ignorance, might have inspired Caliban's fears that Prospero's spirits may "hiss me into madness" (2.2.14), and "will chastise me" (5.1.266).

But as in *The Tempest* Caliban's fears are actually founded in experience, not superstition, his outcry leads some way toward the second type of New World writings. In these the savagery depicted is European, often involving actual ill-treatment and punishment of indigenous inhabitants. Most famous were the condemnations of cruel maltreatment and enslavement in the Spanish West Indies of the 1540s, written by Bartolomé de las Casas, a Dominican bishop, and the Dominican jurist Francisco de Vitoria. Montaigne's essay "Of Coaches" also contains a stomach-churning account of Spanish perfidy and cruelty in the New World,[62] as does Benzoni's book mentioned in connection with pearls in chapter 1.[63] By Shakespeare's time there were many English responses to revelations of a supposed "leyenda negra" of Spanish New World atrocities, usually claiming that the English were kinder.[64]

Thanks to a textual discovery by Eleanor Prosser, a common European interest in the "leyenda negra" can be connected with spiritual and ethical aspects of the wide-ranging allusiveness of Ariel and Caliban. Prosser found a second echo of Florio's Montaigne in *The Tempest*, besides Gonzalo's famous borrowing from "Of the Cannibals."[65] This is from Montaigne's essay "Of Cruelty."[66] I believe that a sharp difference in the two Montaigne essays parallels disjunctions in the symbolisms implied by the characterizations of Caliban and Ariel. "Of the Cannibals" implies an admiring awe at native Brazilians' fortitude and physical courage, but the later-placed essay "Of Cruelty" implicitly downgrades stoical excesses like those of the Brazilians.[67] Thus in "Of the Cannibals" Montaigne recounts how, when expecting to be mangled and eaten, the Cannibals never quailed, but jested with their captors and scorned betraying any desire for escape, and how they admired and imitated Portuguese tortures because they were more "smartfull, and cruell" than their own.[68] "Of Cruelty," by contrast, praises a living virtue sensitive to mental pain, and so capable of voluntary sacrifice.

Ariel makes a lively application of these ideas when he prompts the angry Prospero to forgive his enemies, urging him to allow his "affections" to become "tender." To Prospero's question "Dost thou think so, spirit?," Ariel answers: "Mine would, sir, were I human" (5.1.20). Prospero follows this paradox with the noble passage, "Though with their high wrongs I am struck to the quick," echoing verbally, as Prosser discovered, the opening of "Of Cruelty."[69]

So, with profound ethical insight, Ariel leads Prospero to appreciate, as Montaigne does in "Of Cruelty," a painful "vertue . . . *more noble*" than merely benign "goodnesse," or honorable vengeance, no matter how brave. Although only imagining himself as if a human, Ariel instructs a princely magus, as he had earlier rebuked transgressing nobles. Shakespeare allows this supposedly non-human islander extraordinary scope.

Even passion-driven Caliban, representing the dark side of European perceptions of "native inhabitants," clearly betters in intelligence and focus his fellow conspirators, the drunken renegades Stephano and Trinculo. That he has superior capacities is no imposed modern view,[70] but instead is consistent with Montaigne's admiration of Brazilian mores in which "there is a wondrous distance betweene their forme and ours."[71]

Yet both high-born and low-born rogues of *The Tempest* appraise Caliban in terms of profits to be made from European freak-shows (2.2.27–34, 2.2.68–70, and 5.1.267–69).[72] Caliban is identified as a "salvage and deformed slave" in the First Folio's "Names of the Actors," and he is seven times called Prospero's "slave" in the text. Prospero's and Miranda's attitude toward their "poisonous slave" Caliban, whose material services they "cannot miss" (1.2.312–15), is abhorrence. This may seem to pry earthy Caliban and dainty Ariel even further apart, but are they so distinct?

Certainly Prospero wants to keep them separate. As has been explained at length in the Introduction above, Prospero becomes conspicuously indignant on recalling that the chafing Ariel had called himself his "slave," but he applies that label readily to Caliban. So Prospero implicitly contrasts the mild service he now asks of Ariel with Sycorax's former evil "hests," "earthy and abhorred" (1.2.273–74). As will be seen in chapter 6, the relations between Prospero and Ariel more closely resemble those of a master and grumbling apprentice than of a master and slave. Although autocratic Prospero is harsh and threatening to Ariel on occasion, at the play's end he beautifully expresses regret at their parting: "Why, that's my dainty Ariel! I shall miss thee, / But yet thou shalt have freedom.—So, so, so" (5.1.97–98).

This tenderness presents an extreme contrast to the nauseous epithets Prospero hurls at Caliban: "Freckled whelp, hag-born" (1.2.284); "Dull thing" (1.2.286); "Thou earth, thou" (1.2.316); "Thou poisonous slave, got by the devil himself" (1.2.321); "Thou most lying slave" (1.2.346); "Filth as thou art" (1.2.348); "Hagseed" (1.2.367); "malice" (1.2.369); and so forth until finally "this thing of darkness I / Acknowledge mine" (5.1.278–79).

Yet Caliban reveals the breakdown of a formerly tender relationship with Prospero. Sullenly but beautifully bemoaning a lost family-like mutuality, he complains:

> I must eat my dinner.
> This island's mine, by Sycorax my mother,
> Which thou tak'st from me. When thou cam'st first,
> Thou strok'st me and made much of me, wouldst give me
> Water with berries in 't, and teach me how
> To name the bigger light, and how the less,
> That burn by day and night; and then I loved thee,
> And showed thee all the qualities o' th' isle,
> The fresh springs, brine-pits, barren place and fertile.
>
> (1.2.332–40)

There are many dimensions to this extraordinary lament, and to Prospero's reply. Because in the lament Caliban focuses more on the loss of his place in a Renaissance family-like household than on the loss of his island, readers or hearers must look beyond the limiting strictures of the "discourses of colonialism" school. It is true that Prospero does not respond directly to Caliban's "This island's mine, by Sycorax," but rather flares up to remind Caliban of how he had housed him in his "own cell" and treated him "with human care" until the attempted rape of Miranda. The extreme fury in Prospero's reply is indicated in its inclusion of the most ferocious of Prospero's imprecations, in which he calls Caliban "filth as thou art." Such anger bypasses all proprietorial or colonial questions. It is founded rather on psycho-sexual aspects of the play regarding chastity (to be discussed in chapter 7), and on Prospero's characteristic fury at his slaves' and others' perceived ingratitude. Earlier, when describing Antonio's ingratitude, Prospero even doubted that the term "brother" could be applied to him (1.2.118). And in the dramatic context immediately preceding Caliban's lament Prospero expostulated the grumbling Ariel's ungrateful forgetfulness of benefits, reminding him with bitter vehemence of Sycorax's dire treatment of her servant and of his own contrasting kindness (1.2.270–94).

So Prospero's characterological coherence and current state of mind amply motivate his angry answer to Caliban:

> I have us'd thee,
> Filth as thou art, with human care; and lodg'd thee
> In mine own cell, till thou did seek to violate
> The honour of my child.
>
> (1.2.347–50)

Mutual hatred shines out of this indictment of Caliban, and from Caliban's unrepentant reply to it, indicating a collision of wills and of outlook standing in stark contrast to hopeful English claims that by living alongside Virginia's native inhabitants the English settlers would in the best possible way "bring them to [Christian] conuersion, but by dailie conversation, where they may see the life, and learn the language each of other."[73] Thus *The Tempest*, by subtly articulated dramatic means, throws doubt on one of the chief justifications of English settlement. Far from eluding contemporary questions of justice, it focuses on them.

Most significant here is how closely Caliban's history of displacement mirrors contemporary events in Virginia. The prominence of feeding in his recollection of lost family-like affection recalls how early Virginia visitors like Barlowe movingly described being feasted and caressed by "gentle, loueing" Algonkians.[74] Somewhat later, as Harriot, Strachey, and several others recount, skillful "dams . . . for fish" like those offered by Caliban, and hospitality including much-needed food, were generously given by Algonkians to the English settlers.[75] There is even considerable archaeological evidence, in the form of Algonkian cooking pots at James Fort, "that there were Indians living in the fort and working for the colonists."[76] Some of these people may have lived in domestic relations with the settlers as servants, and there might have been women living as wives or concubines with male settlers.[77]

But, as has been mentioned, before the time of *The Tempest*, the Algonkians of Virginia, like Caliban by the start of the play, had become the forced, reluctant, and necessary providers for European interlopers.[78] By 1610 local Algonkian groups, firmly marshaled under Powhattan, very effectively boycotted Jamestown, denying them their services; this partly parallels Caliban's drunken rebellion against serving Prospero: "No more dams I'll make for fish, / Nor fetch in firing / At requiring, / Nor scrape trenchering, nor wash dish. / 'Ban, 'ban, Cacaliban / Has a new master.—Get a new man!" (2.2.179–84).

Most crucially, in quite another way there is a parallel between Ariel's role and contemporary events in Virginia. The image of Caliban's hopeless revolt cannot evoke the morally instructive actions of the efficient and virtuous Algonkians who had starved and nearly driven away English settlers weakened by their own "ignorant" inabilities (John Smith's word), insubordination, divisiveness, laziness, licentiousness, and mutiny. But Ariel rebuking greedy European "men of sin," while denying them food, may well have recalled the disturbing impact of that.

The fantastic creatures of *The Tempest* thus reflected inner and outer aspects of a crisis of clashing cultures in Virginia. There a decay of former good relations with Algonkians not only imperiled the settlers, but also presented their predicament in an unflattering mirror, showing their folly, blindness, and arrogance.[79] Beyond putative "discourses of power," the symbolic representations in *The Tempest* of encounters between Europeans and exotics involve fury, betrayal, misunderstanding, and unbelief in a shared humanity, but also learning, tenderness, forgiveness, and regret. Thus the play's poetic concerns include the epistemological and emotional, as well as the economic and sociopolitical, challenges of cultural encounter.

4

The Tempest, Atmospheric Science, Prague Magi, and a Jamestown Experimenter

RENAISSANCE SCIENCE, TECHNOLOGY, AND TECHNOLOGIES OF KNOWLEDGE

THIS STUDY WILL NEXT INVESTIGATE A DIFFERENT WAY IN WHICH *The Tempest* responded to issues concerning new knowledge, by locating in both the New World and the Old contemporary knowledge-seekers who could have been precursors of, or even the inspirations for, the construction of the play's central image of an intellectually devoted, power-seeking exile.

These characters left their historical traces chiefly on account of their involvements with the actual technical instruments of scientific study. Consequently, my discussion will first consider some of the ways in which new technologies interacted with the Renaissance expansion of knowledge. Some terminology borrowed from the colorful vocabulary of computer science may help to focus these matters.

"Bootstrapping" is a computer science term denoting the special method whereby a computer can start itself up when it is first turned on. The term alludes to the joke phrase "to lift oneself up by one's own bootstraps," which provides a very apt image to describe the seemingly paradoxical functioning of the self-altering programs that set electronic digital computers initially into motion.[1]

"Bootstrapping" will be used here as a metaphor for the way in which technology and scientific knowledge (or in Renaissance terms, "the arts" and "philosophy") can mutually set one another into motion. Because there are two realms bootstrapping one another, the mutual interaction is complex. The interaction runs in cycles, with no particular starting or ending point, roughly as follows: technological advances facilitate access to new information; new information calls for advances in understanding; understanding facilitates further technical advances, and so on. For instance, early astronomical uses of telescopes stimulated (especially Kepler's) interest in geometrical optics; this (probably) led to the development of better telescopes; astronomy thereby advanced and the new astronomy motivated a search for better optics. . . .

Greater knowledge or access to knowledge resulted from practical (and often economically motivated) Renaissance advances in such areas as mapmaking, glassmaking, lens grinding, metalworking, shipbuilding, instrument-making, and navigation.[2] Renaissance scientific and mathematical instrument-making, which directly enlarged not only knowledge but the field or scope of knowledge, will be a special concern of this chapter and a part of the next chapter.[3] But instrument-making, and all other Renaissance technologies, were of relatively small significance compared with the one technology that most powerfully advanced the creation, distribution, and stockpiling of knowledge in Europe. That was the development of printing. The huge importance of book production for expanding Renaissance learning was frequently commented upon at the time.[4] By way of mutual bootstrapping, printing both depended upon and made possible new industries such as papermaking, typefounding, engraving, professional authorship, and a book publishing industry. A number of distinctly intellectual enterprises were benefited by the availability of of relatively affordable printed books which could standardize texts. For instance, printing encouraged the study, editing, and translation of known and newly discovered classical writings, and this together with biblical translation promoted the development of philology. The availability of printed books also allowed the formation of academic and private libraries, and underlay a huge expansion of both popular and erudite literary cultures.

The crucial information technology of Shakespeare's time was often commented upon in his writing; almost every one of Shakespeare's plays or groups of poems refer to books, and many plays allude to printed poems and ballads (for instance, the idiotic Slender in The Merry Wives of Windsor 1.1.82 mentions Richard Tottel's famous poetic Miscellany).[5] Many Shakespearian references to literacy are positive,[6] but Shakespeare also (often humorously) reflected a view that books, poems, ballads, or even plays could be ridiculous, frivolous, shallowly fashionable, or misleading.[7] Yet the attack on law, learning, book culture—and even papermaking for book production—seen in Jack Cade's rebellion is portrayed by Shakespeare as entirely brutal and ugly.[8]

Actual, and not just historical, threats also abounded. Shake-

speare as a playwright, no less than the religio-political controver-
sialists and pioneering scientists of his age, was constrained by
censorship; the serious scurrility of the English Martin Marprelate
tracts, for instance, and the innovations in Galileo's 1638 *Two New
Sciences* required clandestine publication, or publication out of the
reach of the Holy Office. An increasing flow of new ideas engen-
dered still more ideas, but also entailed new dangers.

THE TEMPEST AND SOME DANGERS OF STUDY

One such danger, several times depicted by Shakespeare, lay in
the possibility of studious sovereigns, excessively devoted to books
and libraries, failing to rule properly. There were actual examples
of overly intellectual rulers in Shakespeare's day, including Charles
V, perhaps James I, and the Holy Roman Emperor Rudolf II who
will presently be discussed.[9] The same sort of failure may seem to
attach to Shakespeare's Duke Vincentio of *Measure for Measure*,
who for fourteen years neglectfully "ever loved the life removed,"[10]
or Shakespeare's King Henry VI, of whom opponents say "[His]
bookish rule hath pulled fair England down."[11] But these impracti-
cal rulers only partly prefigure Prospero, who in Milan had thought
"my library / Was dukedom large enough" (1.2.109–10).

It seems that the books Prospero "loved . . . above my dukedom"
(1.2.167–69), and *his* sequestered time spent "transported / And
rapt in secret studies" (1.2.76–77), were devoted mainly to magic.
These motives in a sovereign may not have been unique in Shakespeare's plays or age,[12] but they do differentiate Prospero's negli-
gence in reigning from that of Shakespeare's Henry VI, Richard II,
Duke Vincentio, or Antony in Egypt.

To pursue that difference, the following several chapters of this
book will address questions concerning magic both in Shakespeare's time and in *The Tempest*, and will inquire particularly into
how such magic connected with or diverged from science. Here, to
begin with, some new and intriguing proximities will be discovered
between the historical background of *The Tempest* and contemporary uses of scientific instruments.[13]

Previous to the present study, only one scientific instrument has
been considered in relation to *The Tempest*: the astronomical telescope. As indicated in the Introduction, the important early modern advances made with that instrument will not be my main focus,
but because of the great interest shown by some critics in the im-

pact of the new astronomy on English literature,[14] a bit of the history of the telescope will be reviewed.

Very near the time of *The Tempest* (probably initially in Holland from about 1608) proper multi-lensed telescopes evolved from medieval spectacle-making technology.[15] In a dramatic sequel, by January 1610 Galileo improved such instruments,[16] then viewed the heavens, and in March 1610 he published his *Sidereus nuncius*. Three different momentous discoveries published in this startling book, and two further major telescopic discoveries made by Galileo in 1610, confirmed that the astronomical bodies are made of matter just like our earth, quite contrary to Aristotelian principles.[17] These discoveries were very well publicized, and soon "Italian dukes, German princes, the queen of France, the holy Roman Emperor, and half the cardinals in Rome wrote to Galileo asking for one of the instruments that made the celestial wonders visible."[18] Although his own planetary theories were disturbed by it, immediately upon seeing an early copy of *Sidereus nuncius* Kepler "was not incredulous . . . his original harmony disturbed, he immediately began to seek for a greater harmony,"[19] and he promptly published a pamphlet supporting Galileo's breakthrough, the first public support it received.[20]

Kepler's public support was a notable act of devotion to truth, but should also be noted because it proves the newness of telescopic observations in 1610;[21] in his pamphlet Kepler explicitly admits that he was wrong in his view held before *Siderieus nuncius*, that lenses could not advance astronomical observation.[22] As the world's greatest astronomer admitted this error in 1610, there is almost certainly no chance that astronomical telescopes were in use in Elizabethan England.[23] Claims sometimes made to the contrary are based on misreadings of the empty boasts of some would-be Elizabethan inventors.[24] Three in particular—Leonard Digges, his son Thomas Digges, and John Dee—made equivocal Elizabethan claims sometimes interpreted as stating that they had made telescopes;[25] it seems more likely, however, that, while alleging to have made impossible improvements on some achievements formerly claimed by Roger Bacon, these men actually described magnifying or image-projecting mirrors.[26] If such optical setups were ever constructed, and not just products of fantasy, they would have been useful only for entertainment or mystification.

The "perspective glasse whereby was shewed manie strange sights," mentioned by Thomas Harriot in his 1588 *A briefe and true report*,[27] was therefore probably also a mirror-type device,[28] or else some kind of a camera obscura. Yet a confused recent tradition holds that it was a telescope. It is worth noting that immediately after mentioning showing this "perspective glasse" to Virginian Algonkians, Harriot listed the further wonders of "burning glasses" (that is, concave mirrors) and "wildfire woorkes." Harriot also lists just before and after these toys European products of much greater utility, including a compass, guns, books, and writing.[29]

The unlikely notion that Harriot had an Elizabethan telescope has been argued pro and con by some historians,[30] but is assumed without argument or reserve in the important college textbook *The Norton Anthology of English Literature*. This assumption, presented as fact, first appeared in the 1993 edition of the *Anthology*, and remains in the most recent edition. The 1993 version boasted on its back cover the new inclusion of Harriot's work; this was an excerpt from *A briefe and true report* of the short passage centrally addressed in Steven Greenblatt's "Invisible Bullets." To provide a context for this passage the 1993 edition supplied a headnote which equated Harriot's interest in the peoples of North America with the freak-show scopophilia of the English masses, and that in turn with the attitude alleged by the drunkard Trinculo of *The Tempest*: "When they will not give a doit to relieve a lame beggar, they will lay out ten to see a dead Indian" (2.2.31–33). This explicit linking of Harriot's supposed cultural chauvinism with *The Tempest* is removed in the latest edition of the anthology, but like its 1993 predecessor the current edition still glosses Harriot's "perspective glasse" as a "telescope," and the headnotes of both editions remark that Harriot used a telescope at about the same time as Galileo.[31] Although this second claim is true, it is misleading, for it fails to mention that Harriot's and Galileo's nearly simultaneous telescopic investigations of the sky date to over two decades after *A briefe and true report*.

Two useful lessons may be drawn from this farrago. One is that exact chronology is a crucial determinant of historical meaning, and must not be overlooked for polemical reasons. Another more specific lesson is that distinctions must be observed between scientific instruments made for different purposes, even if they seem to be based on similar principles.

Both of these lessons have a bearing on the investigation that will now be presented of scientific matters that have hardly ever before been discussed as significant to *The Tempest*. This investigation will scrutinize the growing knowledge in Shakespeare's time not of planetary and stellar phenomena (which are by now quite well understood), but of the phenomena of terrestrial meteorology (which still present our own science with unsolved and pressing perplexities).

ATMOSPHERIC PHYSICS IN THE RENAISSANCE, AND A ONCE-FAMOUS RENAISSANCE TECHNOLOGIST

The Tempest begins with a wild storm, and ends with a promise of "calm seas, auspicious gales" (5.1.318). Both weather phenomena are supposedly produced and controlled by Prospero through the agency of Ariel. To begin a consideration of the issues surrounding Prospero's claims to a "so potent art" capable of raising or settling a storm, it is worth asking if the weather changes in *The Tempest* could have been understood by an original Shakespearian audience as plausibly deriving from any technological or else less natural "art."

The early Renaissance Neoplatonic magus was supposed to have powers over atmospheric phenomena: "Ficino tells us, the perfected magus, as agent of God, can . . . 'command the elements, rouse the winds, gather the clouds together in rain' ."[32] Later in the Renaissance, by Shakespeare's time, the same powers were claimed by, or claimed for, some scientific wonder-workers.

John Dee (1527–1608) was both a magus and a scientist. His famous *Mathematicall Preface* to Billingsley's 1570 edition of Euclid discussed—as aspects of mathematics—a wide range of scientific, technological, and even artistic matters; Dee was also an important contributor to practical sciences (especially navigation).[33] Yet from the beginning, and increasingly in his later years, Dee was also a mystical adherent. John Aubrey reports that Dee was once "troubled and indited" for conjuring, and Aubrey adds immediately after this that "a mighty storm and tempest was raised in harvest time, the country people had not known the like," and that an eighty-year-old lady who had known Dee told Aubrey "he laid the storm by magic."[34] This seems to accord with a notion that adepts (Hermetic or scientific?) could intervene in the causes of the atmospheric "meteors," which earlier astrological belief held depended solely on the stars. Of course these actions were only *attributed* to Dee, who actually, and in common with other scientific observers of his time (notably Kepler), kept a record of current meteorological data alongside astrological data, with a view to their correlation.[35]

Another less-well-remembered contemporary of Shakespeare in England allegedly used some sort of technology (presumably mechanical or chemical, as he was never viewed as a magician) to manipulate local weather. This technologist was thereby able to terrify kings and nobles, very much as Prospero did. He was one Cornelius Drebbel, a trained engraver who became a well-known inventor or "engineer." Drebbel was born in Alkmaar in the Netherlands in approximately 1572, and he remained mainly resident in England from about 1604 until his death in 1633.[36] In his earlier years at least Drebbel was indeed very famous, and numerous seventeenth-century scientific pioneers believed "the famous Drebble" or "very famous Drebble" to have been a credible artificer.[37] From today's perspective, he seems to have been a self-promoting technologist-entrepreneur, but also something of a semi-charlatan given to wild boasting.[38]

Drebbel's supposed weather manipulations have an interesting background. It is perhaps because in 1604 he published a wholly conventional but often reprinted treatise in Dutch entitled *On the nature of the elements and how they bring about wind, rain, lightning, thunder* that Drebbel was credited in the Chronicles of Alkmaar with a patent impossibility, given the knowledge and energy resources available in his time:[39]

> Aided by some instruments of his own manufacture, Drebbel could make it rain, lighten, and thunder at every time of the year so that you would have sworn it came in a natural way from heaven.
>
> By means of other instruments, he could, in the midst of summer, so much refrigerate the atmosphere of certain places, that you would have thought yourself in the very midst of winter. This experiment he did once on his Majesty's request, in the great Hall of Westminster; and although a hot summer day had been chosen by the King, it became so cold in the Hall, that James and his followers took to their heels in hasty flight.

This same story was current in England, and is alluded to by Francis Bacon.[40] But the medieval Westminster Hall, famous in Shakespeare's time for (cacophonously, simultaneously) housing three busy Royal Law Courts, is and was huge. It remains today as a kind of vastly oversized lobby to the left of the entry to the Houses of Parliament; a moment's visit to this impressive space shows that the claims made for Drebbel suddenly refrigerating it using mechanical "instruments of his own manufacture" were absurd.

Yet in Shakespeare's time instrumental science to do with weather and the earth's atmosphere was advancing, and this fact may have an unexpected significance for *The Tempest*.

Although he could not have radically altered the indoor temperature at Westminster, Drebbel certainly did devise (or claimed to devise) many "instruments" that reacted to atmospheric forces. It was mainly for these that he won his wide renown.[41] In fact Drebbel is among several candidates suggested for the first creation of a thermometer, although the story of that invention is most confused.[42] In 1598, in Holland, he certainly did patent a self-winding clockwork driven by atmospheric changes. But it is doubtful if this was a pioneering thermometer in any real sense; pneumatically driven gadgets or temple "miracles" turning temperature changes into motion were described anciently by Philo of Byzantium and Hero of Alexandria, and in the Renaissance by della Porta long before Drebbel. Clearly definitional problems arise. For one thing, mechanical toys may share principles with scientific measuring instruments (and the props of mystical adepts or conjuring cheats may bring in a third category). For another, the physics of heated gasses were insufficiently understood in the early seventeenth century to enable effects of temperature to be distinguished reliably from other phenomena, as will be seen.

Thus one authority investigating competing claims for priority holds that by 1611 "Santorio was the first to make use of the thermometer as a scientific instrument [although] Galileo may well . . . have made an experiment even in the 1590s,"[43] while another authority places Santorio's invention "between 1602 and 1612."[44] Yet another candidate for precedence is Bartolomeo Telioux, who illustrated a graduated thermometer in a manuscript dated 1611 (see figure 8).[45] Another scholar thought that Santorio, Galileo, Robert Fludd, and Drebbel each may have independently invented the thermometer,[46] and indeed chapter 1 has shown that independent rediscovery was not uncommon in Shakespeare's age.

The question of technological priority in thermometry is furthermore complicated because from an early but uncertain date an instrument ambiguously measuring temperature or atmospheric pressure (technically very like a device described by Hero of Alexandria) was widely used in meteorological applications in Holland and England. This device, known as a "weather glass" or "calendar glass," drew the attention of Francis Bacon, who in 1620 gave "lucid directions for its construction,"[47] while indicating it was in general use earlier.[48] This popularity continued; in 1634 a book by the English craftsman John Bate devoted a long section to variants on, uses of, and construction of weather glasses.[49]

Weather glasses were not accurate scientific measuring instruments because, not being sealed like modern bulb thermometers, they are sensitive both to temperature and barometric changes. So

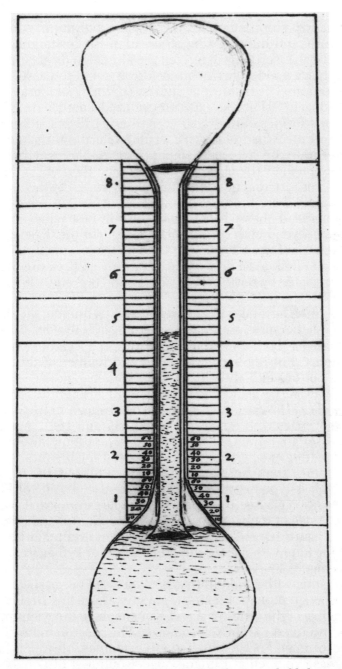

Figure 8. Telioux's thermometer illustrated in the remarkably beautiful
Bartolomeo Telioux, *Mathematica Maravigliosa* (Rome, 1611), 45. MS 8525
in La bibliothèque de l'Arsenal, Paris. By permission of Bibliothèque nationale
de France.

John Bate wrote of their confusing responses: "you may (the time of the yeare, and the following observations understandingly considered) be able certainly to foretell the alteration or uncertainty of the weather a good many hours before it come to passe," where "understandingly considered" means (in today's laboratory parlance) "fudged."[50] For this expert recognized a double functioning, in that "the formes of the weather glasses are divers, according to the fancy of the Artist, yet the use of all is one and the same: to wit to demonstrate the state and temper of the season, whether hot or cold; as to forshew the change and alteration thereof."[51] The deficiency of this instrument was eventually answered by the manufacture of narrow-bore thermometers sealed against air pressure, but these demanded finesse in glass blowing only first achieved in Italy in the later seventeenth century. The reason for the deficiency was first realized by Torricelli when in 1644 he made a practical barometer (the mathematical laws of temperature and pressure in gasses were enunciated by Boyle and by Charles in 1662 and 1787 respectively).

Before those advances in knowledge and technique, the dual action of a weather glass presented something of a mystery. To repeat, it functioned as both a weather-measuring and weather-predicting instrument, showing both "the state and temper of the season, whether hot or cold" and "to forshew the change and alteration thereof." Mystery was no problem for an English enthusiast of the weather glass, Robert Fludd. Fludd, who engaged in methodological controversies with Kepler between 1617 and 1622, was a kind of successor to John Dee in mystical aspirations, although no match for him in science.[52] Fludd adopted for his mystical purposes, from a manuscript derived from Philo of Byzantium, a weather-glass-type instrument (see figure 9).[53] In one of Fludd's many weather glasses the open receptacle is enclosed within a model of a pile of rocks "to make it more wonderful and entertaining" (see figure 10).[54] This sort of instrument eventually became a symbol for Fludd, replacing the monochord of Pythagorean tradition (see figure 11).[55]

Contrasting with Fludd in that he expressed no mystical aspirations, although perhaps seeking to mystify, Cornelius Drebbel used the principle of the weather glass as an engine to drive a number of devices intended to amuse or amaze. The most famous of these were his claimed "perpetual motion" machines, of which the best known was exhibited at Eltham Palace southeast of London from sometime before 1607.

The Europe-wide fame of Drebbel's perpetual motion machines

Figure 9. Robert Fludd's weather glass was derived from a manuscript which he claimed at least seven hundred years old. As was shown in Taylor, 1942, the manuscript was actually Bodleian ms. Digby 40, which is not nearly so old. This illustration of the manuscript is included several times among Fludd's work. It is reproduced here from Robert Fludd, *Utriusque Cosmi Majoris scilicet et Minoris Metaphysica; Physica atque Technica Historia* (Oppenheim, 1617), 31. British Library C79.d.7. By permission of the British Library.

led to speculation concerning the secret basis of their operation. No help was available from Thomas Tymme's 1612 *A Dialogue Philosophicall*, which illustrated the outer case of Drebbel's Eltham device (see figure 12), and described it as a self-driven clock, tide predictor, and astronomical calendar.[56] Tymme claimed that the operation of the device proved a geocentric cosmology, and that an intrinsic "fiery spirit" was its motive principle.[57] However, the real principle of the device was easy to guess, even by those not knowing about Drebbel's 1598 clock patent. Many did correctly guess it, including Constantyn Huygens, Marin Mersenne, Daniello Antonini, and probably Galileo. These saw that Drebbel's perpetual motion shared its motive principle with his proposed self-playing virginals and other self-driven wonders: the principle was the same as in Drebbel's more practical inventions of self-regulating ovens for bread baking or incubating chicken eggs. That principle was that

Figure 10. Robert Fludd's weather glass with a disguised mechanism, reproduced from Robert Fludd, *Integrum Morborum Mysterium* (Frankfurt, 1631), 8, from British Library 30.g.13. By permission of the British Library.

mechanical work could be derived from changes in temperature by means of the thermal expansion of gasses.[58]

Elizabethan and Jacobean literature frequently imaged perpetual motion machines as ludicrous. So Falstaff, playing at the war-weary hero, complains "I would to God my name were not so terrible to the enemy as it is—I were better to be eaten to death with a rust than to be scoured to nothing with perpetual motion" (*Henry IV, Part II* 1.2.217–21). Drebbel's actual engine is named contemptuously in Ben Jonson's Epigram 97, "On the New Motion," as

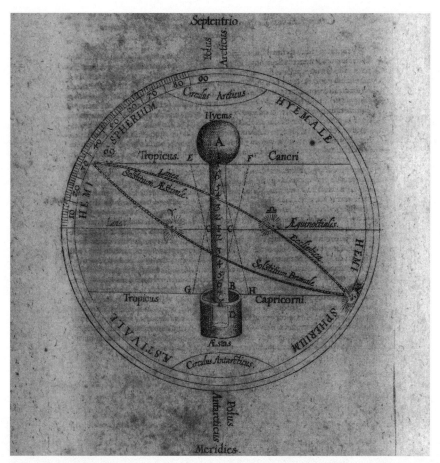

Figure 11. The weather glass as Robert Fludd's symbol of the world, reproduced from Fludd, 1631, 28. By permission of the British Library.

merely "the Eltham thing," while, near the end of Jonson's 1609 *Epicoene*, Morose exclaims in dismay:[59]

> my very house turns round with the tumult! I dwell in a
> windmill: the Perpetual Motion is here, and not at Eltham!

The Eltham device was also noted in the modish Henry Peacham's "Sights and Exhibitions in England," prefixed to *Coryats Crudities*, a cult book that was seen and facetiously praised in advance of its 1611 publication by many in Prince Henry's circle, and which was very probably known then by Shakespeare. The fame or ridicule persisted. In 1621 Henry Farley scathingly bracketed the vanities

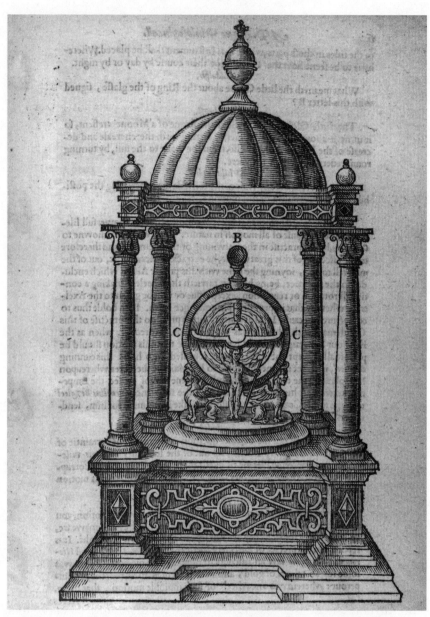

Figure 12. Thomas Tymme's illustration of Drebbel's perpetual motion
engine. Reproduced from Thomas Tymme, *A Dialogve Philosophicall*
(London, 1612), 61. British Library CUP407.kk.11. By permission of the
British Library.

of admiring "A foolish Ingin move alone, / A Morris-dance, a Puppit play," along with going "To see a strange out-landish Fowle / A quaint Baboon, an Ape, an Owle, / A dancing Beare, a Gyants Bone," and also patronizing, among other animated attractions,[60]

> A Rimers Jests, a Juglers cheats,
> A Tumbler shewing cunning feats,
> Or Players acting on the Stage,
> There goes the bounty of our Age.
>   But unto any pious motion,
>   There's little coine, and lesse devotion.

The placing of the "foolish" perpetual motion "Ingin" and other pseudoscientific curiosities alongside staged performances, especially of deceitfully moved "Puppits," recalls Ben Jonson's epigram, and his mockery elsewhere of puppets or "motions," modish collegiate ladies, and pseudosophisticated connoisseurs.

Further investigation of Drebbel's self-advertising showmanship, which proposed other uses for barometric/thermometric-actuated machines, leads to one or more tantalizing connections with *The Tempest*.

THERMOSCOPES AND A VIRGINIA SCIENTIST

After just a little more discussion of early thermometry, this next section will arrive at the starting point for my interest in atmospheric physics and *The Tempest*.

Before the skills needed for making sealed-tube thermometers were developed, other means were available for measuring temperature independently of atmospheric pressure. From an uncertain date there were instruments "lazier and more slothful" than the weather glass,[61] operating on a different principle. These were called "thermoscopes," but that same term is also sometimes used for other types of thermometer.[62] To distinguish them from others, these "lazier" instruments may be called "buoyancy thermoscopes." These consisted of a glass vessel filled with a transparent liquid, usually spirits, in which were placed a number of weighted floats distinguished from one another by shape or color, and having varying weight-to-volume ratios. The floats and their attached weights rose or fell in the fluid according to the varying density of the fluid, thus indicating temperature.[63] The response of these devices was slow, but it sufficed to measure ambient temperatures and it was even used to provide small strap-on-the-arm clinical thermometers called "tadpoles" (see figures 13 and 14).

Now, claims to what Harriot in 1588 described as the "holsome" climate of Virginia,[64] presumed to be a climate in accord with the southerly latitude, were of great importance to those who promoted the desirability of settlement there, and particularly to those who from 1606–1607 established the first English New World colony destined to endure. In fact, the Jamestown settlers did not find as mild and equable a climate as they might have hoped for when they compared the English and Virginian latitudes.[65] Perhaps not coincidentally, atmospheric phenomena play a prominent part also in

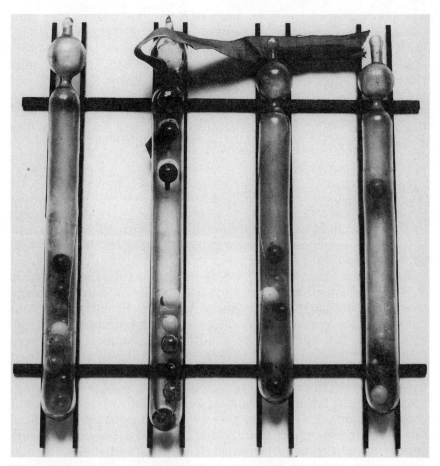

Figure 13. Florentine thermoscopes, called *infingardi,* or lazy ones, because of their slow response. Mid seventeenth century, Inv. 184 from the collections of the Institute e Museo di Storia delle Scienza, Firenze.

Figure 14. "Tadpole" thermoscopes, used as clinical thermometers by the Florentine Academy del Cimento in the mid seventeenth century. Inv. 2449, 2450 from the collections of the Instituto e Museo di Storia delle Scienza, Firenze.

The Tempest. A question of some interest is how precise the Virginian settlers, and in another sense Shakespeare himself, might have been in their approaches to climate and weather.

While on a visit to the newly excavated site of Jamestown at the end of 1995, and coincidentally just before a terrific winter storm struck, I saw three glass artifacts recently excavated in a pre–1610 context by the archaeological team of William Kelso (see figure 15).[66] These fragments of small figurines were kindly shown to me by the curator Beverly Straube, who has since then published an account of them.[67] As Beverly Straube informed me, a large collection of similar glass figurines were found in Amsterdam in an early-seventeenth-century context by Dr. Harold Henkes (see figure 16). I have since been able to see these latter, kept at the Museum Boijmans Beuningen Rotterdam, thanks to the kindness of Dr. Henkes, who has made a connection between the Dutch objects and those found at Jamestown. He has identified all of these as the glass weights attached to the floats of thermoscopes, thus suggesting that a thermoscope was used at Jamestown.[68]

Here evidence of the material culture of the Virginian settlers may have startling implications for students of *The Tempest*. For events concerning Jamestown are an acknowledged source for *The Tempest*, while newly identified facts now include the presence at Jamestown of a colonist, as Straube puts it, "interested in scientific investigations."[69]

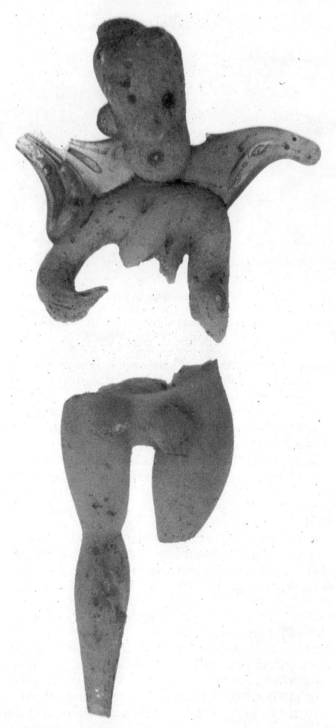

Figure 15. Glass "angel" or figurine excavated at Jamestown. By courtesy of Jamestown Rediscovery, APVA.

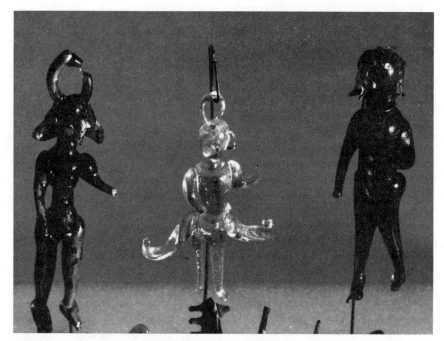

Figure 16. Glass figurines, possibly thermoscope weights, seventeenth century, excavated at Prinz Hendrikkade, Amsterdam. By courtesy of the Boijmans Van Beuningen Museum, Rotterdam.

Whoever did these scientific investigations, motivated by curiosity about the new-found world, used instruments that indicate the application of methods in the newer style, not derived from enthusiastic esoteric beliefs, but conforming with sober, careful, measurable, experiential approaches. It is fascinating to wonder if Shakespeare could have had knowledge of such a scientist at Jamestown, and if he was in consequence influenced in his handling in *The Tempest* of the theme of human knowledge.

The records and artifacts of Jamestown have not as yet provided information sufficient to determine the identity of such a proposed scientist.[70] But both historical records and the artifacts excavated do show that despite hardship and widespread ill-discipline leading to crude conditions there, the colony was not primitive in terms of material culture, and that far more than the basics of life were enjoyed by some settlers.[71]

About eighty percent of the names of settlers in Virginia between 1606 and 1608 are known.[72] Of these one in particular may possibly have been a gentleman scientist. This was George Percy, the youngest brother of the "wizard" Earl of Northumberland.[73] Percy filled several prominent offices at Jamestown between his arrival with the first sailing of 1606/1607 and his departure in 1612. During 1607–1608 he kept a (now lost) journal of the events of the first voyage and the early colony. This was later partly published in *Purchas his Pilgrimes*.[74] Philip Barbour comments that it is "regrettable that Percy's writings were so manhandled by Purchas," for valuable "ethnological detail" was likely lost.[75] I, of course, wonder what else was lost.

What Purchas did publish includes Percy's description of the West Indian climate ("wee lost none but Edward Brookes Gentleman, whose fat melted within him by the great heat and drought of the Countrey"), and of the many subsequent deaths in early Virginia, including one of a settler "starved to death with cold."[76] These and others of Purchas's extracts show in general Percy's intelligent curiosity about the New World's climate, natural history, and people.

Accounts of money paid in England by the wizard Earl to supply his younger brother George Percy at Jamestown show mainly the costs of sumptuary food and clothing, and of trading goods.[77] But one entry shows an outgoing of over 67 pounds paid to "Sondrie other persons, for sondrie provicons, necess. and readie monie by them delivered to the said Mr George Percye in Virginia and repaid here in England by his Lo";[78] could some of this have been for a scientific instrument? The likelihood of this is enhanced if D. B. Quinn's well-reasoned beliefs are accepted that Percy was briefed by Thomas Harriot before he went to Virginia; that Harriot personally oversaw (on behalf of the Earl imprisoned in the Tower following the Gunpowder Plot) the payments made for Percy's provisions while he was in Virginia; that Harriot may have encouraged Percy's journal writing and read it; and that "When Percy returned in 1612 the two men [he and Harriot] are likely to have reinforced each other's knowledge of the North American scene." Quinn concludes that "We may see George Percy, though still rather dimly from the existing evidence, as a significant continuing link between Harriot and the early settlement of Virginia in which he had been so important as a precursor."[79]

Given his interests and contacts, Harriot was likely to have known that one or more men "starved to death with cold" in early Jamestown, and that Percy, who gave up the governorship, had to resume it again after a new appointment, Lord de la Ware, left Jamestown after less than a year (in March 1611) because the climate disagreed with him.[80] If so, Harriot would have been surprised, and been led to doubt his earlier assessment of the Virginia climate (which had been based on the exceptionally mild winter he had passed there).[81] As has been argued in chapter 2, a surprised or doubting Harriot would have investigated if at all possible. And, as shown for instance in his pioneering optical, astronomical, and cartographical work (involving improvements to telescopes and other instruments), Harriot was both an extremely ingenious and rigorous instrumental scientist, and an extraordinarily "persistent and accurate" empirical observer.[82] If an accurate method of measuring Virginian climatic conditions were available, Harriot was among the most likely of men to encourage its use; the speculation that George Percy (the brother, in Virginia, of Harriot's patron) might have been his agent in this is therefore not very wild.

One further clue possibly indicating George Percy's interest in science is a record dated 18 August 1607 mentioning a recent letter from Percy in Virginia to the English scientist Walter Warner.[83] Warner was in the service of the Earl of Northumberland, with "a special responsibility for the care of" the latter's (largely scientific) books.[84]

These hints together do not make a firm case for George Percy as an amateur scientist or user of a thermoscope, and there may have been another as-yet-unidentified practitioner of scientific observation at Jamestown.[85] There was a precedent, as Raleigh's 1585 Virginian ventures based at Roanoke had included two scientists, Thomas Harriot and Joachim Gans. The latter was a mineralogist from Prague who had a brother who was a mathematician and astronomer with a wide European reputation.[86] In its first years the Jamestown settlement also included eight medical men,[87] and a group of Germans who conducted experimental glass manufactures during 1608–1609.[88]

There are, on the basis of the evidence just presented, and also on the basis of additional archaeological material to be discussed in chapter 5, indications of the presence of scientific interests in early Jamestown.[89] If there was a proto-scientist there, Shakespeare may well have known this, as he was connected through friendship with many Virginia promoters.[90] That in turn might have partly inspired the creation of a Prospero more sober and thoughtful and less mystical than the character found in many readings of *The Tempest*.[91]

By way of contrast, the next part of this chapter will consider a real-life model for the more usual conceptions of Prospero as an adept, or as an artist, showman, wonder-provoker, manipulator, illusion-maker, or as a man of the theater. Strangely, the study made so far of early modern instrumental science will provide an excellent basis for doing this.

DREBBEL AGAIN, AND WIDER TRAVELS

Several writers on Cornelius Drebbel have suggested in effect that his "social role" as "one who had provided amusement for the king" was reflected in his supposed placement, in the 1625 funeral procession for King James, "between Baston le Peer, the dauncer, under officers of the Mynte, Actors and Comedians."[92] This attractive theory, however, is based on an error in the interpretation of historical records, which probably arose from misleading line breaks in a standard printed reference work on Jacobean ceremonial processions.[93] Not as transcribed there, but in the original manuscript record of James's funeral procession (PRO SP 16/2/ fol.61, in the State Papers for 7 April 1625), "Dreble ye Enginier" is not grouped with stage artistes, but is listed in a series of separate lines together with them and a whole miscellany of yeomen, grooms, housekeepers, clarks, tailors, messengers, wardrobers, and other underlings.

Yet, even if Drebbel was not neatly slotted into a social category of entertainers (if any such existed; there was no legal basis for one), there is no doubt that he practiced his own sorts of showmanship. For his public career was based on publicity; his aims were to attract celebrity, mystify rivals, and (by doing famous things in their name) gratify noble patrons. (Galileo was not wholly different in naming the moons of Jupiter that he discovered as the "Medicean Stars.")[94]

Drebbel achieved some real advances in often quite mundane technologies (including chimney design, cloth dyeing, and as we have said, bread making and chicken hatching).[95] His supposed advanced glass-working skills were not capable of producing promised telescopes enabling the reading of handwriting at seven leagues or a light-gathering mirror allowing reading at night and illumination of a space thirty paces around,[96] but he did produce various impressive optical toys.[97] In addition, Drebbel encouraged or allowed to be spread incredible rumors of his technical achievements (for instance, that at age seventeen he had devised a practical submarine), and claimed knowledge of numerous "secrets of nature."[98] Some achievements claimed for him were based on (for then) impossibilities, for instance that he could make an "artificial sun that would be always lit, day and night" or a central "artificial sun, that is to say perpetual fire" to heat all the houses of London.[99] Such proposals, intended to win credulous financial backers (dot-commers), made for a rocky career containing one notably precarious adventure.

The Holy Roman Emperor Rudolf II asked Drebbel to come to Prague to re-create his perpetual motion and pursue further researches. Drebbel arrived in October 1610, following the footsteps of the likes of Giodorno Bruno and Rudolf's English magi John Dee and Dee's roguish medium Kelly.[100] In fact the reclusive Rudolf was besotted with all the arts and sciences; his expensive obsessions included wonders of natural history, clockmaking, cabbala, magic, music, musical instruments, painting, gems, astrology, alchemy, medicine, and ciphers.[101] Since 1600 Rudolf had been sequestered in his Prague castle, which was filled with books, rarities, artworks, scholars, magi, artists, and artisans.[102] More or less in consequence of this, by 1608 Rudolf had been usurped of his Austrian, Hungarian, and Moravian possessions by an ambitious and more hard-headed younger brother, Mathias. In May 1611 the Archduke Mathias also replaced his brother as King of Bohemia, and so effectively deposed him as the Emperor. This outcome was indeed predicted in newsletters sent home to England by Sir Henry Wotton. The similarities of the situation Wotton reported to that prefacing *The Tempest* are very great. Thus Ambassador Wotton wrote in March 1608 and November 1609: "Our news of Austria inclineth to some notable divisions between the Emperor and his brother Mattias" and then "I am forced to end in the contemplation of a Prince, highest in name and least in virtue, punished from heaven most justly by the fatal lethargy of his own affairs."[103] So, as Robert Grudin has suggested, and E. H. Gombrich and Barbara Mowat had earlier hinted, Rudolf's history in Prague would have provided a model for Prospero's history in Milan, and been known in time to inspire *The Tempest*.[104]

Moreover, according to Grudin, Rudolf was addicted to mystery, intrigue, and "occult means for enlarging personal power," and once having been usurped he sought "various stratagems for regaining power and revenging himself upon his brother" which involved his occult advisors.[105] Prominent among the latter was Drebbel, who had been maintained in some splendor.[106] The contrastingly ill-paid (or irregularly paid) Imperial mathematician Johannes Kepler, in a very different sort of service to Rudolf, expressed grave doubts about Drebbel's abilities.[107] He was right, for Drebbel and his ilk failed to reinstate Rudolf, who instead died soon after.

The sequel was sad for Drebbel. In 1612 he was stripped by the usurping younger brother Mathias of all the property and commandeered luster of his glory. Even worse nearly befell him, as Drebbel's two sons-in-law told the French savant de Peiresc (as recorded in manuscripts at Carpentras):[108]

> When the archduke Mathias surprised Vienna and captured the Emperor his brother, he made prisoner all those who were of the Council of the Emperor, and among others Drebbel, whose house was pillaged and all his furnaces and instruments broken. The house was returned to Cardinal Clesel, to whom it had belonged. The archduke condemned all the Council to death and had the scaffold for their beheading erected in a place in front of the Palace of the Emperor. He, seeing the preparations from the window of his room, asked his guards why that was done, and having learnt that this was to kill Drebbel was greatly afflicted. The archduke coming to visit him and finding him so sad, asked what was the cause of his extraordinary affliction and was answered that this was because he was going to put to death the most important person in the world.

Mathias then released Drebbel, and asked him to join his own service. Having had enough of the continental high life, Drebbel argued that due to his being, as it were, on loan from the King of England he was bound to go back to him. This was backed up by letters requesting his return, which he had urgently and covertly solicited from England. And so, in 1612, Drebbel with his family and an assistant traveled back to England, with a typically empty Imperial promise of a honorarium of two thousand crowns.

This evidently did not materialize, for upon arriving in London Drebbel ran across an old familiar enemy, poverty.[109] He petitioned his erstwhile patron Prince Henry to persuade Lord Treasurer Salisbury to allow him to conduct a lottery for his own benefit, but in vain. Soon after, following the Prince's death, Drebbel wrote a beseeching letter in Latin to King James, containing typical wild proposals, which deserves quotation at some length:[110]

> Some years ago, sublime and mighty King, I have journeyed to Prague in order to make for your Majesty an apparatus according to that which your Majesty had seen, while with the approval and promise of your Majesty to the exalted [P]rince Henry, of blessed memory, the solemn promise being (myself taking this very much to heart) that I should return within six months. But His Imperial Majesty found much unusual pleasure in my inventions, of which he had seen an example so that in such a short time I could not detach myself from him but he retained me up to the time of his death. Meanwhile the Emperor's death came

to the ears of Prince Henry (whose memory can never be fully valued). Therefore I urged him earnestly by letter to ensure that I should return to him. In consequence I besought Emperor Mathias urgently that he would give me permission so that I could travel back to Great Britain but he would not grant my request, alleging that he had need of my help in other things, and under no circumstances would he let me leave his court, unless I obtained from Prince Henry, of blessed memory, a warrant. Finally, I received this, and gave this letter to his Imperial Majesty to read, and he, after reading it, gave me permission to return home, while he made me happy with a favourable present of money for my journey. While this was happening I heard to my unbelievable grief and sorrow of the death of Prince Henry. Therefore, because I have always burned, and still burn, with a great desire to serve your gracious Majesty and to divert you with my inventions, I offer you with humble respect, again with humility, my services and achievements in the highest expectation that your Majesty will derive much exceptional pleasure from them. Of these things I shall here make brief mention.

In the first place I have a means whereby all forms of clockwork are given a continual motion, so that this is self regulating and automatic, or to explain more clearly—if the hour hand is about two or three hours late in the morning or evening—when the sun shines it will go back to the true hour of the day and even to the minute, of which invention Emperor Rudolf has seen an example.

Secondly, I can make an instrument by which letters can be read at a distance of an English mile, and I do not doubt that your Majesty . . . will support me with money, so that I may be in a position to construct something so large that by this it will be possible to read letters at a distance of about 5, 6, or 7 miles, the letters being no bigger than they usually need be. . . .

Thirdly I have the skill to construct all kinds of musical instruments which will play themselves by the rays of the sun, and then a very pleasant sound will be heard, of which invention your Majesty has seen only a very incomplete example, that I, as I say, had determined to bring to a more completed condition, namely with an arrangement whereby when the sun shines the curtains and doors of the said instrument would open of their own accord and a beautiful music would be heard, after which when the sun was hidden behind the clouds, curtains and doors would close themselves again. In addition I had resolved to connect a fountain to this musical instrument (usually called the "virginals") from which continuous jets of water would come, and from which when the sun shines, a hundred various rivulets would appear—all very pretty to be seen. Furthermore, Neptune would appear from a grotto of rocks accompanied by Tritons and sea-goddesses, bathing in the water which surrounds the altar of Neptune. Furthermore I shall display a glass filled with water which in a fixed period flows backwards and forwards like the sea, running to and fro in about 40 minutes each 24 hours, with such perfection that from the rise and fall of the water one can estimate the hours and minutes of the day, it being completely self-regulating. But if the sun is over-clouded or has sunk, then the fountains cease to flow, except the two first named which would continue to play. And Neptune would retire into the grotto of rocks accompanied by his following as he sadly laments the absence and the loss of the splendour of the sun. Moreover, Phoebus appears from the clouds, playing on his zither, and seated on his coach with his four galloping horses, and it shall seem as if these are floating on their wings in the air, and the wheels of the said coach shall turn. And all this shall be accomplished by the rays of the sun alone, without any help. In case your Majesty might wish to feast your eyes for a moment on these ingenious movements when the whole sky is clouded, then you will nevertheless be able to do this by simply touching a small glass vessel with a warm hand. If I might be so bold—as most courtiers usually are—to bring to your Majesty's remembrance the promise which you have earlier graciously made to me [etc.] . . . To conclude, oh King, I would respectfully advise Your Majesty that you will have already appreciated how much inconvenience and loss I have suffered by the death of Prince Henry when I left the position of paid servant of His Imperial Majesty.

The proposed decorative antics of Neptune and company are consistent with Drebbel's association with Balthasar Gerbier d'Ouvilly, who was to become responsible for the Duke of Buckingham's sumptuous theatrical entertainments.[111] Some scholars have suggested that earlier Drebbel himself designed stage or scenic effects.[112]

However, Drebbel's proposed warmth-animated musical instruments may not have amused as promised. They clearly shared their motors with his ovens and his "perpetual motion" machines. For thermodynamic reasons it is far easier to construct a temperature-driven flue regulator for a hot oven than to extract power from small fluctuations in ambient temperature or air pressure. So it may be doubted if many of Drebbel's gadgets worked for long, or worked at all.

But one low-friction pneumatic device, a lunette-shaped or curved glass tube in which a liquid was seen to rise and fall with no apparent cause except time itself, was likely to have been actualized successfully by Drebbel. Diagrams of its construction are included in the de Peiresc manuscripts at Carpentras.[113] This same *"mouement perpetuel"* was also described and properly analyzed in two letters of Antonini to Galileo in February 1612; through the subsequent century Drebbel's often-remarked device was repeatedly re-analyzed and rediscovered to be an ingenious variation of the familiar weather glass type of barometer-thermometer, despite claims that it was a magical tidal predictor.[114] Here a possible confusion arises between the identities of Drebbel and of Thomas Harriot himself: an anonymous Roman Catholic account of the wizard Earl of Northumberland's scientific associates claimed that "Mr Heriot" had "presented Queene Anne with a viol of water which ebbed and flowed at the same time as the Thames."[115] Harriot of course connects directly to the Virginian enterprise, but I have come across no definite connection between that New World venture and Drebbel, except for the information given to de Peiresc that Drebbel was an extreme tobacco addict.[116]

It is interesting to ask how much Shakespeare might have known of the linked matters adumbrated here, concerning Virginian science, the usurpation of a European would-be princely magus by a younger brother, and a conjurer/showman/engineer concerned with weather magic. Before writing *The Tempest* Shakespeare certainly knew some of Virginia's chief promoters; it is evident he had access to private Virginian communications in Strachey's unpublished letter. The reputation of Rudolf II was universal, and the reputations of both Cornelius Drebbel and King James's favorite mountebank magician Hocus Pocus were often noted in literary and theatrical London (both are alluded to in Ben Jonson's writing).[117] Moreover, Rudolf II's woes were known in English governmental circles and could have been transmitted to Shakespeare before 1611 through either Hugh Holland, Thomas Coryate, or John Donne, so that "Shakespeare had ample opportunity to give birth to a Rudolfian Prospero."[118]

So part of Shakespeare's inspiration for the story of Prospero could have come from quite *outré* parts of the contemporary European scene, involving modish mystics or mystical impostors. The modish and *outré* was often treated satirically by Shakespeare: so the world-defying philosophical intentions of the young adepts of *Love's Labour's Lost* or Lucentio at the start of *The Taming of the Shrew* are merely spoofed, and the Italian-leaning tastes of an English artistic avant-garde with regard to statues are more subtly mocked in *The Winter's Tale*.[119] However, there is no explicit satire attached to the fact that the structure and language of *The Tempest* reverberate with images and the vocabularies of astrology, natural magic, and alchemy. To the contrary, a notion that Shakespeare may have had no reservations at all about Prospero's magic may seem implicit in Barbara Traister's comments that the perfect magus Prospero stands apart from all earlier English stage magicians because his magic is fully successful. But Traister adds that Prospero "makes no mistakes as a magician, has no flaws in his magic that might explain why magic does not make him forever omnipotent."[120] Whether or not Traister's claim that Prospero's success derives from his great self-knowledge and self-control is to be accepted, her other remarks undoubtedly leave a riddle and imply a question of great importance. This is the question of why Prospero eschews or abjures the permanent omnipotence seemingly within his grasp; this question, or a question of why omnipotence in general should be restrained, will be borne in mind through the remainder of this book.

However, the matters just discussed do not concern magicians alone, for they reveal possibilities of connections between Shakespeare's Prospero and a genuine scientific practitioner in contemporary Virginia, as well as between Prospero and European mystical adepts, or even showmen/conjurers like Hocus Pocus. These varied possibilities for the image and origins of Prospero will be found in the following chapters to be enclosed within the complex construction of the magus of *The Tempest*, and the dynamic between them will be traced.

5

"The Strong Necessity of Time"

—Antony and Cleopatra

THE TEMPEST AND TIME PRESSURES

A NEWLY PRECISE CONSIDERATION OF TIME WAS CRUCIAL IN THE DEVEL-
opment of early modern science.[1] Time also plays a prominent part
in *The Tempest*, in several different ways. To explore a possible conjunction of these facts, it is worth investigating which (if any) new
ideas about time appeared in the Renaissance, and whether Shakespeare expressed or implied awareness of any such ideas.

I will begin by considering if there were novel outlooks in Shakespeare's age on the time allotted for work, because "work" in relation to *The Tempest* will be a major theme of the concluding
chapter 7 of this study. Did a rising "puritan work ethic" of late-
sixteenth- and seventeenth-century England produce a new kind
of focus on time? The comical laziness of the always-indigent and
always time-defying Falstaff,[2] and the disastrous consequences of
Milton's industrious Adam and Eve failing in punctuality for their
lunch appointment (*Paradise Lost* 7.839–61), might tempt one to
think that by then beliefs were held that "time is money," and that
"the Devil makes work for idle hands." However, these do not seem
to have been proverbs of Shakespeare's age.[3]

It is certainly true that by the time of *The Tempest* idleness was
seen as sinful and socially dangerous, but that was not a new view,
nor one held exclusively by those avid for reformed religion. Idleness
had been condemned in many orthodox and mainstream Elizabethan texts such as the official "Homilie against Idlenesse," the poor
laws, conduct books, and social-political commentaries. Early Jacobean men of affairs with no puritan leanings also favored industriousness. For instance, in a 1608 letter from Virginia, Captain John
Smith despised the would-be-gentlemen of the settlement whose
unwillingness to stir themselves would soon help bring Jamestown to
the point of collapse; Smith eagerly encouraged the London Virginia

Company to send instead settlers possessing, and willing to use, practical skills.[4] But, despite this, there was no strongly marked coupling in Shakespeare's lifetime between ideals of industriousness and such practical behaviors as good time-management, punctuality, or steady assiduousness. Productivity did not then generally demand adherence to fixed working hours extending throughout the year. Appointment-keeping for business purposes was also generally very loose until well after Shakespeare's time.[5]

So, even if, as Andrew Gurr argues, *The Tempest* presents an "Industrious Ariel and Idle Caliban" modeled on a virtuous apprentice and unworthy waged household servant respectively,[6] this distinction may not have much to say about the treatment of time in the play. Indeed, Prospero assumes that Ariel and Caliban are both constantly at his disposal, permanently, as it were, "on call" (so Ariel is frequently summoned and Caliban grumbles he is not given time to eat his dinner).

In the social reality of Shakespeare's London as well, apprentices and household servants alike were expected to be available for any kind of task (however menial) at any time of day or night, and sometimes quite unreasonably so.[7] Although some early modern trades, including seafaring, required timekeeping for changes of shifts, the concept of the "working hours" of a "working day" came mainly with mass industrialization, well after Shakespeare's age. So a newly arising work ethic was not likely to have been highly relevant to the obsession with time in *The Tempest*.

THE TEMPEST AND "REAL TIME"

Nevertheless, if not to reflect a new work ethic, then for another reason or reasons, *The Tempest* dramatizes heavy pressures placed upon Ariel to perform certain specified tasks within the short span of one late afternoon. One reason, which will be discussed shortly, may be to emphasize certain limitations placed upon Prospero's "art" or "project." Another may be to help foreground the play's peculiarly exact observance of the unity of time.

As has often been noted, the play's dramatic action occupies a segment of time hardly any greater than its staged running time. The passage of time indeed becomes an obtrusive factor in *The Tempest* because the play text includes a running commentary on the passing time unique in Shakespeare. When asked "What is the time o' th' day?" near the play's start, Ariel replies "Past the mid season." This rough estimate is more accurately adjusted in Prospero's: "At least two glasses. The time 'twixt six and now / Must by us both be spent most preciously" (1.2.240–2). Toward the play's end, as his "project gather[s] to a head," Prospero again seeks a time check from Ariel in "How's the day?" and receives the reply "On the sixth hour" (5.1.1–4). And then, their senses just recovered, several of the play's characters exclaim about the amazing things that happened within a mere three hours (5.1.138, 5.1.189, 5.1.226), further reinforcing an audience's awareness of the brief duration of the whole action.

Moreover, if seen on the Globe stage in an afternoon performance, the often-commented-upon stage time of *The Tempest* would have nearly coincided with the actual diurnal time during the play's running. To borrow another expression of computer-engineering, the play was programmed to run in "real time." This in effect made an unusual meta-theatrical gesture; by eliminating the convention that stage time is *not* the same as real time, the temporal structure of *The Tempest* perhaps partly dissolved the distance between the play's fantastic action and the "real lives" of its first spectators.[8]

SHAKESPEARE'S IDEAS OF TIME

Come what come may,
Time and the hour runs through the roughest day.

—Macbeth

Before further examining the peculiar treatment of temporality in *The Tempest* it will be useful to review some of the leading studies of Shakespeare's representations of time, or his expressed or implied ideas about it.

Several such studies have suggested that Shakespeare reflects multiple kinds of time. A book by Frederick Turner, for instance, finds nine "aspects" of time reflected by Shakespeare,[9] which is a larger number than is found in rival research.[10] Also unusually, Turner does not claim that any of these nine aspects were newly "discovered" or formed as concepts in the Renaissance.[11] Far more often among critics, allegedly innovatory ideas about time have been traced in Shakespeare's period to supposed Renaissance shifts of outlook on one or more of history, fate, providence, human possibilities, or the purposes of life.[12] For instance, for D. L. Peterson time as "merely the measure of transience" is an "old Augustinian view" that is superseded by a "twofold conception of time that is new in the Renaissance," in which time is either duration or positive opportunity.[13] Conversely with regard to transience and opportunity, David Scott Kastan claims that: "Through lenses

ground by the reformation and the Copernican revolution, time appears more as the measure of movement toward dissolution than
as the medium in which God's creatures fulfill their potentiality."[14]

Other studies allege there was a new seventeenth-century conception of "universal" time running uniformly through all places at
once. Such a conception is often associated with the work of Isaac
Newton as a physicist, or sometimes as a biblical and historical
chronologer.[15] So, when lecturing on *The Tempest*, Northrop Frye
suggested that Newtonian time has nothing to do with Shakespeare: "Thinking in terms of time and space . . . is post-Newtonian
rather than Shakespearean."[16] This distinction is at least partly be-
lied by several close historical studies of concepts of time which
find that supposed "Newtonian" ideas of universal time were actually derived before, or even long before, Newton.[17] Yet I would
partly agree with Frye insofar as I find no sign in *The Tempest* of
later-made subtle distinctions such as those between concepts of
the temporal moments as either mathematical points on a line
charting a universal flowing stream, or as sets of simultaneous
events not requiring a uniform flow (Newton versus Leibniz).[18]

This, however, does not mean that a substratum of "uniform"
time is not crucial in the play; nor does it mean that simultaneity is
not important in it also. Barbara Mowat has noted that "Prospero's
sudden recollection of Caliban's conspiracy during the wedding
masque . . . [creates] for us the sense that disparate actions are oc-
curring in the play simultaneously."[19] Indeed, in this and other instances the distinctive dramaturgy of *The Tempest* unmistakably
presents time as a single stream running beneath diverse se-
quences and actions. In fact *The Tempest* multiply presents both
the isolation of some outcomes from other streams of events, and
the consequences of some prior events in particular outcomes.
That is to say, the dramatic construction of *The Tempest* images
both of the two counterbalancing factors, causality and contingency. Here I mean "contingency" in the sense of undetermined
fortuitousness, as it is defined in *OED* II.3,[20] or possibly (as will be
later discussed) as it is imaged in the long-awaited "accident most
strange" mentioned in 1.2.179 by Prospero.

In relation to Shakespeare's concerns, and also to those of science,
perhaps too much exclusive emphasis has been placed on time as
"the medium of cause and effect." This, Turner's sixth "aspect" of
Shakespearian time,[21] connects with only one side of the causality/
contingency pair. It is the aspect of time that has often been held to
be the only one of importance for scientific investigation and explanation, but in fact an awareness of the possibility of temporal contin-

gency is also crucially important for science. For one thing, a measured appreciation of *un*connectedness allows science at particular times to understand that it can within the current "state-of-the-art" address some questions satisfactorily, but must defer from addressing others.[22] For another, science has often been most successful in finding satisfying explanations of phenomena when limiting circumstances exist, or can be contrived, that allow the phenomena in question to be isolated (in terms of cause and effect) from other simultaneous phenomena which then can be disregarded or discounted in terms of causal determination of outcomes.[23]

In accord with this last point, the dramatic structure of *The Tempest* (in which various plot threads are run out, and not tied together until the end) depends vitally on the possibility of chains of events evolving simultaneously yet unconnectedly or disjointly. Just as in a laboratory, or at a well-managed experimental station, the isolation of parallel experiments on Prospero's island is carefully managed. Parallel, artificially devised, testing ordeals (for example concurrent temptations to seize power or usurp) are kept strictly apart, as if to test for any diverging results. As in a laboratory, so on the island, supervision is used and precautions are employed to contain or protect against explosive mishaps. As in a laboratory also, much of what is learned in *The Tempest* requires a keen double awareness of the counterbalancing aspects of time involved in causality and contingency.[24] This double awareness leads to two ethical perspectives crucial for *The Tempest*. One is that even in controlled conditions outcomes are partly determined by human volitional acts; this implies that free agents must always take responsibility for the effects of their actions or inactions. The other is that there is always a possibility of the disjunction of some outcomes from controlling causative acts; this suggests that any claim to magical omnipotence is a fantasy, and possibly a dangerous delusion.

MYSTICAL *KAIROS* AND RATIONAL TIME

Yet another range of Renaissance notions about time may have had a bearing when dramatized repetitions in Shakespeare's plays allowed re-enactments of the past, in some cases permitting reversals of past errors.

It has been argued that in the sixteenth and seventeenth centuries formerly optimistically viewed cyclical or circular models of time were becoming more frequently related to mutability or decay, and so were viewed more pessimistically.[25] But there was still available an earlier concept of certain unique moments of repetition in time, or possibly of momentary timelessness, which might offer special opportunities for spiritual refreshment or advancement.[26] Such singularities of time (neither periodic nor regular) were associated with the Greek god *Kairos*, as opposed to *Chronos*.[27] I have argued that *The Winter's Tale* crucially portrays precisely such singular moments, as for example when Leontes is given a second chance to woo his wife.[28] Such moments are, however, rare and unusual; *The Winter's Tale* quite clearly portrays irreversible losses in the aging process and in the deaths of Mamillius and Antigonus.

On further consideration I would revise my former views of the overarching importance of time as *Kairos* for *The Tempest* (even though *Kairos* is closely associated with the Latin *tempestivitas*). For, in *The Tempest*, when opportunities are offered for re-enactment—as when Antonio has a second chance to engage (or not engage) in usurpation, or Gonzalo has a second chance to calumniate (or not) the Boatswain, or Caliban can use his regained "freedom"—typically worse rather than better choices for re-enactment are taken.[29]

The great predicament of the play in terms of the use of time's gift of an opportune moment lies, however, in the decision Prospero has to make about the use of what he calls the "zenith" of his "fortunes" (1.2.182–84). In the moment of the reunification in a testing wilderness of all the important persons of his former life, a chance for some sort of re-enactment does arise, but, as will be argued in the next chapters, the choices that Prospero makes in his moment of opportunity may have a more natural and less a mystical complexion than I had previously supposed.

Far from being mystical, the obsessive treatment of time in *The Tempest* seems to accord with an Aristotelian emphasis on time being (using G. J. Whitrow's word) "fundamental" to all sane thinking.[30] It is true that Shakespeare portrays the island sojourners as hardly believing that only three hours have passed there, and Shakespeare also generally appreciated that inner perceptions of the duration of time are subjective (as is humorously pointed out in *As You Like It*, 3.2.301–24). It might be further conceded that some aspects of Shakespeare's plays suggest that "in human relationships to see the person rather than the thing is to see something which is not entirely of the temporal world, something not completely limited by the confines of time."[31] But such qualifications only modulate, and do not deny, the centrality for Shakespeare of temporal reality. For instance, he typically portrayed the consequences of the disregard of time in the tones of Richard II's chagrined "I wasted time, and now doth time waste me" (5.5.49), and even comically time-defying Falstaff[32] becomes a victim of time (and the changing times) when he dies or fades away "at the turning o' th' tide."[33]

Time-denying approaches to history were also becoming extinct in the late sixteenth century; as C. A. Patrides put it, historians tended to move from "the supernatural to the natural, from the universe to the nation or to the principality or to the city, and finally as hagiographies were displaced by biographies — to individual members of the *civitas terrena*."[34] Despite some artistic time-condensation and deliberate anachronism, Shakespeare's history plays and many of his tragic dramas also reflect such a movement.

Perhaps in respect of this students of Shakespeare should be wary of a nonchalant disregard for temporal sequence. A recent not untypical monograph considering *The Tempest* in relation to New World encounters notes and frankly accepts that its "analysis is not concerned with the play as a reflection of historical events in Virginia."[35] Why this is acceptable is not explained, while much is made of historical events in an oddly anachronic way. Thus Columbus encountering the native people of Hispaniola in the 1490s and the economics of Virginian tobacco plantations that began (well) post–1616, and various historical points in between, are joined seamlessly and seem equally to have a bearing on the "discourses" governing a 1590–95 poem (*The Faerie Queene*) and Shakespeare's 1611 *The Tempest*; moreover these "discourses" identified in the monograph touch distinctly on condemnations of twentieth-century mass consumerism, marketing directed at women or other "gullible consumers," and even a fifteenth-century non-European woman degraded as "a fashion model."[36]

In earnest of a promise to avoid such confusions and to seek the historically concrete, another archaeological discovery recently made at Jamestown will be discussed next.

TIME-TELLING IN SHAKESPEARE'S AGE AND AT CONTEMPORARY JAMESTOWN

"There's no clock in the forest" (*As You Like It* 3.2.295) *versus* "And then he drew a dial from his poke" (*As You Like It* 2.7.20).

the seventeenth century was the great age of sundialling.—Keith Thomas

How did one tell the time in Shakespeare's age? In an inquiry into this, many of the characters so far met in this study can be called as witnesses, and so can most of Shakespeare's works.

In 1578 the Emperor Rudolf II and his younger brother Mathias each bought "elaborate and precious globe-clocks" from one Georg Roll (1546–92), a guild-defying freebooting clockmaker and clock merchant. In an interesting adjunct to this story, noted by David Landes, when Rudolf learned that Roll had charged him less for his clock than he had charged the hard-headed Mathias for his identical copy, Rudolf became convinced that Mathias had been supplied with a better model, and so threw the haplessly protesting Roll into prison! After being released Roll later supplied further timekeeping devices to Rudolf II and other German nobility, no doubt ensuring that they were suitably costly.[37] Indeed Rudolf bought many other clocks from various makers, and in 1609 he sent a gift of a clock and a celestial globe to James I of England.[38] R. J. W. Evans uses the latter fact to support his view that James and Rudolf were closely similar in interests, temperaments, and outlooks; this affinity may help explain why these two monarchs borrowed from one another the famous Cornelius Drebbel, and why in 1620 James made a bid for Rudolf's former astronomer and Imperial chronologer, the mathematician Johannes Kepler.[39]

Now, as has been seen in chapter 4, Drebbel sent a begging and wildly boastful letter to King James claiming among other things to have made for Rudolf II self-correcting clocks activated by the rising or setting of the sun. These were proudly claimed to be capable of eliminating on each day accumulated time errors of "two or three hours."[40] Such appalling inaccuracy seems to have been typical of many timekeeping devices before the mid-seventeenth-century invention of a theoretical (by Galileo and Huygens) and then a practical (by Coster) pendulum clock. Before that, clocks had to be regularly readjusted astronomically.[41] It is also extremely unlikely that the mechanism Drebbel claimed to have manufactured could have done that automatically, for before (at least mechanical) computers no machines could have calculated the changing length of days.

Shakespeare referred very frequently to time-telling and its instruments. Dials, clocks, or watches are mentioned in the majority of Shakespeare's plays, as well as in *The Rape of Lucrece* and Sonnets 12, 57, 77, and 104. In addition, Shakespeare often alluded facetiously (perhaps on account of their notorious unreliability) to contemporary clocks, watches, or sundials. So in response to an absurd Falstaffian request for the time of the day, Hal proposes the use of time-telling dials as the signs for "leaping-houses" or bordellos;[42] seeking a wife is compared to acquiring an unreliable German clock;[43] the bawdy hand of the dial is placed upon the prick of noon;[44] and in *The Tempest* Gonzalo's wit is compared to a watch wound up and apt to strike later without cause (2.1.13–14).

Yet these mocking usages do not indicate that Shakespeare took time-telling lightly. In *The Tempest* especially there is a sense of time, "the hour . . . the very minute" (1.2.36–37), being a crucial factor.[45] The instruments of its measurement are also important. Near the start of the play Prospero refers to the time as "At least two glasses," implying the nautical method of time measurement by use of an hour glass. In other Shakespeare plays various public clocks, including a good number heard in the ancient worlds of Britain, Rome, or Athens before their medieval invention,[46] strike tragically, ominously, or fatally.

As just mentioned, such instruments had to be regulated in relation to astronomical movements, which was usually achieved by observing the shadow of a gnomon on a sundial. A time-telling sundial is indeed mentioned in nine of Shakespeare's plays and two of his sonnets.[47] Even for philosophical reasons "Dyalling" was an important early modern pastime.[48] In an age of travel and exploration it was also quite fashionable to carry a portable sundial like the "dial" attributed to Touchstone by Jaques in the epigraph above. Such a dial would have to be much more complex than a fixed one, of course, as it had to be adjustable with regard to latitude and orientation.

The Jamestown Rediscovery project has recently excavated a large fragment of one of these portable dials. This is in fact a fragment of more than a time-piece; it is an example of the ivory "compass dials" that were complex early modern mathematical, astronomical, and geographical instruments. Its discovery therefore offers further indication of possible scientific interests at Jamestown, although compass dials were more common than thermoscopes, and were perhaps less likely to be used in serious researches.

It is possible that the ivory dial recently excavated is the very one that Captain John Smith demonstrated to the "king" of the Pamunkey Indians in December 1607, and by this means saved his own life.[49] Smith's two accounts of this use of his "Dyall" are fascinating. The first account, dated 1608,[50] has been mentioned in relation to Caliban's education in the Introduction above. Smith's second account, published in his 1623 *The Generall History of Virginia*, is not a likely source for *The Tempest*, but is a fine evocation of the epistemological wonders of scientific and cultural encounters. Smith, having surrendered to Pamunkey warriors, and:[51]

demanding for their Captaine, they shewed him Opechankanough, King of Pamaunkee, to whom he gave a round Ivory double compass Dyall. Much they marvailed at the playing of the Fly and Needle, which they could see so plainely, and yet not touch it, because of the glasse that covered them. But when he demonstrated by that Globe-like Jewell, the roundnesse of the earth, and skies, the spheare of the Sunne, Moone, and Starres, and how the Sunne did chase the night round about the world continually; the greatnesse of the Land and Sea, the diversitie of Nations, varietie of complexions, and how we were to them Antipodes, and many other such like matters, they all stood as amazed with admiration. Notwithstanding, within an houre after they tyed him to a tree, and as many as could stand about him prepared to shoot him, but the King holding up the Compass in his hand, they all laid downe their Bowes and Arrowes, and in a triumphant manner led him to Orapaks, where he was after their manner kindly feasted, and well used.

Here Smith emphasizes the Native Americans' capacity to appreciate complex new ideas, including cultural relativity, or "the diversitie of Nations, varietie of complexions." There is no evidence of the trickery or bamboozlement of "savages" by sophisticated Europeans so often recently imagined.

There was clearly at least one "Ivory double compass Dyall" at Jamestown, whatever the particular provenance of the instrument recently excavated. The probable origin of such dials is well understood; they are a type of instrument that had been manufactured at Nuremberg since at least 1500, and widely sold. The cultural, economic, artistic, and scientific aspects of such Nuremberg dials have been closely studied by Penelope Gouk. She remarks that the complex construction of the better sorts:[52]

reveals a commitment to accuracy wherever the instrument might be used. In other words, they were the product of an age of expanding horizons and new understanding.

Thus Gouk suggests that these devices reflect an age of exploration. It should also be noted that the main practical function of such dials, to determine the local time wherever they were used, implies that time passes steadily through all places uniformly, and such an implication places this idea in pre-Newtonian Europe.

In the views of the archaeologists who excavated the partial compass dial at Jamestown, time-telling had little if any "pressing social or economic" use in the seventeenth century. And so they argue that its use would have been rather to provide an "astronomical model of the celestial sphere" in order to allow the contemplation of our earth in its cosmos,[53] and place this in the context of "an age of exploration and discovery, of scientific inquiry that is as much philosophy as it is science."[54] Yet Gouk identifies important practical secondary uses of compass dials in orientation, surveying, and astronomical observation,[55] and so the scientific uses of the Virginian example may not have been limited to speculative contemplation alone. Certainly mapmaking was an important activity in early Virginia, linked to hopes of economic gain through food production, mining, and the discovery of transportation routes.

With such material and practical historical matters borne in mind, it will next be asked to what extent time-telling is seen in *The Tempest* as a necessary concomitant to knowing the natural or unnatural causes of things.

TIME, WEATHER, AND WONDER IN *THE TEMPEST*

In Shakespeare's age weather phenomena or "meteors" were often linked to (astronomically measured) time, and indeed a functional dependence of weather on the stars was sought empirically by as serious-minded an investigator as was Kepler.[56] Partly in consequence, although disappearing banquets, mysterious music, mistake-based resurrections, and the like may have been familiar to Jacobean audiences, the conjuring of the sea-storm that initiates *The Tempest* may have occupied a special category with regard to its acceptability as a theatrical ploy.

It is worth returning briefly to claims that some scientists or technologists were able to raise sudden storms. Francis Bacon clearly was inspired by these sorts of claims when he furnished his *New Atlantis* of 1624 with "great and spacious houses where we imitate and demonstrate meteors; as snow, hail, rain, . . . thunders and lightnings,"[57] but that of course was in a fictional work. In the nonfictional writings of Bacon, among *Great works of nature for the particular use of mankind*, Bacon listed many "anticipations" borrowed from Agrippa, including "Impressing of air, and raising of tempests."[58] The term "anticipations" is important, as it implies moving events forward in time (as in *OED* 4), rather than overruling or counteracting any natural processes. Bacon's list of "anticipations" included also "Acceleration of time in maturation," "Acceleration of germination," and "Making of new species";[59] Drebbel hatching eggs in winter in thermostatically controlled incubator ovens thus would fall into Bacon's category of artificial anticipations.

Earlier Renaissance intellectuals attributed capabilities such as that of meteorological manipulation to a "natural magic" that employs only natural means and so, in the words of Paolo Rossi, produces "miracles only in the etymological sense: things worthy of admiration."[60] Cornelius Agrippa wrote that in "natural magic":[61]

> incredible miracles are often accomplished not so much by art as by nature . . . magicians are like careful explorers of nature only directing what nature has formerly prepared . . . so that these things are popularly held to be miracles when they are really no more than anticipations of natural operations; as if someone made roses flower in March or grapes ripen, or even more remarkable things such as clouds, rain, thunder . . .

Here again weather manipulation is described among "anticipations of natural operations."

An article by J. P. Conlan offers an alternative way of seeing the "unusual meteorology of *The Tempest*" as "more plausible than wondrous."[62] This article argues that in the play "Shakespeare set up an interrogation of Anglican rational storm phenomenology" concerning electrical discharges seen in masts and rigging. It continues that this phenomenology was (in 1555 by Robert Thomson and in 1589 by Richard Hakluyt) identified with Anglican rationality, as opposed to Roman Catholic superstition. Furthermore, according to Conlan, by describing as harmless Ariel's forms of Saint Elmo's Fire (1.2.197–207) *The Tempest* implicitly critiques these Anglican theories, which would have been available to Shakespeare in Eden's and Martyr's *The decades of the newe worlde*.[63] These are recondite and debatable matters, but it is refreshing to see early modern scientific theories linked to the question of possible natural causes underlying Prospero's apparent magic.

A yet more radically naturalistic way of understanding the storm in *The Tempest* and its setting in time can be highlighted by posing two questions regarding coincidence. These questions are: could there have been any conceivable naturalness for Shakespeare's contemporaries, firstly, in a story of a wild storm bringing a shipload of passengers and crew all into a safe haven, or, secondly, in a story of unexpected encounters between nationally related Europeans in a wild and remote place? Of course, put this way, a description of the chief events accompanying Prospero's "zenith" is also a description of the actual 1609–1610 experiences of the Gates and Summers party. They were indeed first shipwrecked in a hurricane without loss of life, and then saved at the last possible moment from disaster at Jamestown by the timely and improbable appearance of Lord de la Ware's relief ships on the James River. But, if these actual near-miraculous events were the model for *The Tempest*, why would they have been chosen as the basis for a play? One reason could have been to present in a patriotic way a dramatized counterpart of the providential salvation of Virginia and its new settlers. But, as has been seen in chapter 3, that salvation was by no means certain in 1611, and besides the whole European contingent in *The Tempest* finally sails home; as has been mentioned, this hardly lauds a successful settlement.

Moreover, the *Sea-Adventure* story would have been a poor basis for a play according to Aristotle's opinion that representing possible yet implausible events, such as may unusually uniquely occur, is unsuited to poetry.[64] Aristotle thought poetry should represent only general and likely truth, but Shakespeare may have intended to portray a different kind of truth when he echoed well-known, if extraordinary, actualities in the fantastic-seeming plot of *The Tempest*. Shakespeare's purpose may have been specifically to dramatize the collapse of one or more seeming miracles into the plausible. For, while Prospero's actions are at first dramatized with an intent to maximize wonder in accord with certain Renaissance aesthetic doctrines (traceable to classical sources),[65] there still may have been built into the trajectory of *The Tempest* an eventual opposite intent, deliberately to disabuse audiences of wonder and disillusion them concerning magic.[66]

THE TEMPEST AND DISILLUSIONMENT

> Be collected.
> No more amazement.
>
> (*The Tempest* 1.2.13–14)

Although the term "a coincidence" denoting a merely temporal conjunction having no causal connection was not yet in use in Shakespeare's time, its meaning was available. I may thus posit the radical hypothesis that, in order to pursue his long-awaited project, Prospero simply waited for an appropriate coincidence involving a just-strong-enough storm, and all his enemies on a ship nearby. The problem with this hypothesis, and also with its opposite, is that there is a contradiction built into the play regarding Prospero's agitation because "my zenith doth depend upon / A most auspicious star."[67] Prospero's admission to Miranda of a strong dependency on time (his "star") may seem paradoxical when placed beside his debriefing of his potent agent Ariel (1.2.194–207), his later claims to having "raised the tempest" (5.1.6), and especially his soliloquy on the "so potent art" he is about to abjure. Prospero says that, with the "aid" of "demi-puppets," he has:

> bedimmed
> The noontide sun, called forth the mutinous winds,
> And 'twixt the green sea and the azured vault
> Set roaring war—to the dread rattling thunder
> Have I given fire, and rifted Jove's stout oak
> With his own bolt; the strong-based promontory
> Have I made shake, and by the spurs plucked up
> The pine and cedar . . .
>
> (5.1.41–48)

along with doing even wilder necromantic work. And yet again, Prospero tells Miranda of his reliance on an "accident most strange" and "bountiful Fortune" when she, with her long experience of him, simply assumes that his powers are equal to "raising this sea-storm" (1.2.178–79). Which is the truth: does Prospero have the power to raise an earthshaking storm at will, or is he dependent for his enemy-gathering storms on the accidents of time and the bounty of fortune?[68]

It was a common, if waning, belief of Shakespeare's age that the godly might obtain through their prayers a divine intercession to change or allay bad weather or storms.[69] However, the Boatswain of *The Tempest* does not spend crucial time in prayer. He also insubordinately mocks any notion that overweening "authority" can control a wild storm. Authority itself may doubt it too; it is not known if King Alonso's unheard prayers during the play's storm are petitionary for his safety, or if they seek grace for the salvation of his uneasy soul.

The Boatswain, who believes in the efficacy of "labour" or "work" as long as there is any hope in these, knows also that work has its limits in the face of insurmountable ill-fortune. So he sees the possibility of "the mischance of the hour, if it so hap" (1.1.24–25). His outlook accords with important views of the age, in which human agency may be effective, or equally may be overwhelmed, and so strenuous efforts are justified, but not by certainties.[70] This

connects with an ancient questioning of the extent of the dominance over human freedom of either fate or providence; this has
received valuable critical treatments in relation to medieval, humanist, and Renaissance thought,[71] and to Shakespeare's ideas
about time.[72] A relevant view is seen also in the famous penultimate
section of Machiavelli's *The Prince*, which reserves some effectiveness to human efforts, but concedes an equally often overwhelming
power to "fortune."[73] For Machiavelli, fortune is a woman to be
wooed, but is not the "strumpet" or "rebel's whore" bitch-goddess
of two Shakespearian tragedies,[74] nor the source of universal tragedy as in Sir Walter Raleigh's pessimistic *History of the World*.[75]

In the light of mixed contemporary ideas about the relative efficacy of human will in the face of chance or fortune, it is difficult to
judge the meaning of Prospero's admission of his dependence upon
a "star" or "bountiful Fortune." Does he need the help of time and
fortune to raise his storm, or does he possess the powers sometimes
attributed to Renaissance magi or scientists, described in chapter
4, to raise storms at will? That is to say, what are the implied limits,
if any, of Prospero's power?

Here comparison with *The Winter's Tale* may be useful. When
Paulina animates the statue of Hermione (mimicking another traditional power of magi) she says "'Tis time. Descend. Be stone no
more" (5.3.99).[76] By mentioning a special time she adds porten-
tousness to her music and crowd-control effects, in all these seeking to maximize the wonder-evoking qualities of the moments
leading up to a perfectly secular event, a merely theatrical coup.
Yet in another sense Paulina's "'Tis time" can be interpreted not
just as deliberate mystification, but also as correct, for it can be supposed that she has sensed that the precise moment has arrived that
will allow Leontes' inward realignment.

This interpretation provides a natural rather than mystical foundation for the above-mentioned concept of tempestuous time or
Kairos, which concerns rare moments allowing weighty human
changes. Time fit for such change or self-transcendence is in biblical or classical contexts often identified as a God-given "season" (is
this why Ariel says the time at *The Tempest*'s outset is "Past the
mid season"?). But in *The Tempest*, as in many other Renaissance
contexts, time-as-opportunity is often conversely represented as
enabling an opportunism that serves egotistical, villainous, vindic-
tive, expedient, or deceitful purposes.[77] It has already been pointed
out that *The Tempest* presents repeated images of those who would
misuse or abuse opportunities.[78] Correspondingly, words concerning time often reference opportunism. So even virtuous Miranda

grasps that fratricide, infanticide, and regicide are the likely outcome of an opportune political "hour" (1.2.138–39). According to
Antonio, almost all the Italian courtiers will accede to the plot described in Ariel's warning song wherein "*Open-eyed conspiracy /
His time doth take* (2.1.306–7); they will all "tell the clock to any
business that / We say befits the hour" (2.1.294–95). Caliban likewise tries to warn his confederates how crucial it is that they do not
delay and "lose our time" (4.1.246), while Prospero, referring to
this "foul conspiracy," says the "minute of their plot / Is almost
come" (4.1.139–42).

In all these instances, words in *The Tempest* immediately concerning time ("hour," "clock," "time," "minute") refer to open-
eyed conspiracies and murderous plots. This accords with the opinion of many critics that this play tends toward a disenchantment
with all that magic, or time, or the times had to offer. W. H. Auden,
for instance, alleged that *The Tempest* "ends much more sourly"
than *Pericles*, *Cymbeline*, and *The Winter's Tale*, and identifies a
"world of difference" between Cymbeline's "Pardon's the word to
all" and Prospero's:

> For you, most wicked sir, whom to call brother
> Would even infect my mouth, I do forgive
> Thy rankest fault, all of them, and require
> My dukedom of thee, which perforce I know
> Thou must restore.

> (5.1.132–36)

Here Prospero seems still embittered ("all of them") and is surely
menacing ("perforce I know / Thou must"); here and in general
Auden senses a deficiency of symbolic musical "harmony and con-
cord" at the end of the play.[79]

My own impressions are not so negative as Auden's in response
to the seeming lack of harmonious universal solutions at the end of
The Tempest when compared with the transcendental endings of
other Shakespearian Romances. Such a lack may even be positive.
I thus tend to accept David Scott Kastan's view that *The Tempest*:[80]

> is the great Renaissance *comedy* of lost illusions. Certainly limits are
> discovered and exposed . . . but knowledge of these limits does not im-
> press us with the sense of irretrievable loss or desolating waste that
> tragedy imposes. Here loss gives way to gain; the "lost illusions" make
> possible the discovery of truth.

Kastan adds that this truth is primarily "the truth of a flawed humanity that can be redeemed not by power but by prayer," and this

may well be so, as Thomas McAlindon has just argued in detail.[81] But discoveries of other sorts of truth may be referenced in the play as well, in particular the sorts of truth that allow uncertain and limited, yet still plausible and definite, gains in the power of human agency.

Northrop Frye has claimed in his Shakespeare lectures that merely human limitations of power apply precisely to "Prospero's work," which is:[82]

> entirely "sublunar": he works within our world and is human himself. In the final scene Alonso speaks of needing a goddess and an oracle to explain what's happening, and goddesses and oracles have turned up on the other three major romances. But *The Tempest*, except for Ariel, does not move out of the normal natural order: even Caliban, though the son of a witch, is human. The action of the play is transformation within nature.

Frye goes on to illustrate this by claiming that the deaths in *The Tempest* are just like Hermione's in *The Winter's Tale*, theatrical shams backed up by strategic lies. So Alonso is no more drowned, despite the testimony of "One of the most beautiful songs in the world," than is Miranda or Ferdinand dead. This very song's balance of truth and falsehood has been considered in chapter 1. As for the death of Miranda, as Frye reminds us, Prospero only suggestively "speaks of Miranda to Alonso in a way that gives Alonso the impression that she is dead." Although Prospero ambiguously equivalences his "loss" of Miranda with the supposed death of Ferdinand (5.1.143–50), both deaths are soon disproved. Frye concludes, "We can say here, as in *The Winter's Tale*, that people die, but only metaphorically."[83]

An implication of the circumstances remarked upon by Frye is that when Shakespeare's audience is shown the staged "High miracle" of the resurrection of Ferdinand and Miranda, they must realize that this cannot substantiate Prospero's claims (made just before) to have powers to raise the dead. Because they are granted knowledge of his manipulations, the audience is thus forced to realize, as Frye puts it, the "sublunar" quality of "Prospero's work."[84]

RECAPITULATION

What is gained in disillusionment is a possibility of alternatives to illusion. These alternatives need not all be materialistically reductive (even now)—they certainly were not so in Shakespeare's time. A loss of belief in omnipotence and omniscience leaves an awareness of a great deal that is unknown; there is no premature or totalizing closure implicit in that.

I want finally to recap in different terms some of what this chapter has discussed. In relation to time and tempest, it might be noted that the single Latin word *tempestas* denotes both weather and time (as does *temps* in French). Aside from verbal ambiguities, scientifically sought (and not yet found) dependencies left open questions about the implications of time in relation to Prospero's storm. At one extreme Prospero could be understood as simply awaiting the "influence" of a "most auspicious star" to provide his tempest. At another, he could be understood to have raised his storm using diabolically black,[85] or some sort of paler-colored, magic, or even some miraculous-seeming technology. The differences between these understandings are important because they reflect differing kinds of emotional investment by Prospero in his "project," ranging from a real or presumed omnipotence like that of a Sycorax, to a radical humility like that expressed in Viola's "O time, thou must untangle this, not I" (*Twelfth Night* 2.2.40).

In between these extreme positions lay more than one possible intermediate. One, concerning only-seeming magic, time, and storms, is seen for example in George Gifford's 1593 *A Dialogue Concerning Witches and Witchcraftes*:[86]

> In Germany and other countries, the deuilles haue so deluded the witches, as to make them beleeue that the[y] raise tempests of lightenings and thunders. For the deuils do know when these things be comming, tempests of winds, and thunders, and faine would he make the blind world beleeue that those great works of God, be not Gods but his . . . These deuils make the witches beleeue, that at their request they kil both men and beasts, and many waies afflict, when as many of the things fal out naturally, which they would seeme to doe.

Here the witches are led to believe, falsely, that they control tempests, and the devils' work is to persuade the credulous witches that perfectly natural events are of their making.

The next chapter will explore many more intermediate notions that provided bases in Shakespeare's period for beliefs in continuities or intermediates between the natural and supernatural realms.

6

The Natural and the Supernatural

THE RENAISSANCE STATUS OF THE SUPERNATURAL

DESPITE THE EXISTENCE OF AN EXTENSIVE BODY OF SCHOLARSHIP ON the supernatural in Shakespeare's period, or on the supernatural as it is reflected by Shakespeare,[1] there is still room for a better understanding of Prospero's magic. Such understanding might help to answer crucial questions for students of *The Tempest* including: what sort of beings were Ariel and Caliban respectively; why would Duke Prospero, intending to return to Italy, "discase" himself of his "magic garment"; and what is meant by Prospero's release of Ariel, and his abjuration of "rough magic"? Those questions in turn bear on yet another question essential for the present study: what affiliation, if any, did Prospero's abjuration of magic have with a new deflation of intellectual presumption, a repudiation of omnipotent dreaming, that arguably was the mood required to advance a nascent scientific movement?

It has often been alleged that theater audiences of Shakespeare's time would have had no troubles of belief concerning magicians on the stage, because actual encounters with the supernatural were widely accepted as plausible. Some critics have simply claimed that such encounters were an accepted part of popular everyday experience.[2] Others have presented an intellectual background to Renaissance "high magic," describing the alliance of the "New Learning" with a "vigorous efflorescence of forbidden or phantasmal arts" involving a multitude of non-demonic spirits intermediate between man and God.[3]

Indeed, intermediate or middle spirits encountered in the Renaissance came in many diverse forms, ranging from English village fairies to classical sylphs and local genii.[4] Such spirits have been discussed at great length by William Empson, whose interest was in what English theater audiences "would think about magicians."[5] Empson claims that the daemons (and probably not

demons) who were the middle spirits held a prominent place in
both popular and learned imaginations, and were particularly prev-
alent on English stages around 1590.[6] He also comments that the
Church's objections to beliefs in these spirits were eventually
"merged into a general common-sense rejection of spirits," yet
"revival of the belief in spirits coincided with the unique West-
European breakthrough into genuine science," finding this a coincidence "which must always remain a matter for curiosity."[7] This
comment indicates Empson's unusual degree of honesty in recognizing historical paradoxes, even where they tend to go against his
own strong commitments to rationalist anti-clericism.

To expound further on Church doctrines, it should be noted that
any acceptance of traffic between the natural and the supernatural
would have been contrary to officially sanctioned beliefs. St. Au-
gustine had condemned all kinds of magic without distinction, and
Jean Bodin and King James VI of Scotland, among many others,
vehemently did the same.[8] Moreover, Protestant theologians including Calvin, and to a lesser extent Luther, held that after the
time of Christ all miracles had ceased.[9]

That particular Protestant belief is reflected even by Shakespeare's pre-Reformation Archbishop of Canterbury, who says: "It
must be so, for miracles are ceased, / And therefore we must needs
admit the means / How things are perfected" (in *Henry V* 1.1.69–
71). The context to which the Archbishop replies indicates that by
"admit the means" he signifies "admit that there are natural
means"; this remark has been associated with the rise of scientific
rationalism by a number of Shakespearian commentators.[10] However, the same rationalist position is challenged by the clown Lafeau of *All's Well That Ends Well*:

> They say miracles are past, and we have our philosophical persons
> to make modern and familiar things supernatural and causeless.
> Hence is it that we make trifles of terrors, ensconcing ourselves
> into seeming knowledge when we should submit ourselves to an
> unknown fear.
>
> (2.3.1–6)

Yet this is a clown who is given to paradoxical banter using inverted
reasoning, and also to travestying theological differences between
opposed Catholic and Protestant positions.[11]

The whole affair that Lafeau refers to, the curing of the King of
France by the medical art of Helena, has important resonances for
the present discussion. For Lafeau the cure is effected by a "mira-

cle," or the "Very hand of heaven" (2.3.32), but the "remedy" that was bequeathed to Helena by her physician father is not heavenly but of this world. Admittedly, when advertising her cure to the skeptical Countess, and then the doubting King, Helena says her "legacy" will "be sanctified / By th' luckiest stars in heaven" (1.3.243–44), and that even the likes of her modest self may present "miracles" (2.1.140), and moreover she will depend on "the help of heaven" (2.1.152). But in soliloquy Helena admits that her reliance must be on her skill alone, beginning:

> Our remedies oft in ourselves do lie
> Which we ascribe to heaven. The fated sky
> Gives us free scope, only doth backward pull
> Our slow designs when we ourselves are dull.
>
> (1.1.212–15)

It seems that only she herself, using solely natural means, will be the full cause of what will be only apparently miraculous.

The difficulty of distinguishing the truly magical from "miracles only in the etymological sense"[12] (that is, wholly natural if extremely surprising events) is resolved if it is supposed, as della Porta and others would have had it, that any effective, or allowable, "natural magic" is actually arcane technology.[13] This sort of notion, naturalizing all apparent magic, is echoed in Polixenes' famous remark on advanced horticultural technology in *The Winter's Tale*:

> Yet nature is made better by no mean
> But nature makes that mean. So over that art
> Which you say adds to nature is an art
> That nature makes.
>
> (4.4.89–92)

Perdita's rejection of this proposition, showing her alarm over rivalry with "great creating nature" (that is, *natura naturans*), retains a repugnance against "nature's bastards" reflecting moral suspicions of a fallen world and man's misdeeds in it. Her fears were not untypical, and despite the influence of Calvinism, rationalism, skepticism, or official attempts to quell superstitious panics and persecutions, anxieties concerning the unnatural or supernatural persisted in Shakespeare's England.

Shakespeare's mixed way of dealing in such matters accords with the tendency of the age for beliefs in the supernatural to assume an irrational half-and-half character.[14] There was, in fact, even a degree of persistence within early modern science of analogical, mystical, and magical thinking, as may be seen in the controversies just after the time of *The Tempest* between Robert Fludd and Kepler,[15] and in the cosmology developed by Francis Bacon in his later career.[16]

The next four sections of this chapter will discuss various aspects of the typical half-and-halfness of early modern attitudes concerning the magical—or various ambiguities, intermediates, and continuities arising from "the permeability of the boundaries between the natural and the supernatural."[17] The first three of these background discussions are of specific ideas and practices relevant to the content, structure, and poetic temper of *The Tempest*. The fourth discussion concerns the self-perceptions that differentiated the pursuit of *virtu* from scientific attitudes in the Renaissance. This will lead on to the final section of this chapter, in which the departure of Ariel from Prospero, and the latter's repudiation of magic, will be related to contexts of a newly sober intellectual outlook of Shakespeare's time.

BETWEEN THE NATURAL AND THE SUPERNATURAL (I): SHAKESPEARE AND THE HUMANIST ONTOLOGICAL PERSPECTIVE

A notion of an intermediate realm between the natural and the supernatural may seem extraneous to any modern viewpoint, but in *The Psychopathology of Everyday Life* Freud showed that various manifestations of the unconscious mind—such as fulfilled premonitions, *déjà vu*, and "parapraxes" or "slips"—may suggest such a realm.[18] Actually, Freud himself was highly skeptical of beliefs in the supernatural, although he did not deny that some phenomena seen as "superstitions" might possibly attain eventual scientific confirmation.[19] It is a fact somewhat uncanny in itself that Freud's wry remark, "To my regret I must confess I am one of those unworthy people in whose presence spirits suspend their activity and the supernatural vanishes away, so that I have never been in a position to experience anything myself which might arouse belief in the miraculous,"[20] echoes in tone and content a passage of Montaigne's "Of the Lame or Crippel" beginning: "All these miracles and strange events, are untill this day hidden from me. . . ."[21] The reason for this uncanniness will be revealed at the start of the next chapter; here it suffices to note that even a strict determinist and rationalist like Freud accepted that the seemingly supernatural, albeit always with a deep-rooted natural explanation, has an important place in human experience and thought.

Returning to Shakespeare's time, it may be remarked that even for the highly educated—for whom fairies, Pucks, nymphs, sylphs, or hobgoblins may have had more frisson-value than truth-value—there were widely accepted beliefs involving middle spirits inhabiting both the natural and the supernatural realms. In the official scale-of-being ontology of the age the supernatural realm could include only God, the angels, the fallen angels, and a divine image in the human soul. But, as C. S. Lewis and many others have noted, these narrow limits were greatly widened in Renaissance "dignity of man" arguments. So Lewis has explained that a plethora of non-demonic spirits intermediate between man and God, first conjured up by Florentine Neoplatonism, allowed "innocent traffic with the unseen and therefore high magic or *magia*."[22] Neoplatonic Humanism and allied philosophical traditions also held that mankind itself occupies an intermediate—and perhaps ambulatory—ontological position between the divine and the earthly;[23] according to the influential (if unorthodox) arguments of Pico della Mirandola, man's soul partakes of all natures and so mankind is free to define itself anywhere between the "material" and "invisible" extremes of the traditional scale of being, or is perhaps off that scale (for some of Pico's ideas even challenge the existence of a chain of being).[24]

However, Shakespeare seems to have mainly aligned himself with Montaigne's sort of skepticism regarding theories that there are paths whereby men may approach divinity. Declarations of post-lapsarian human perfectibility are enunciated in early Shakespeare plays only to be mocked soon after, as is seen in the rapid collapse of several faddish Shakespearian youths' missions to become the philosophical "heirs of all eternity," or to leave "A shallow plash to plunge him in the deep."[25] In later plays such as *Julius Caesar*, (*Hamlet?*), *Measure for Measure*, *Othello*, and *Coriolanus*, identifications of mortal selves with exalted ideals cause only blunders, downfall, and tragedy. It seems that for Shakespeare a name like "Angelo" cannot suggest the nature of the man; for him man cannot be a near-heavenly creature. And, as I have argued elsewhere, when this same Angelo of *Measure for Measure* eventually says that the illusion-wielding Duke Vincentio seems to him "like power divine" (5.1.366), the structure of the play makes this opinion a case of high irony;[26] it will be argued here that in *The Tempest* the flawed Prospero likewise cannot retain his apparently divine omnipotence.

BETWEEN THE NATURAL AND THE SUPERNATURAL (II): EARLY MODERN VIEWS OF THE PRETERNATURAL

There was undoubtedly an early modern obsession with the preternatural nature of magic, freaks, exceptions, portents, and marvels.[27] According to Lorraine Daston, throughout Shakespeare's period preternatural phenomena "constituted a third ontological domain" aside from the natural and supernatural.[28] She also asserts that in the sixteenth century preternatural phenomena "came to be ever more closely associated with the dubious and possibly demonic activities of magic and divination";[29] magicians, then, would operate in an intermediate "ontological domain."

Daston's main point is that historically evolving modes of dealing with the preternatural moved it toward the natural, and that this process was crucially important in the development of notions of scientific evidence.[30] Such an argument places Daston at one extreme of a range of differing historical views in which interests in marvels or the preternatural are seen to have been either highly important, or else not at all important, in the development of early modern science. At the opposite extreme from Daston many historians of science have been dismissive of magical enthusiasts like Cardano, and of fashionable (often wealth-flaunting) collectors of curiosities like Rudolf II, because such *virtuosi* were not concerned that *real science* pursues general rules applicable to typical, rather than exceptional, phenomena.[31]

Daston's contrary view, that an obsession with seeming miracles motivated the development of a concept of objective scientific evidence, matches in some respects Lynn Thorndike's much earlier attribution of the origins of experimental science to various magical enterprises.[32] In both these formulations an historical path is posited to have been followed between the occult and latterly the rational, that is, between concerns with occult causes and abnormal instances and concerns with physical causes and general laws. Even though the progression along such a path may have lacked intent, the existence of such a trajectory still implies a kind of continuity between realms bordering the supernatural and the natural.

Objections are available to views like Thorndike's (and, I think, Daston's also) in terms of a need for the verification of generalities in case-by-case studies.[33] Yet in one particular instance discussed at length by Daston, the example of the scientific epistemology of Francis Bacon, her claim for strong interests of early modern scientific thought in the preternatural seems well borne out. Daston holds that in his later works Bacon "handpicked" facts "for their recalcitrance" in order to challenge "glib rules."[34] Thus Bacon's reasons for his late special interests in "rare or strange phenomena and experiments that probed nature's hidden secrets"[35] could have been epistemological.

A general principle that may lie behind this is that exceptional cases can be generally instructive if they are used to disprove false generalities. That is, a pursuit of paradoxes leading to the discovery of error and elimination of falsehood constituted a path to knowledge for Renaissance thinkers who were precursors of twentieth-century falsificationist epistemologists.[36] Bacon could well have been among such precursors, despite his undeserved later reputation for employing only positive inductivism.[37]

In fact, even from early on, Bacon was interested in unaccountable and aberrant phenomena. His 1605 book *Of the Advancement of Learning* accepted that there were "works of nature which have a digression and deflection from the ordinary course of generations, productions, and motions; whether they be singularities of place and region, or the strange events of time and chance, or the effects of yet unknown properties, or the instances of exception to general kind."[38] In response, Bacon insisted on a thorough and methodical investigation of aberrant or preternatural phenomena using sound tactics and an analytical outlook. So, later in *The Advancement*, by lamenting a deficiency in the literature available in his time, Bacon set out a task:[39]

> It is true, I find a number of books of fabulous experiments and secrets, and frivolous impostures for pleasure and strangeness; but a substantial and severe collection of the *heteroclites* or *irregulars of nature*, well examined and described, I find not: especially not with due rejection of fables and popular errors . . .

The procedure Bacon specifies here, involving a large "collection" of instances, appears to use neither mathematical methods nor explanatory hypotheses. A long tradition of nineteenth- and earlier-twentieth-century commentary has held that this sort of apparent lack meant Bacon's methodology was not a true precursor of "the scientific method." But more recently scholars, paying closer attention to texts and contexts, have determined that Baconian methodology does indeed employ hypotheses, experimental testing and rejection, and other complex features, and so have overturned these views.[40]

In any case, carrying out Bacon's program for the "severe" and rational investigation of "*heteroclites* or *irregulars of nature*" would demand a sober and methodical temper of mind contrasting with the typical enthusiasm of those having magical interests in his age.

That attitudinal demand is crucial, but in terms of content it is hard to determine if Bacon's program to investigate the preternatural does or does not imply intermediates between the supernatural and natural realms. It is very tempting to suppose that Bacon was a supporter of belief in such ontological intermediates, for Graham Rees has identified "a characteristic Baconian intellectual reflex, his tendency to assume the existence of in-between states poised between any two antithetical ones."[41] But, although Bacon's own late-developed cosmology involved "spirits" infusing the material world,[42] it probably did not allow for vertical commerce between higher and lower realms; in the opinion of Graham Rees, Bacon's own background was too Calvinist to allow for such a possibility.[43] Also, as Rees shows,[44] Bacon's late cosmology elicited very few responses in its own time; thus, for chronological and other reasons it was unlikely to have had an impact on Shakespeare or his audiences.

BETWEEN THE NATURAL AND THE SUPERNATURAL (III):
THE INTERMEDIATE STATUS OF WITCHCRAFT,
NATURAL MAGIC, AND ASTROLOGY

There was a very peculiar aspect to the frequent early modern official discouragements and suppressions of witchcraft-persecutions: the support of simple rationality (Empson's "common-sense") was not made explicit when the Church or state, as they often did, attempted to quell or moderate witch-hunting crazes.[45]

It was, instead, exceedingly rare to find any explicit early modern disavowals of the reality of demonic witchcraft.[46] This tricky area of ideology was typically approached with deliberate ambiguity, and unresolved contradictions were common. For instance, the reality of witchcraft seems unquestioned when Prospero describes "The foul witch Sycorax" in *The Tempest* 1.2.259–60, yet witchcraft-accusations are seen to be deluded or malicious in *Othello* 1.3.64, *Pericles* S.9.49, and *The Winter's Tale* 2.3.68. There are many other—often highly complex—references to malefic witchcraft in other Shakespeare plays,[47] and especially in *Macbeth* witches are portrayed with an astonishingly rich ambiguity.[48]

In a particular real world instance of self-contradictoriness, King James's 1597 *Daemonologie* argued that melancholy delusions cannot explain witch-phenomena,[49] yet, following the 1602 Mary Glover case in London, James apparently approved of (or may have inspired) Edward Jordan's 1603 thesis that her possession by witchcraft was a medically explainable mental delusion.[50] Indeed it has long been noted that James changed his focus from the pursuit of Scottish witches to the pursuit of witchcraft-impostures and false accusations soon after he arrived on the English throne, or perhaps even earlier.[51]

It is not surprising, since even King James silently vacillated in attitude, that the less high-placed were mainly cautiously discrete. And so in early modern Europe there were extremely "few examples . . . at each end of the spectrum ranging from total acceptance of all demonic claims—where we find only Bodin and perhaps Remy . . . —to total rejection—where we find only Reginald Scot and his English followers."[52] The fact that almost all other views touched neither extreme, which Stuart Clark finds "striking," suggests that the actual norm in thinking was middle-of-the-road or fence-sitting on questions of witchcraft. This again implies there were beliefs in some kind of a middle station, or perhaps a continuity, between converse positions.

The Renaissance practice of "natural magic," mentioned above, also attracted the status of an intermediate activity despite the fact that its practitioners were supposed to use only natural means. For some of these practitioners intended their beholders to be as astounded as if genuine miracles had been performed. Although they may have had economic motives, these practitioners need not have been complete charlatans, as has been seen in the case of the showman-technologist Cornelius Drebbel who set out deliberately to amaze and to disguise his natural means. For the less wise in the age a goal of amusement rather than profit sometimes inspired spooky impostures or "miraculous" showmanship, although this was far more dangerous then than now.[53] And some impostures had a philosophically illustrative intention, as has been seen above in Robert Fludd covering and dressing up the working parts of a weather glass in order "to make it more wonderful and entertaining."[54]

The Renaissance faced several problems with regard to the status of astrology. These were sometimes sidestepped by the familiar means of giving an intermediate status to a magical-seeming practice. Thus Keith Thomas describes several ways in which astrology was given qualified or partial credence by its early modern practitioners and even some early scientists.[55]

Before turning to some of the ramifications of that, it is worth noting that there was frequent Shakespearian ambiguity on this topic as well as on witchcraft. Prospero's trust in a "most auspicious star" in *The Tempest* may be juxtaposed with Edmund's scorn seen in *King Lear* 1.2.101–35 for a reading by his father Gloucester of portents into "These late eclipses in the sun and moon." Edmund further asserts that the effects of ill "fortune" are most often due only to "our own behaviour," but his is hardly a doctrine of responsibility (for Shakespeare designated his viewpoint as reductive).

The underlying perplexities for the Renaissance about astral determinism did not offer a simple choice between Gloucester's superstition and the converse cynicism and materialism of Edmund. Contemporary debates over astrology considered more profound alternatives, and the main issue involved was human freedom. The kinds of "skyey influences" which in *Measure for Measure* 3.1.9 are alleged to render mankind "Servile" were vigorously denied such dominance in Pico della Mirandola's famous attack on astrology.[56] Pico's humanistic defense of the untrammeled power of human choice connected with a wide range of early modern doubts about the reliability of signs, prodigies, or auguries. Although opposed to Pico's arguments, religious authorities mounted a long if sporadic campaign against "judicial" if not "natural" astrology (only the first sort alleges the power of astral determinism over human free will).[57]

On another basis again, Montaigne was sometimes explicitly skeptical of astrology (as well as of all reported miracles, monsters, and wonders). This was mainly because he was greatly impressed by human tendencies to frail reasoning, fantasy, credulity, fearfulness, and especially love of self-generated opinion.[58]

For all that, and although belief in its usefulness in medicine, statecraft, and other spheres was beginning to wane, early modern astrology was still a flourishing industry.[59] So sovereigns like Rudolf II eagerly sought the stars' advice (using the unwilling Kepler as his guide), while James I of England feared horoscopes (accusing Harriot of casting them), very near the time when Shakespeare wrote *The Tempest*.

The decline of belief in astrology did not have to await the development of a rationalistic model of a clock-like mechanistic universe. Moreover, to suppose that such a model of the universe was assessable and fully formed (rather than nascent or incipient) at the moment of *The Tempest*, as some literary critics have done, is to anticipate;[60] the clock-like universe belongs to the later seventeenth century and beyond.[61]

Yet physics had some bearing on questions of determinism by Shakespeare's time, for, as has been discussed in chapter 5, there was a beginning then of an idea of the dependency of all physical effects on a substratum of uniform, universal, forward-flowing, and astronomically measured time. To expand on that in terms of historical sequence, the conception of "linear" time as an "independent variable" (as we now call it) was fully implied in Galileo's terrestrial kinematics (published in 1638),[62] but was also anticipated for instance by Kepler, both generally and in the form of his "second law" of planetary motion, first published in 1609.[63] However, although some historians have made suggestions tending toward the converse,[64] there was probably little chance that Shakespeare knew in any detailed way of Kepler's revolutionary thinking regarding planetary physics.

It is, however, plausible that Shakespeare was responsive to new attitudes abroad corresponding with Kepler's solution to questions of question of astrology and historical causation,[65] and in this solution time also has the quality of a substratum or independent variable.[66] As has been mentioned in chapter 2, Kepler tried to avoid astrological prognostication, but he did employ astrology in a sophisticated way in order to structure and organize psychological and historiographic insights. In this guise astrology was not predictive, but instead provided a framework for the analysis of evidence.

Most interestingly, Kepler also used his own horoscope similarly, employing it as a means to express his personal psychological insights and self-analyses. In keeping with the trend of his remarkable scientific achievements, here also Kepler was unsparing in his adherence to exact observations even where these produced personally unpalatable or disruptive truths.[67]

Kepler's uses of the structures and vocabulary of astrology to record profound autobiographical insights into the mind of a practitioner of the new science, were truly remarkable.[68] Taking passing note of them brings this discussion to the point of considering the attitudes towards their own practices of magi, wonder-workers, scientists, and other early modern agents—attitudes which have a great deal of bearing on the meanings in The Tempest.

BETWEEN THE NATURAL AND THE SUPERNATURAL (IV):
THE RENAISSANCE "RATIONAL ARTIST" AND HIS SCIENTIFIC RIVAL

The sub-heading of this section alludes to a 1986 article by the distinguished historian of science Alistair Crombie entitled "Experimental Science and the Rational Artist in Early Modern Europe."[69] Crombie's article identifies an Italian Renaissance view (having classical antecedents) in which a *virtuoso* or man of *virtu* can overcome *fortuna* by "aiming at reasoned and examined control alike of his own thoughts, intentions, and actions, and also his surroundings."[70] This conception, Crombie holds, "points to the essence of the moral and intellectual commitments by which the Western scientific movement was generated."[71] In this claim Crombie paints a more heroic picture of the origins and the originators of science than do the earlier chapters of the present study. In the particular instances examined in those chapters, sixteenth- and early-seventeenth-century science was seen to have had a more haphazard or incoherent progress, and a more curiosity-driven rather than loftily interventionist motivation, than is implied by Crombie's conception.

There is, however, more overlap between Crombie's and the present study's account of early modern Western science than might at first appear. For one thing, in accord with the main theme of the present book, Crombie does not view an argument of "two cultures" as relevant to the European Renaissance, but rather finds there was a common basis for advancements in science and concurrent achievements in the visual, musical, and literary arts.[72] For another, Crombie does not find in *virtu* a flawless guide to truth. He claims rather that it produced an abundant supply of instances of misleading rationalizations of reality or "failures of European vision to comprehend what existed, because it was unexpected."[73] In the present study European misapprehensions of the unexpected are equally seen to have been frequent; in particular my chapters 2 and 3 have discussed instances of the sort of failures of comprehension of "the intellectual and pictorial records of European expansion overseas" that are mentioned by Crombie as examples of the failures of *virtu*.[74]

The present study, however, suggests there were alternatives to the outlook of *virtu*. It has been observed historically that clearer or more comprehensive views of the world often did eventually correct former blindness or error, for an often painful overcoming of misapprehensions characterized the growth of scientific knowledge. Indeed, in all the diverse examples offered above of advances in scientific illustration, instrumental science, natural history, ethnology, political arithmetic (demographics and economics), jurisprudence, and other matters, the effective outlook implied was quite distinct from that of a *virtuoso*. For in these examples an arduous dedication to precision and logic often indicates much less arrogance, and much more diligence, than is implied by the overweening assumptions of *virtu*, as described by Crombie.

Moreover, those who advanced scientific knowledge in the ways instanced in the above chapters were often able to confront openly what could not fit common preconceptions, and evolve new concepts and thought processes able to encompass new realities. I have also suggested above that Shakespeare demanded a similar degree of receptiveness of the disruptive and unexpected from the audience of *The Tempest*.

In fact, in stage portrayals by Shakespeare and some of his contemporaries, the *virtuoso*, a fashionable icon of the time,[75] was typically an unpleasantly presumptuous figure, fit for derision.[76] For there was much to ridicule in the supposition that *virtu* could neatly arrange or dispose of all things, and overcome all obstacles, even those of *fortuna*. On the contrary, for the likes of a Harriot, a Kepler, or a Rondelet—or in some of the viewpoints implied by Shakespeare—an honest aspiration to address enigmas was not accompanied by the arrogant assumption that immediate and complete answers could or would be readily available. The alternative viewpoint to that of the *virtuoso* held rather that it was often necessary to pursue laborious investigations with no certainty of answers, and to restrict efforts to solving only what Crombie in another essay called "limited and clearly defined problems."[77]

In a fine instance of this, in 1604 Kepler sensationally advanced optics by putting aside the question of how the brain receives visual images (which had confounded all former investigators), and instead for the first time he correctly geometrically traced the paths of light rays into and through the eye, up to the retina.[78] Again, in a crucial instance in the history of science, Kepler's tremendous 1605 success in determining the true orbit of Mars "illustrates a modern scientific tendency toward limited and specific investigations."[79] But among Kepler's other quests, many of which cost enormous efforts, some remained unfulfilled. A perfect combination of appropriate intellectual humility, firm faith that an order exists that may be sought after, exceptional talents for speculative and practical ingenuity and for dedicated close observation, courageous readiness to sacrifice comfortable neatness or familiar doctrines to even minutely contrary facts, and logical and sometimes mathematical precision and inventiveness, is an ideal that hardly any artist or any scientist has fulfilled. But even fulfilled this ideal would not equal *virtu* in terms of the idealization of mankind's abilities. It would still, for instance, leave the artist vulnerable to *fortuna* (and not its master), just as Machiavelli's most astute Prince must be.

On the other hand, rational humility and an acceptance of limited goals, as opposed to inflated goals and magical thinking, did increasingly advance the study of nature, and some in Shakespeare's age recognized this. It has long been remarked, for instance, that Francis Bacon's objections to magical thinking were of a sort to encourage the intellectual atmosphere necessary for scientific furtherance, even if Bacon himself failed to respond to some of the best science of his own time.[80] So even Frances Yates, the great champion of Hermeticism, approved heartily of Paolo Rossi's interpretation of a Bacon:[81]

> in reaction against the Renaissance magus ideal largely on moral grounds. He deplores the self-centredness and spiritual pride of those who use their knowledge and powers for self-glorification. The works of God in nature must be approached with profound humility; scientific knowledge should not be kept secret while its possessor glorifies himself with pretensions of omniscience and power. The work of those who seek into the truths of nature must be shared with others; only through collaboration of many workers can advances be made, and these advances are to be made in the interests of mankind at large, and not for individual aggrandizement.

Rossi's ground-breaking *Francis Bacon: From Magic to Science*, just then translated from its 1957 Italian original, indeed richly substantiates the deflationary character of Bacon's views of an appropriate scientific attitude. This attitudinal position of Bacon is described by Rossi in a recent summary:[82]

> Bacon condemned magic and alchemy on ethical grounds. He accused them of imposture and of megalomania. He refuted their non-participatory method and their unintentional unintelligibility, their attempt to replace human sweat by a few drops of elixir.

However, Rossi adds that Bacon himself "borrows from the magio-alchemical tradition the idea that man can attempt to make himself the master of nature."

Now it may seem that Prospero at first has made himself the "master of nature," yet later he abandons this. Accordingly, many critics have seen *The Tempest* as a play of disillusionment, with the repudiation of magic at its end symbolizing a "farewell of the human imagination to magic and all its ways."[83] But an unanswered question remains as to whether that farewell is really a great loss. It must be so for critics who assume that power of any sort is worth having, or that seeking absolute control over nature is identical with the Western scientific enterprise. For instance, Marco Mincoff, who sees Prospero's art as a "benevolent" art of manipulative illusion-making,[84] yet with some elements "more suggestive of witchcraft than of theurgic magic,"[85] holds:[86]

> There is no justification for identifying Prospero with the neo-Platonic theurgist and all that he implies. Nor can he be identified, as some have tried to do, with modern science harnessing the forces of nature, for then the breaking of his magic staff becomes inexplicable.

An aim here will be to show how it may well be explicable.

It is useful to return briefly to Francis Bacon, who did prefer "experiments of light" to "experiments of fruit," that is, those that gave valuable insights to those that gave only an immediate profit.[87] Yet for Bacon there was a primary ethical value in the human production of "works," a value that has been explained by Antonio Pérez-Ramos as belonging to a "maker's knowledge tradition."[88] So in 1605 Bacon mentioned nobility when he wrote that "the sciences themselves, which have had better intelligence and confederacy with the imagination of man than with his reason, are three in number; astrology, natural magic, and alchemy: of which sciences, nevertheless the ends or pretenses are noble."[89] It would seem that Bacon's "noble" ends are enlargements, through knowledge, of human power. Moreover, the three sciences that Bacon names are the very ones that permeate much of the language referring to the magic actions in *The Tempest*. A repudiation in the play of means to such "noble" ends may seem "inexplicable," as is claimed by Mincoff.

However, Bacon's *Advancement* later reproves hollow magical pretenses:[90]

> as for natural Magic whereof now there is mention in books containing certain credulous and superstitious conceits and observations of sympathies and antipathies, and hidden properties, and some frivolous experiments, strange rather by disguisement than in themselves; it is as far differing in truth of nature from such a knowledge as we require, as the story of King Arthur of Britain, or Hugh of Bordeaux, differs from Caesar's Commentaries in truth of story. For it is manifest that Caesar did greater things *de vero* than those imaginary heroes were feigned to do; but he did them not in that fabulous manner. Of this kind of learning the fable of Ixion was a figure, who designed to enjoy Juno, the goddess of power; and instead of her had copulation with a cloud, of which mixture were begotten centaurs and chimeras. So whosoever shall entertain high and vaporous imaginations, instead of a laborious and

sober inquiry of truth, shall beget hopes and beliefs of strange and impossible shapes.

The myth of Ixion reconstructed in this splendid *locus* represents
a psychological and epistemological pitfall in the form of a self-de-
lusive deviation from the path to true knowledge. Such deviations
were the subject on which Bacon was most acute. Bacon's parable
also suggests that false claims to wondrous achievements may have
results not only wasteful, but monstrous. Asking why fantasies of
reaping omniscient or omnipotent power may have seemed monstrous to a Jacobean, and indeed procreatively monstrous, will lead
in the next section, and even more in the next chapter, to the conclusion of my discussion of *The Tempest*.

The Naturalization of Magic:
Symbolic Time Intervals in *The Tempest*

The evidence in the preceding sections confirms that there were
varied sorts of early modern beliefs in intermediates between, or
continuities between, the natural and supernatural. This background will now be seen to supply grounds for an actual movement
across that scale, traceable in *The Tempest*.

It will be remembered that Ariel and Caliban were treated as representing something apart from middle spirits in chapter 3, in
which emphasis was placed on the correspondence of their shared
uncanniness with the experiences of Europeans in their encounters with cultural others. But the figures of Caliban and Ariel are
notoriously unfixed in signification. I would extrapolate beyond the
suggestion of A. D. Nuttall, made in rejecting a "stony" allegorical
reading of *The Tempest*, that although "Ariel and Caliban of all the
characters in the play come nearest to being allegories of the psychic processes," yet "it would certainly be a mistake not to realize
that they are very much more besides."[91] Enlarging also on Frank
Kermode's view that "Many elements are mixed in Ariel, and his
strange richness derives from the mixture,"[92] I would include in
the "very much more besides" so much more as to suggest not only
ampleness or copia but even a localized principle of plenitude that
is palpable in the nature of these two imaginary characters.[93]

Therefore no final summing up of them will be offered here. Yet
there are indications in the play of their places on the scale of
being. Caliban is said to be a half-witch and half-devil (1.2.321–32),
while Ariel, repeatedly addressed as "spirit," promises to do his

"spiriting gently" (1.2.299). So Ariel, at least, must be a spirit of the middling sort. According to the scheme expounded by William Empson,[94] he would be mortal but very long-lived, and would have no soul; this scheme also allows traffic of elementals with humans—and indeed Ariel learns to empathize with human souls in the subjunctive mood, "were I human" (5.1.20). Again in the scheme outlined by Empson, Caliban contrastingly would have a soul, because one at least of his parents was human (and the other, if the devil, would have had a soul also). As Empson puts it, Ariel "positively wants to dissolve into the more handsome parts of nature, and renounce all contact with mankind,"[95] but we see that Caliban in his last lines intends to "seek for grace" and be more wise in his dealings with Europeans (5.1.298–301). If representing cultural others, this difference of outcomes might correspond to Caliban becoming more assimilated or better adjusted to humanity, and Ariel being allowed freedom in a natural realm cleared of human or European intruders.

However, many more meanings may be suggested by the outcomes for the two characters. In this section Ariel's changed status in *The Tempest* will be investigated, while the changing destinies of Caliban, Prospero, and Ferdinand (and their Miranda) will be studied within a new framework in the following chapter.

It should first be emphasized that structural oppositions or actual contests between "white" and "black" magicians, such as were represented in many English Renaissance stage plays,[96] must be distinguished from symbolic enactments of the deflation of magical claims. A question of great interest thus arises: is the first sort of opposition (seen in the Sycorax versus Prospero distinction) or the later kind of enactment (seen in Prospero's abjuration of magic) more significant in *The Tempest*?

There is an historical complication of the "theurgy" versus "geoty" opposition often discussed in relation to *The Tempest*. This arises because the distinction between a "white" magician (or "white witch") and a "black" magician was often not clearly made in Shakespeare's England. Highly ramified confusions or blurred distinctions between demonic witchcraft, malefic witchcraft, sorcery, and the benign or useful activities of "wise" men or women were expressed in widespread English popular practices, and in English witchcraft laws, accusations, and prosecutions.[97] Thus it is not entirely clear what contemporaries of Shakespeare would have made of Frank Kermode's contention that "the relationship between Prospero and Ariel is perhaps not theurgically pure."[98] Kermode suggests that this was "due to the element of popular demonology in the play." But social historians have shown that in the popular beliefs of Shakespeare's time there was much less tendency to view supernatural powers as demonic than there was to domesticate them and see them as practical, effective, and in a sense natural.[99]

For the more intellectual outlooks of the age, naturalization could have been alternatively based on skeptical views of the supernatural. These tendencies may underlie Shakespeare's various dramatizations of only seemingly supernatural manifestations, which are actually manipulated illusions (as in the resurrections of Claudio, Hero, or Hermione), and his staging of apparitions as mental delusions (as is suggested in "Or have we eaten on the insane root / That takes the reason prisoner?" in *Macbeth* 1.3.82–83, and seen in Banquo's ghost's return in *Macbeth* 3.4 or the Ghost appearing to Hamlet in *Hamlet* 3.4).

However, in *The Tempest* the naturalization of the supernatural seen toward the play's end is not implied, but rather involves an explicit repudiation of magic such as is not seen elsewhere in Shakespeare. For this reason it may convey uniquely complex ethical-epistemological implications.

If Prospero had used the full powers of his magic vindictively when "At this hour / Lies at my mercy all mine enemies" (4.1.260–61), would he have made good use of his "zenith"? It is widely agreed not, and that to the contrary Prospero's unique chances would have been misused opportunistically and destructively had he chosen to allow vengeance to dominate forgiveness.[100] Many, but far from all, critics agree also that Prospero must struggle in order to make this choice, and that when he chooses to restrain vengeance his non-magical action may be spiritually restorative and creative of new possibilities for order.

Something additional can be added to back up that not-uncommon viewpoint. This is that Prospero's crucial choice between alternatives is symbolized in *The Tempest* by his explicit actions concerning Ariel's period of servitude.

Ariel's first interchange with Prospero reveals that he has served his master for twelve years. Twelve was a highly symbolic number, most often related to time.[101] But twelve years was neither the customary nor the legally sanctioned period of contemporary employment contracts, either for waged servants or for apprentices.[102] For that or other reasons Ariel appears to be "moody" or testy. But grumbling and complaint was wholly typical of the servants depicted in contemporary popular literature, and was also likely to have been quite typical of actual servants of the time.[103] Then Prospero threatens Ariel with physical discipline if the latter disobeys him—which discipline was allowed masters by contemporary law if it remained proportional and within reasonable limits. But such limits are exceeded in Prospero's menace, merely "If thou more murmur'st," to inflict on Ariel twelve years of torture pegged in an oak, overgoing the twelve years he had groaned in a pine tree because he would not do Sycorax's "grand hests" (1.2.295, 1.2.275).

So Prospero at first resembles an excessively harsh master, and Ariel a typical servant. Legally, masters could beat, but not torture or imprison, unwilling servants.[104] Prospero's tyrannous threats against his servant, exceeding an exiled witch's, imply another evil which also could result from his strength; this would be to continue to tyrannize over "all [his] enemies" (4.1.261), and perhaps the undeserving Ferdinand as well.

His strength allowed Prospero to free Ariel from Sycorax's cloven pine (1.2.287–94). Yet freed Ariel is not as free as he would wish, and is portrayed as still eager for full liberty. This, at last, he will obtain "Within two days" (1.2.242) after the play's action, having provided Alonso's Italians with "calm seas, auspicious gales / And sail so expeditious that shall catch / Your royal fleet far off" (5.1.318–20). But if Prospero had not "pardon'd the deceiver" (in or around him), then Ariel would still have been needed on the island, and so would have been denied the "full year" (1.2.251) abatement of his period of service promised him.

Collecting numbers scattered in the play, the sums show that Ariel's original indentures to serve Prospero must have been for the unusual period of twelve plus one, or thirteen years.[105] This unlucky number was traditionally associated with "doom and evil."[106] In consequence, Cornelius Agrippa's 1651 translator John French was unwilling even to name it, and uses a circumlocution to indicate this (and no other) number.[107] The crucial question then becomes, just what was potentially so unlucky?

It is true, of course, that had he not curtailed his powers over hated enemies, Prospero would have gone the way of Sycorax. It is thus possible to suppose that by reducing Ariel's thirteen-year term to twelve, manumitting the servant spirit ex-gratia, Prospero mainly preserves his theurgy from geoty. However, I would prefer a somewhat different reading of the early release of Ariel, not emphasizing that Prospero chooses to avoid geoty, but rather that he chooses to move from magically inflated epistemological outlooks and aims toward the naturalization and deflation of these.

For Prospero does more than release Ariel, drown his book, and break and bury his staff. He also permanently puts aside his cherished "magic garment," about which he has said tenderly "lie there my art" (1.2.24–25). He assumes instead the natural costume of a duke, his "hat and rapier" (5.1.84); this costume, although brave or "fine" (5.1.265), involves the weather-protection and mainly ceremonial weapon of ordinariness.

Prospero's explicit purpose in re-costuming himself is to "myself present / As I was sometime Milan" (5.1.85–86), that is, make himself recognizable to his countrymen who are just recovering their senses. Then, following their recognition, Prospero becomes newly highly effective, but in pursuit of strictly limited goals, and in ways quite other than magical. Having realized that he cannot have reconciliation and revenge at once, Prospero sets about to regain, by only natural means, his former position and sovereignty. Faced with the unresponsiveness of Sebastian and Antonio to his bringing forth of "wonder" (as he calls it), Prospero applies methods more convincing to them than illusions. Thus, in tones of renewed but only human authority, and with only limited aims, he threatens the two usurping younger brothers with the exposure to King Alonso of their assassination plot:

> But you, my brace of lords, were I so minded,
> I here could pluck his highness' frown upon you
> And justify you traitors: at this time
> I will tell no tales.
>
> (5.1.126–29)

He thereby wrests back his dukedom from an usurping brother, "which perforce I know / Thou must restore," using quite another kind of subtlety from that of the younger-brother-deposed Rudolf II and his purveyors of magical illusions.

7

Why Prospero Abjures "Rough Magic," and What He Must "Acknowledge"

And images of selfe-confusednesses,
Which hurt imaginations onely see;
    And from this nothing seene, tels newes of devils
    Which but expressions be of inward euils.
                        (Fulke Greville, *Caelica* 100)

WHEN FREUD WAS UNCANNY

As I mentioned in the last chapter, in a passage of *THE PSYCHO-pathology of Everyday Life* Freud may have echoed a dry disclaimer of any personal acquaintance with wonders and marvels made by Montaigne in his essay "Of the Lame or Crippel." Montaigne began: "All these miracles and strange events, are untill this day hidden from me. . . ."[1] In Freud's heavier-handed version, a similar mock-innocent disavowal runs: "I am one of those unworthy people in whose presence spirits suspend their activity and the supernatural vanishes away, so that I have never been in a position to experience anything myself which might arouse belief in the miraculous."[2] I suggested that Freud's version bore the prospect of being rather uncanny, and promised to indicate why later. This is because, if Freud did in fact half-recall Montaigne's context, he could have had at the back of his mind the phrases immediately sequent to Montaigne's remark. These are:[3]

I have seene no such monster, or more expresse wonder in this world, then my selfe, *"With time and custome a man doth acquaint and enure himself to all strangenesse*: But the more I frequent and know my selfe the more my deformitie astonieth me: and the lesse I understand my selfe.

163

Freud himself did not follow up his own adoption of a feigned regret with any similar reference to the strangeness of the up-close personal unconscious at work. Nevertheless, *The Psychopathology of Everyday Life* is full of evidence of such strangeness. In effect, Montaigne, in his version of the denial, was more like a Freudian than was Freud.

Montaigne's remark expresses a mind equally skeptical of the possibilities of true knowledge of the very close at hand as of true knowledge of the impossibly remote or extraordinary. It also aligns with its author's beliefs that almost any degree of inherent weirdness can disappear from whatever becomes customary.[4] But most interesting in the remark is its gesture toward extending the field of inquiry and knowledge in the inward direction, toward an examination of the monsters, wonders, deformities, and mysteries of the interior self that exceed any outward ones.

This final chapter will be following a similar tack with regard to *The Tempest*. Montaigne's and Greville's vivid phrases cited above show that no anachronism vitiates this attempt. Indeed, *The Tempest* itself is amongst the best evidence for the proposition that advancing knowledge over "selfe-confusednesses," gaining a grasp of "that within which passeth show" (even "show" to the self), was the furthest frontier imagined in the bold pursuit of knowledge of Shakespeare's age.

In particular, in this chapter three important themes of *The Tempest* will be investigated in relation to a master theme of the pursuit of self-knowledge. These are the themes of anger, of work, and of licit or illicit sexuality. Although at first I will treat them sequentially, it will be seen that these three themes are interlocking.

The interconnectedness of these very themes is implied, but not pursued, in an essay by Maurice Hunt on "work" in late Shakespeare plays. This essay begins by associating contexts involving "work" or "stir" in these plays with a long list of vigorous activities or mental states, including "coming to life," "violence," "turbulent passion," and "sexual arousal."[5] The essay also contains a direct association of "work" with "anger" (at least as a central issue for *Cymbeline*).[6] Hunt's suggestive observations point in the direction of my own quest to understand how a pursuit of knowledge connects with what is stirring, psychologically dynamic, and in some cases transmuting, within *The Tempest*.

From this quest the concluding proposition of this book will emerge: that the relevance to *The Tempest* of matters concerning struggles for knowledge is most compelling in relation to the fruitful "plantation" of a "brave new world" within. In the metaphor of a "fruitful plantation" I do not refer to Gonzalo's idle dreams for Prospero's island, nor even Thomas Harriot's rational economic plans for Virginia, as have been analyzed above. I refer rather to something allied to the "maker's knowledge" tradition mentioned in the last chapter in relation to Francis Bacon's 1605 view on the "noble" if deluded aims of astrology, natural magic, and alchemy. In this tradition, knowledge is understood in terms of capability for doing: the tradition claims in effect that those who do something are those who know it.[7] It will be argued here that, from the perspective of the outcome of *The Tempest*, the pursuit of knowledge can strive for nothing better than the greater understanding or self-understanding equivalent to being more humanly effective.[8]

The *Nosce Teipsum* tradition was of course a commonplace of Shakespeare's culture, but the notion I have in mind goes further than that. The reflection of this notion in *The Tempest* is anticipated in Sir Philip Sidney's *Apologie for Poetry*. This devotes several sections to arguing that "In the promotion of the final end of all knowledge Poetry may be shewn to be superior to all sciences."[9] That final end, called by Sidney "the highest end of the mistres Knowledge," is defined by him as "the knowledge of a mans selfe, in the Ethicke and politick consideration, with the end of well dooing and not of well knowing onely."[10]

ANGER AND GUILT IN *THE TEMPEST*

The tigers of wrath are wiser than the horses of instruction.
(William Blake, *The Marriage of Heaven and Hell*)

It is evident, however, that increments of the self-knowledge making one more effectual are not universally attained at the end of *The Tempest*. Indeed the play seems to make a point—albeit implicitly—of indicating that both the personal capacity and the will to gain self-knowledge are highly variable. Antonio, in all accounts I know, and most movingly in W. H. Auden's poem *The Sea and the Mirror*,[11] is seen to have learned nothing, and to have changed not at all, at the play's end. Old Gonzalo, as will be argued below, possesses little capacity for personal insight and consequent change.

Conversely, however, chapter 1 has already made a case, based on a poetic use of a new scientific image, for King Alonso undergoing a personal transformation deriving from an acknowledgment of previously denied self-knowledge. In parallel with this argument based on imagery, there is also considerable textual evidence for such a change in the guilt-stricken king. Most poignantly, just after being rebuked by the playlet of Ariel and his "islanders," Alonso says:

> O, it is monstrous, monstrous!
> Methought the billows spoke and told me of it,
> The winds did sing it to me, and the thunder,
> That deep and dreadful organ-pipe, pronounced
> The name of Prosper. It did bass my trespass.
> Therefor my son i' th' ooze is bedded, and
> I'll seek him deeper than e'er plummet sounded,
> And with him there lie mudded.

(3.3.95–102)

Alonso also says he wishes he could abdicate to Ferdinand and Miranda (5.1.150–52), and later he indicates his guilty grief in "But O, how oddly will it sound, that I / Must ask my child forgiveness!" (5.1.200–201). Nevertheless, one critic (with an agenda of reading *The Tempest* as cynically as possible) has expressed some mild doubt over the evidence for the King's sincere penitence,[12] and another has characterized such doubts in a rather exaggerated way as a part of a "critical commonplace" concerning an "unrepentant Alonso."[13] This progression demonstrates how *The Tempest* has been a rich source of sometimes bizarre literary critical misperceptions.

More materially, misperceptions are common within the play itself. For instance, not only the "most poor, credulous monster" Caliban of 2.2.145, but even kingly Alonso, noble Ferdinand, and near-divine Miranda, erroneously identify mortal creatures on the enchanted island as heavenly or immortal spirits. But these initial misjudgments do not indicate that those exposed by Prospero's contrivance to misinterpretations, illusions, and surprise are unable to advance in knowledge. On the contrary, their experiences of confusion can help them to attain better knowledge. For, as has been mentioned in chapter 6, resolution of paradox and recognition of falsehood were among the chief means of the advancement of knowledge in Shakespeare's age.

This provokes the question of what kinds of falsehood could conceivably have been recognized and corrected by a Prospero. He is first posited to be a master of liberal arts and learning, and on his island omniscient and nearly omnipotent. How, then, can an audience see that there is anything for him to learn? They can in fact see this, because they frequently witness distempered anger evidencing Prospero's deficient self-awareness.

The Tempest repeatedly provides clues to the dynamics, origin, and teleological purpose, or final cause of Prospero's anger, and so this anger should be closely observed, and not dismissed. Dismissing Prospero's anger has more than once been attempted.[14] An interesting instance of this appears in an historically informed study by David Woodman of white magic on the English Renaissance stage. This finds parallels to Prospero renouncing magic and burning his books, and thus makes a valuable contribution to the contextual understanding of *The Tempest*,[15] but it also claims that the exiled Duke's irascibility is always "Righteous anger," and is always controllable, because "His dedication to white magic does not permit Prospero to lose control of his passions for long."[16] However, Prospero is palpably often furiously out of control, and remains in that state with regard to Caliban, for instance, for very long. The wording of Miranda's remark "Never till this day / Saw I him touched with anger so distempered" (4.1.144–45) clearly indicates that Prospero has at last exceeded himself in distemper, not that he was never angry before.[17] Ariel's long experience also leads him to fear his master's wrath (4.1.169), and of course Caliban does so often. It is not necessary to further detail Prospero's anger in the play, since Peter Lindenbaum gives an excellent survey of the many places in which it is expressed directly or indirectly.[18]

At this point a brief excursus may be useful. It is instructive to consider why David Woodman, while tracing white magic on the English Renaissance stage, became so apparently insensitive to Prospero's anger. This seems to have been because, after observing Cornelius Agrippa's requirements for "vertue" and "holiness of life" in white magicians, a conclusion was drawn that "Prospero suitably exhibits the virtues of piety, temperance and discipline."[19] This suggests an overly blunt reliance on contextual patterns, leading to the overlaying of an unique dramatic representation.

Many external patterns have been imposed on *The Tempest*. The critics in search of Henry James's "Questions" (mentioned in the Introduction) have read the play allegorically, drawing a welter of incompatible conclusions. With more uniformity, from the 1930s through the 1960s critics often followed G. Wilson Knight in finding the play an "amazing work" fully transcending the pain of Shakespeare's tragic phase, and crowning his life's achievement by celebrating a resounding triumph of forgiveness and reconciliation over disorder and vice.[20] More recently, and by contrast, numerous critics have claimed there is in effect no virtue shown in the play, or in its protagonists (except possibly in Caliban, the earlier group's erstwhile villain).

In view of such differences, I believe that the anger seen in *The Tempest* raises highly pertinent questions. Can it allow a vision of *The Tempest* as a reparative comedy? Can themes of forgiveness and reparation be poised against the frequent betrayals of hatred and disgust in the play?

It is worth noting that much of the play's anger is manifested in the more or less oblique forms of impatience, distrust, sarcasm, denigration, or a seething contempt. In particular, Prospero's fully straightforward anger is presented only when Caliban is in question. Symmetrically, Caliban's and his fellow renegades' rebellion expresses explicitly, without reserve, the motives of their social "betters." Many of the aristocratic characters of *The Tempest* exceed the frankly appetitive Caliban in their sly or covert rapaciousness, illustrating how appetite can be dressed up in civility. But, it will be argued here, hidden appetite appears most poignantly, and most dangerously, in the mage Prospero, whose anger and sufferings in despite of his omniscience and near-omnipotence express a guilty mind.

I would thus argue that Prospero's omnipotence in *The Tempest*, and his apparent knowledge of all significant circumstances, are themselves illusions presented by the play specifically to be seen through; how they are seen through generates their meaning. That is to say, the true purpose of the presentation of Prospero's knowledge-based omnipotence in *The Tempest* is to enable a discovery of the invisible limits that lie within such power. To illustrate this, Prospero's anger will next be traced in detail in an early scene of the play.

PROSPERO'S ANGER IN THE PLAY'S ESTABLISHING SCENE

A serene *Tempest* would be worse than an oxymoron. That such a view of the play has been taken is a result of confusions of omnipotence and magical power with wisdom and inward spiritual poise.[21] It is not surprising that power is all-important for critical assessments that (Antonio-like) deny reality to all human relations other than relations of power.[22] But equally, many critics whose thinking is quite contrary to hard-core materialist reductivism have also sometimes simplified the play by assuming Prospero's overarching wisdom and certainty pervades it from the start.[23] From one extreme position or the other, such views make an enigma of why Prospero, entirely lacking practical impediments and never seriously threatened by external revolts, clearly undergoes an emotional struggle. The choice of a dramatic structure that replaces traditional plotting with a myth of omnipotence, omniscience, and reunion in itself points to the questions of what Prospero really fights against, and what he overcomes.

I propose that he in fact battles with dangerous inner rebellions. These rebellions urge him to deny or disown knowledge of his own temptations toward tyrannical and criminal acts; his impatience and anger arise from struggles with these temptations. Prospero's turmoil and rage thus suggest a far less shimmery and indefinite understanding of his knowledge-based magic, and of his enchanted island, than is common in many older or newer interpretations.[24]

On the surface, Prospero's repeatedly implied urgency may be connected with his explicitly expressed desire to complete a project of spiritual alchemy time-constrained by "a most auspicious star" (1.2.183). But the pressure of a tight time-limit does not account for all of Prospero's expressions of anxiety, many of which suggest he is straining against some other kind of odds. In fact, despite announcing within it that he has less than four precious hours for his project (1.2.241–42), Prospero actually wastes time during the play's long establishing scene 1.2. This is especially true in the sub-scene Prospero plays with Miranda, 1.2.1–187. My view is that Prospero's halting communication arises in this section from averted scruples and convenient lapses of memory; for these reasons he mixes a harsh urgency to impart knowledge with a tense reluctance fully to disclose it. So I hold that when in his revelation of the past Prospero communicates to Miranda inefficiently and quite badly this "badness" is a deliberate gesture of the play, and not, as has been claimed, an instance of "bad" writing on Shakespeare's part.[25]

Shakespeare was a master of exposition, and so he could have established the prequel to *The Tempest* succinctly had he wished. He chose instead to display a Prospero who becomes so passionate in telling his tale that his sense falters and his language becomes repetitive, clogged, and turgid. At the least his first audiences would have noticed that Prospero's embittered attitudes ill serve a rationally justified aim to inform Miranda of her background.[26] Perhaps this would have suggested an ambivalence in Prospero's purpose to educate and prepare her for contact with Italian society; because he distrusts and dislikes so many in that society, Prospero might be hesitant about introducing her to it. Indeed later he describes her debut as a case of his beloved daughter becoming "infected" with a plague-like "visitation" (this is his metaphor for Ferdinand's effect on her). If Prospero fears that Miranda is dangerously naive about the outside world (and it seems he undertakes to supply a crash course to correct that), what degree of additional danger will threaten a Miranda-in-love?

At the play's outset, however, audiences can observe only a range of extremely confusing gestures. After seeing the crisis of his victims, they learn that Prospero has arranged a terrific storm, making him seem a powerful mage. But Prospero immediately after presents himself to Miranda as a scholarly contemplative recluse, and implies that this sort of man is far superior to men of power. And although Miranda seems to know fully of her "dearest" father's magical "art," he puts her to sleep before he summons his assistant Ariel (she indeed never witnesses any interchange with Ariel). But these oddities seem to me far less notable than the simple fact that, following the wild storm, Prospero tenderly says to a "piteous" Miranda that he acts only "in care of thee," yet soon after he exhibits repetitive verbal harshness, some of it directed at her.

It is not plausible that Prospero's hectoring of Miranda is motivated only by an exasperated concern that she will remain too innocent, and thus naively gullible. For Miranda is neither blandly nor obstinately over-assured of human goodness. It is true that she assumes that the mainly false-dealing shipwrecked Italians are "poor . . . fraughting souls," and at length, despite Prospero's tutoring about human depravity, will greet them with the, for the Renaissance, highly questionable emotion of "wonder" (5.1.184).[27] Yet Miranda is not an unapt pupil; on the contrary she is seen as quite capable of well-appreciating her father's descriptions of sophisticated evil.[28]

In fact, even before Prospero describes their usurpation and exile, Miranda anticipates it in asking "What foul play had we that we came from thence? / Or blessed was 't we did?" (1.2.60–61). This appreciation of the possibility of evil (and her characteristic and not illogical apprehension of an alternative better view) elicits warm approval in Prospero's affectionate, and unusually softened, response: "Both, both, my girl. / By foul play, as thou sayst, were we heaved thence, / But blessedly holp hither" (1.2.61–63).

Slightly later, Miranda goes beyond simply accepting the rhetorical-pedagogical point of Prospero's "then tell me / If this might be a brother," replying:

> I should sin
> To think but nobly of my grandmother:
> Good wombs have borne bad sons.
>
> (1.2.118–20)

Here (unlike married but naive Desdemona) she shows a capacity to imagine sexual infidelity, and shows moreover an understanding that evil need not be mechanical or hereditary. On other occasions Miranda's *nous* gratifies Prospero: when she asks why fratricide and child-murder did not serve the purpose of the usurpers better than exile, she draws his applause: "Well demanded wench . . . Dear, they durst not" (1.2.139–40).

Such responses prove that anxious parental care to impart a useful understanding of evil cannot wholly explain Prospero's repeated, battering, staccato (and unnecessary) demands for Miranda's better mindfulness. The demands instead imply undercurrents unconnected with a motive of care. While Prospero continues to speak of deceits and misfortunes, Miranda repeatedly inquires for the evidence of the loyalty and concern that countered ill-treatment. Her cross-questioning elicits Prospero's admission of the love of his people for their Duke, of the "cherubin" behavior of her baby self, of the charity of old Gonzalo, and of the providence that brought them safely ashore. But Prospero repeatedly returns to bitter recollections, dwelling on his brother's ungrateful and underhanded behavior, the perfidy of the King of Naples, the ungenerous reason that they were exiled rather than assassinated, and even the wretched boat given them on their expulsion.

Prospero being overwhelmed by his own memories produces a palpable injustice near the play's start, implying a danger to his project.[29] For while Ariel is at least a bit indocile in 1.2.247–51 (and just before that Caliban was infuriating) Miranda by contrast is totally undeserving of the harshness in her part of the same scene. Yet Prospero barkingly repeats "Dost thou attend me?" and "Thou attend'st not?" and many similar injunctions (1.2.38, 1.2.67, 1.2.78, 1.2.87, 1.2.88, 1.2.106, 1.2.117, 1.2.135, 1.2.171). He demands her attention so excessively that even Miranda-her-gracious-self sounds slightly testy in her: "Your tale, sir, would cure deafness" (1.2.106).

It is not an attempt to cure deafness or any other incapacity of Miranda that causes Prospero to be so peculiarly insistent. His fractious tone here expresses rather his own incapacitating conflicts. Divisions within Prospero are also expressed by his use in the establishing scene of several distinct voices. With one he lushly recalls his lost dignities, describing himself (in the split-off third person) as "A prince of power" and as "Prospero the prime duke, being so reputed / In dignity, and for the liberal arts / Without a parallel" (1.2.55 and 1.2.72–74). As is theorized very adequately by the psychoanalyst Melanie Klein, the self-idealization that proceeds by retaining only wanted parts and psychically splitting off unwanted parts of the self typically results in a violent denigration of the projective recipients of those unwanted parts.[30] Therefore Prospero's idealization of himself finds an inevitable inverse in a second voice of belittlement, heard first in the tones of his carping against Antonio, and soon after in his furious dealings with Caliban and in his violent irritability with Ariel.

Thirdly, Prospero uses a language of deliberate obliquity, half-hiding the shame of his own downfall. He tells Miranda, for instance, how Antonio:

> Being once perfected how to grant suits,
> How to deny them, who t' advance and who
> To trash for over-topping, new created
> The creatures that were mine, I say—or changed 'em
> Or else new formed 'em; having both the key
> Of officer and office, set all hearts i' th' state
> To what tune pleased his ear, that now he was
> The ivy which had hid my princely trunk
> And sucked my verdure out on 't. Thou attend'st not!
>
> (1.2.87–97)

Despite his demand that Miranda "mark" him well, Prospero's language here is characterized by a choppy rhythm, neologisms, and a constant preference for metaphor. This style helps the passage to detail the faults of Antonio's "man management" while glossing over Prospero's own failure to govern. It is also inappropriate to an intimate conference with a daughter, and pedagogically very poor.

Moreover, Prospero's explanations themselves half-imply a deceiver within himself in league with his ambitious brother's deceptions, or which even "did beget [it] of him" (1.2.94). A collusion of deceivers must have gone into making a "confidence sans bound" (1.2.97). In the style and framing of his own history Prospero thus suggests that he has long been self-thwarting, and a self-deceiver, with tendencies to self-idealization and evasions of responsibility.

This reading largely agrees with an astute analysis of "Prospero's Anger" by Joseph Summers, but goes further in seeing the angry Prospero as damaged and dangerous at the play's outset. For Summers, Prospero "with the possible exception of Lear, shows the shortest temper of any admirable character in Shakespeare."[31] Yet, according to Summers, he is harsh with Miranda in the establishing scene only because he is a "nervous narrator";[32] "irascibility could hardly be the natural temperament of the good father, the white magician. . . ."[33] So Summers gives Prospero a "normal" motive:[34]

> Prospero, like most fathers standing before their children awaiting judgement, feels anxious, vulnerable, tempted to assert his authority. He is testy, on the edge of anger.

This normalization is strange, since Summers very sensitively reads the initial Prospero-Miranda interchange as potentially theatrically rich because emotionally revealing, and moreover he sees clearly that Prospero's self-exoneration does not hold water. But he does not place these factors in confrontation with one another: notice is not taken of the fact that unlike "most fathers" Prospero has not only formerly done his child and himself harm, but in addition in the present he attempts to conceal that fact both from himself and from her. It is also not noted that Prospero steers clean away from his acknowledged aim to serve only his daughter's needs, and instead indulges in denial, or disowning, of self-knowledge.

WORK AND KNOWLEDGE

The fact is the sweetest dream that labor knows.
(Robert Frost, "Mowing")

Wonder derives from a degree of ignorance, while work involves the understanding that comes from direct experience.
—Maurice Hunt

Several commentators have remarked on the importance of the concept of "work" in *The Tempest*.[35] Particularly interesting ideas are presented in an essay by Ronald Bond, which contrasts a fixation on "Labour" in the play with the generic assumptions of the "Pastoral Romance." Bond shows that, as opposed to the truly idle courtiers of *The Tempest*, Prospero is a hard mental worker, and that in contemporary views mental workers were "not to be accounted idle."[36] I have no quarrel with this, except that I will presently emphasize that Prospero's hard mental efforts of the years before the storm, his studies of magic books, are implicitly as nothing compared with the mental work that he must do within the few hours of the play's action. I would also mention that the mental work Prospero should have done when he neglected his duties to the state in favor of his private study presents a paradigm case of a mental worker evading his duty, a paradigm to which these discussions will return.

It is pertinent to begin by discussing physical work and physicality in *The Tempest*. One critic has pointed out that Prospero "has a fairly unhealthy attitude toward labor—toward good clean manual work," but puts that observation only to the use of carping against the moral standing and good faith of Prospero, and indeed of the play itself.[37] There is, however, much more to see in it.

Prospero is not alone in *The Tempest* in his oddly angry-seeming disdain for the physical generally, and for physical work in particular; it is mirrored also in the attitudes of the Italian courtiers. Almost at the play's start, contempt for physical labor or laborers links with a peculiar remark of "the good old lord Gonzalo," a remark in which he reveals himself as a ribald old man. Gonzalo's off-color remark is especially peculiar because searchers after sexual innuendo in Shakespeare classify *The Tempest* as one of the very "cleanest" of the plays, a play with which "bawdy has little to do."[38] Yet, in the storm scene, the "honest old Councellor" Gonzalo (as he is listed in the Folio) makes the only misogynistic reference to menstruation in all of Shakespeare.[39] This indecent sexual reference is juxtaposed, in a way familiar from *Measure for Measure* 4.2, with a jocular reference to death by hanging; Gonzalo appends it to gratuitously "merry" predictions that the hard-laboring Boatswain is destined for hanging, not drowning: "I'll warrant him for drowning, though the ship were no stronger than a nutshell and as leaky as an unstanched wench" (1.1.44–46).

The obscenity here is not a throwaway ribald gesture, but rather it serves multiple, serious, theatrical functions. (This functionality makes performances of 1.1 with crashes or loud howling drowning out speech theatrically inadequate.) For one thing, this obscenity culminates the repeated crudeness, in the storm scene, of the court party—the officiousness, rudeness, and interference that at length provoke the angry responses of an at-first polite Boatswain.[40] For another, its joking about bodies and executions realistically portrays fear-driven bawdy gallows humor; this enhances the sense of verisimilitude in a scene that seems overall more accurate than the eyewitness account of a shipwreck which is its likely source.[41] Moreover, Gonzalo's obscenity conveys his double denigration (through sexual and social innuendo) of the Boatswain's occupation; this connects with an important theme concerning physical work in the play. And finally, Gonzalo's reference to the leaky body of a "wench" initiates a theme concerning sexual maturity, which is of great importance in the play, and which will receive attention presently.

However, the question of physical work must be considered first. Chapter 3 has argued that the Virginia-voyage background to the composition and reception of *The Tempest* most saliently involved a near-disaster caused mainly by what Philip Edwards has called "the disinclination of the many gentlemen among the voyagers to erode the privilege of their status by actually working."[42] Yet an important difference is seen between Shakespeare's shipwreck scene in *The Tempest* and the actual shipwreck described in the just-mentioned probable source of the scene, William Strachey's letter concerning the 1609 wreck of the *Sea-Adventure*. In Shakespeare's scene Alonso and his courtiers, the leading men on board a foundering ship, are (in the apt words of Ronald Bond) idle "busybodies" who only annoy the truly "busy."[43] In the words of the play, they "mar" the mariners' efforts, even "assist the storm" (1.1.12–13).[44] The Boatswain's most effective retort to the foul imprecations of some of the courtiers is "Work you, then" (1.1.41). In the scene's real-life precedent, however, far from hindering the struggling sailors, the high-born on board the storm-beset *Sea-Adventure* were reported by Strachey to have helped to bail the ship out, while one of the expedition's leaders, Sir George Summers, was first to sight landfall, and the other chief, Sir Thomas Gates, was said to have undertaken on land a share in "every meane labour" avoiding "no travaile of his body."[45]

This contrast with his likely source cannot have arisen because the late Shakespeare subscribed—together with Castiglione, Leonardo da Vinci, Sir Philip Sidney, and many others—to a Renaissance aristocratic distaste for physical work. For in *Pericles* (published in 1609, before any reports of the *Sea-Adventure* shipwreck), Shakespeare's Marina is proud of her princely father who, in a wild storm:

> did never fear
> But cried "Good seamen" to the mariners,
> Galling his kingly hands with haling ropes.
>
> (Scene 15.103–5)

Gonzalo and his fellows are galling in quite another sense when they harass the Boatswain. Worst in language are Sebastian and Antonio, who cry out "A pox o' your throat, you bawling, blasphemous, incharitable dog!" (1.1.39–40) and "Hang, cur, hang, you whoreson insolent noise-maker" (1.1.42–43). Here they project their own uncharitable tendencies into him; while their objections to a sailor's salty language are dressed up as pious, they themselves are full of profanity (and at the same time they simply ignore Gonzalo's suggestion that they join the King in prayer below). By contrast, Gonzalo's extemporaneous prayer in the storm, concluding "The wills above be done, but I would fain die a dry death" (1.1.63–64), shows a superior courage, resolution, and humor. If only relatively, Gonzalo is seen as "A noble Neapolitan," as Prospero will tell Miranda (1.2.162).

But still, amidst the reuniting and recognitions at the end of *The Tempest*, Prospero's "Holy Gonzalo" (5.1.62) behaves most peculiarly. Just after pronouncing a moving blessing on Ferdinand and Miranda, to which King Alonso says "amen," Gonzalo sums up the whole island adventure by expressing gratitude for its closure in Claribel's marriage, the recovery of all the lost selves, and the crowning restoration of Duke Prospero and his daughter (5.1.207–18). Then, wreathed in so much new dignity, the formerly facetious "Councellor" (in 2.1.182 he has admitted his "merry fooling") encounters and greets a miraculously restored, now gently-spoken, Boatswain. Gonzalo promptly abandons his praises of reconciliation and resumes the raillery of the storm scene: "I prophesied, if a gallows were on land / This fellow could not drown" (5.1.220–21). In addition to some insensitivity to the occasion, his remark conveys further incongruities. He asserts a gallows awaits the Boatswain, but the Italians' ship is still believed lost. Thus Gonzalo assumes that there will be gallows on Prospero's island (as there were indeed on Gates's and Summers's Bermuda). His capacity for sudden sheering away from a solemn spirit of thanksgiving, to a relief-based levity involving a punitive fantasy, may help explain why, although Gonzalo receives no outward punishment,[46] yet he suffers inwardly: "His tears run down his beard like winter's drops / From eaves of reeds" (5.1.16–17).

I think we are meant to understand that although Gonzalo's tears may be "penitent," as Prospero says (5.1.28), they are still ineffectual. Gonzalo has been a relatively good man within a corrupted milieu, and of course he could not have resisted the command when he was "appointed / Master of [the] design" to destroy innocent Prospero and Miranda (2.1.163–64).[47] He indeed risked as much charity to them as he dared. But twelve years later he still leads in witty abuse of the Boatswain. An appropriate final response to Gonzalo requires a balanced attitude; although as "Sir Prudence" he was unique in not being predictably compliant with Antonio's and Sebastian's murderous scheme (2.1.291–95), in a mild sense he resembles them in clinging to fallen courtly modes in a wilderness.

"Gonzalo's paradox," discussed in chapter 3, in which he imagines himself "king" of a Golden Age commonwealth with "No sovereignty," comically shows his limited social conceptions. Also, although not sinister, Gonzalo's utopian fantasies are evocative of the sin of accidie or torpor;[48] they entirely lack any idea of arduous virtue. He would have in his imaginary commonwealth "No occupation, all men idle, all," and all good things come "Without sweat or endeavour" (2.1.160 and 166). This dream does not call for a pastoral or a philosophical *otium*, but merely for elimination of all effort. Later, after Gonzalo's actual tears and perhaps sweat have been extracted on the magic island, he seems only pathetically exhausted, begging: "Some heavenly power guide us / Out of this fearful country!" (5.1.105–6).

What I am suggesting is that Gonzalo, although instinctively loyal, may be seen partly to shirk the mental work (work that strives for understanding) required of men in a governing class. The younger Prospero's similar disgrace was that, unlike Hamlet, he allowed himself to not notice when efficient administration took the place of justice. Widespread collusion with unjust efficiency is still rife at the play's start, for Antonio's crime of usurpation has been conveniently forgotten. Moreover, Antonio confidently expects all the courtiers except Gonzalo readily to accept a repetition of the usurpation: "They'll take suggestion as a cat laps milk" (2.1.293). Collusion with or acceptance of a "deceiver" can also point inwards rather than outwards. How this is represented in *The Tempest* as countered by extremely difficult mental work is my next concern.

Sexual Knowledge and Chastity in *The Tempest*

Increases in Prospero's self-understanding in *The Tempest* have sometimes been connected with a rather simple psychomachia involving Ariel and Caliban, but that will not do. Although Prospero at first shows scant respect for physical work, or indeed for the physical realm itself, his autobiographical account of an all-dominating pursuit of knowledge cannot mean that he has habitually acknowledged only that part of himself which resembles an incorporeal Ariel. For important textual evidence denies that Caliban and Ariel actually can be simply opposed as figures of matter versus spirit, of the vegetative versus the sensitive soul of faculty psychology, or of the id versus the superego.[49]

For one thing, as has been argued in chapter 3, on close inspection many disjunctions between Caliban and Ariel tend to dissolve. For instance, log-bearing, fire-making, food-loving, sex-craving Caliban displays great sensitivity to Ariel's music; indeed the master Henry James has judged that Caliban's "conception and execution" shows the height of "ineffable delicacy."[50] Moreover, Prospero does not employ Ariel in any sense immaterially. In fact, Ariel is commanded to deal with all four physical elements on Prospero's behalf; his master insists that Ariel must not think it too "much":

> to tread the ooze
> Of the salt deep,
> To run upon the sharp wind of the north,
> To do me business in the veins o' th' earth
>
> (1.2.253–56)

while Ariel also must "dive into the fire" to "flame distinctly" (1.2.192 and 201).

Prospero even uses Ariel's spirits to provide gross effects to enslave Caliban (2.2.3–14). Indeed, through much of *The Tempest*, Prospero, who sees servile grotesqueness in physical activities, delegates these to Ariel. Even important artistic activities are imposed on what he calls denigratingly a "rabble" of Ariel's "meaner" assistants (4.1.35–37).[51]

A notion of Ariel as a psychomantic representative of pure thought or disembodied imagination is further vitiated by his readiness to deal in stinks as readily as in purifying fires.[52] Virgil's harpy was, after all, a filthy creature. Also it has been noted that Ariel uses some of the "coarsest imagery in the play";[53] he does seem to relish saying "belch" in 3.3.56, and "the foul lake / O'er-stunk their feet" in 4.1.183–84.

I can go further to prove the peculiar materiality of Ariel (whose gender is ambiguous). The menstrual theme that first appears in Gonzalo's simile of an "unstanched wench" is curiously echoed in the interchange between Ariel and Prospero in the play's establishing scene. Prospero complains that "once a month" Ariel becomes restive and impatient, and so requires a weary reiteration of the stories of pregnant Sycorax, his imprisonment, and Prospero effecting his release (1.2.263). So the play presents first a "Moody" Ariel (1.2.245)—moody, it is said, on a monthly basis—yearning to terminate a long-term commitment to remain with his master. Possibly for this sort of reason, Prospero later describes Ariel as "My tricksy spirit!" (5.1.229). For here an ambiguity in an affectionate epithet may imply a new genial toleration of the erratic: at around 1611 "tricksy" meant "spruce, fine, smart," but also "sportive; mischievous, capricious" (*OED* 1 and 2).

The noteworthy referent of a theme of menstruation in *The Tempest* is not, however, the materiality of Ariel, but rather the implied menarche of Miranda. She too becomes a bit erratic under the urgent demands of her burgeoning womanhood, and here too Prospero eventually shows evidence of toleration. This is negative evidence: Prospero views, but does not comment upon or show any affronted reaction to, Miranda's implicitly forbidden, very forward wooing of Ferdinand in 3.1.77–86, and her disobedience in 3.1.36–37 to his, her father's, explicit "hest."[54]

Both of Prospero's "loved darling" Miranda and his "chick" Ariel require independence from him after twelve years of intimacy, and both are set free. In the latter case this evokes explicitly expressed tender regrets: "But yet thou shalt have freedom.—So, so, so" (3.3.93, 5.1.320, 5.1.98). However, there are also important disjunctions between Miranda's new connections to the wider human world and Ariel to "the air at freedom."

These may be pursued by considering the inimical powers in *The Tempest* of trees and logs. The complex Greek word *"hyle"* means wood, timber, firewood, fuel, physical (or mental) material, and primordial matter.[55] With clear contempt, Prospero commands the log-gathering labor of Caliban with physical threats (1.2.368–73). On Ferdinand he imposes log-carrying as an undeserved (in Ferdinand's terms) "baseness" or "mean task" (3.1.1–5), or in Prospero's word a punishment (4.1.1). Punishment for what? And why, when Shakespeare's Pericles is praised for haling ropes, is Ferdinand's labor degrading? Moreover, if timber in the play represents brute matter, as in the image of the pine tree that imprisoned the spirit Ariel because he would not do Sycorax's "earthy and abhorred commands" (1.2.274–82), why were those commands, clearly distinguished from those of Prospero, so abhorred?

Toward answering such questions, I would suggest that timber in *The Tempest* symbolizes something more specific than the whole material world.[56] For a start, it is notable that the collection of Prospero's "fuel" represents for him something degrading yet necessary, and connected with despised Caliban: "We cannot miss him. He does make our fire, / Fetch in our wood, and serves in offices / That profit us" (1.2.313–15). Here another mystery arises: what can the play's log-carrying represent that has such necessity that it justifies the retention of Caliban, despite his indubitable attempted rape of Miranda?[57]

This necessary thing is, I think, a kind of "work" linked with Prospero's idea of a "fire i' th' blood" (4.1.53), the "work" of sexual desire and arousal. That is, for Prospero, timber or "fuel" points symbolically toward a dangerous-seeming sexualized world, somewhat similar to the "bawdy planet" of Leontes' paranoid fantasies in *The Winter's Tale* (1.2.201).[58] So Prospero would damp down desires in the engaged couple (4.1.14–28); he even banishes Cupid and Venus from their marriage masque (4.1.86–101).[59] But of course, in order to achieve the very fruitfulness that the masque celebrates, the young couple have need of strong sexual desire.

It is left to Miranda herself to assert the importance of sexual attraction. She does this both directly (when Ferdinand is said to be like a Caliban, she says, in 1.2.485–86, "I have no ambition / To see a goodlier man"), and indirectly. Sexually equivocal talk by virginal heroines is common in Shakespeare, but none stress the value of sexual arousal as she does when commenting on Ferdinand's painfully carried "log." She says: "When this burns / 'Twill weep for having wearied you" (3.1.18–19), leading on to talk of "striving" and "discharging" and her desire, "Pray give me that; / I'll carry it to the pile" (3.1.24–25).

Here Miranda is not obliquely bawdy, but utterly frank about desire. She has formerly seen that her "trifling" impulse to dissemble her attraction to Ferdinand was impure, and so she said (and acted on): "Hence, bashful cunning." Besides that, she observed of her desire that "all the more it seeks to hide itself / The bigger bulk it shows" (3.1.79–81). Her imagery of "bulk," as in *The Winter's Tale* 2.1.21, may imply pregnancy. If so, this and the menstrual theme of *The Tempest* would belie a frequently heard suggestion that the play entirely denies the presence of the female reproductive or maternal body, a claim expressed in Janet Adelman's: "*The Tempest* answers [Shakespeare's] need for a bodiless father immune to the female, able at last to control her unweeded garden."[60]

And so, although not wholly immaterial, Ariel is differentiated from Miranda in being unsexual.[61] Miranda, on the other hand, is a fully sexual being, desirable in varying ways to Caliban, Stephano, Ferdinand, and others. The sexual maturing adumbrated in Gonzalo's jocular "an unstanched wench" is re-echoed in 1.2.139 and 1.2.415 where Prospero also uses the term "wench" fondly (and less fondly in 1.2.482) to address Miranda. This shows that from the start he is well aware that it is time she is married. So Prospero raises a tempest to bring Ferdinand to her.

And yet Prospero's anger makes the path toward this marriage far less smooth than it need be. This anger is stated by Prospero himself to be only a sham intended to test the suitor Ferdinand (like the put-on anger of good King Simonides in *Pericles*). I will, however, argue that it is no such thing, but rather expresses a real reluctance of profound importance for the play.

PARENTHOOD AND MARRIED CHASTITY IN *THE TEMPEST*

> I have done nothing but in care of thee,
> Of thee, my dear one
>
> (1.2.16–17)

Prospero in some ways matches the witch Sycorax; he too is an exiled single-parent, and like her is the magician-employer of Ariel. Perhaps on account of recognizing some kinship, Prospero seems to change his tune somewhat in the course of the play regarding Sycorax and her child. The tart description, near the play's end, of a Caliban "as disproportion'd in his manners / As in his shape" (5.1.294–95),[62] although hardly complimentary, is certainly more moderate than the earlier wild abuse in "poisonous slave," or "filth that thou art." This change might be evidence of an enlargement of Prospero's control over intemperate thinking and speech, but the modulation of Prospero's tone regarding Sycorax is more complicated. His first description of her expresses loathing and scorn (1.2.259–67), but, near the play's end, he more emphasizes Sycorax's great strength (5.1.272–74). But a complication of this progressive pattern or evolution lies in the fact that, even in Prospero's first account of Sycorax, specific mention is made of the mitigation, on account of her pregnancy, of punishments due her (1.2.267–68).

So it seems that the bad and illegitimate mother in the play is still afforded some privileges belonging to motherhood. An even worse witch-mother than Sycorax is later alluded to when Prospero closely follows the words of Ovid's Medea in his abjuration speech. Despite the fact that this borrowing has worried some commentators,[63] the worst of Medea's powers claimed by Prospero, that "graves at my command / Have waked their sleepers, oped, and let 'em forth / By my so potent art" (5.1.48–50), turns out to be only illusory necromancy (this has been discussed in chapter 5). The image, however, of a magus who can awaken the dead, open graves, or release life (Ariel's) from constraining *hyle*, may suggest a certain rivalry between Prospero and a mother-figure. But, as has been seen, Prospero is able to describe, without evident disapproval, how Sycorax's (even bastard-producing) procreative status allowed the remission of her punishment to an exile much like his own. Again, a sometimes-claimed "erasure" of mothers in *The Tempest* does not seem at all complete.[64]

A theme of licit or illicit sexuality, or chastity, arises also in the contentions heard in the play over Gonzalo likening the newly married "paragon" Claribel with the classical "widow Dido." Many explications of this episode have been offered. For instance, the link Gonzalo makes between Claribel's marriage to a North African king and the virtue of "widow Dido" (2.1.75–81) has inspired discussions of a Virgilian imperial and interracial subtext.[65] According to a typical such reading, Sebastian's racial "sneer" in 2.1.129–33 concerning Claribel's non-European marriage evokes Virgil's "tragedy of Dido."[66]

Significantly, Dido's tragedy elicits only Antonio's and Sebastian's snickeringly ribald repartee, such as in " 'widower Aeneas' too? / Good Lord, how you take it!" (2.1.84–85). They scoff at Gonzalo foolishly likening the king's daughter Claribel to Dido, because for them Dido was Aeneas's notorious strumpet. Recent scholars have shown, however, that, despite these courtiers' sneers, Gonzalo had sound support in contemporary knowledge for his points both on the near-identity of ancient Carthage and modern Tunis, and on the notion of Dido having been a sexual "paragon." For there were authoritative books indicating that Dido was actually exemplarily chaste,[67] and that Tunis did nearly equal Carthage geographically.[68]

In one sense these matters concern only "book-learning," the sort of learning that some critics have argued is shown to be of little profit to Prospero in the play.[69] However, more is at stake than an exhibition of learning; the contrast of the attitudes of Gonzalo, who would find a gracious historical comparison to praise the new-married Claribel, and of Antonio and Sebastian, who are obscenely churlish (and possibly racist too) in their views of her marriage, touches deeper streams in the play.

Polar attitudes of graciousness and churlishness concerning marriage concern Prospero also, in relation to his need to allow Ferdinand his manhood and Miranda her womanhood. To a degree, Prospero suffers from a problem common to middle-aged fathers in all four of Shakespeare's last plays, the problem of imagining any suitor worthy of their marvelous daughters. Details included in these plays in a sense collude with such doubts: the future son-in-law Lysimachus in *Pericles* is first seen in a brothel;

Posthumus in *Cymbeline* is first boastful, then gullible, mistrustful, and murderous; Florizel in *The Winter's Tale* affronts his father and then becomes uselessly seasick; while Ferdinand arrives on Prospero's island literally all wet, being the first to jump overboard from the wreck.

In parallel with this pattern, a more or less shadowy incest motif also appears in each of Shakespeare's four Romance plays.[70] Thus Gower's *Confessio Amantis*, the explicitly identified source in *Pericles*, gives a much fuller account of Antiochus's incest with his daughter than does Shakespeare's play; the incest motif is also attenuated in *Cymbeline*, where Imogen flees the advances of her stepbrother Cloten only to arouse desires in her unrecognized real brother Guiderius, but the attraction that would have made Guiderius "woo hard" is sublimated because Imogen cross-dresses as the boy Fidele; similarly, in *The Winter's Tale*, in comparison to the source novel Greene's *Pandosto*, the prominence of Leontes' desire for his unrecognized daughter is greatly understated.

Thomas Aquinas extended the principle prohibiting incest to forbid intercourse also between those "who have to live in close intimacy with one another,"[71] and subsequently such principles were in varying ways expressed in the often-shifting rules creating legal impediments to marriage on account of degrees of "affinity."[72] Therefore, a kind of incest is suggested in *The Tempest* where Caliban is seen to have partly reiterated the frankly expressed intention to rape of the coarse stepbrother Cloten of *Cymbeline*.

But Cloten's and Caliban's intentions are gross instances. In my belief, Shakespeare's more typical application of discretion in presenting an incest theme acts like a homeopathic dose, becoming paradoxically most potent where it is actually most dilute or attenuated. This is because the dramatization of a displaced or half-denied wish may adumbrate psychological repression. Therefore I think incestuous wishes may be powerfully represented in *The Tempest*, in a negative form, when Prospero expresses his absolute disgust at the sexual attempt on Miranda by her foster-brother Caliban. This fury, joined with Prospero's general scorn for physicality, combine to silence any deviant desires of his own. Thus the play, I think, represents a skillful ploy of denial, and in Prospero's hatred of lustful Caliban represents psychological projection.

For structural reasons, *The Tempest* differs from Shakespeare's three other Romance plays, in which the errant males (except for the storybook villains Antiochus and Cloten) are ignorant of their family relationships with the women whom they incestuously desire. A displacement of incestuous wishes into an 'accident' of mistaken identity is not sustainable in *The Tempest* because of the central premise of Prospero's magian omniscience. But there is more than one "accident most strange" (1.2.179) in the play: these include Prospero's and Miranda's isolated life together in a single "most poor cell" on a desert island. This circumstance may bring to mind the biblical account of Lot and his daughters, or other legends and true stories of castaways or exiles, in which the outcome is paternal incest. For a number of psychologically oriented readers, such associations have long pointed to an "image" of incest in the play.[73]

And indeed many details of the play suggest a possibility that Prospero possesses a repressed desire to found, with Miranda, a "brave new world" by "peopl[ing] / This isle with Prosperos" (as the despised Caliban would say). So Barbara Melchiori argued that "Caliban is within [Prospero]," and that "Caliban the beast, the physical and incestuous love of Prospero for his daughter, becomes more disgusting with age."[74] She thus claimed that Prospero needs to "struggle" against "his flesh" and "evil thoughts."

I would add to that description some further epistemological and dynamic elements. I believe that Prospero is presented at first as unaware of his own "struggle," and especially unaware that it has caused in him a strong and cruel repression of sexual feelings. To succeed with his project he must first come to know his rivalry over Miranda, and then must overcome both this possessiveness and his cruelty by means of "nobler reason."

Prospero's cruelty is made manifest when all of his physicality is thrust by projection into his "poisonous slave" Caliban, and later in the substitute "log-man" Ferdinand, to be scorned and punished. Punitive attacks on sexuality are seen from the first encounters of Prospero with Caliban, and also the vigorous swimmer Ferdinand. When the Prince honorably objects to being called a "traitor,"[75] Prospero's retort is: "What! I say, / My foot my tutor?" (1.2.471–72; this may be a reply to Miranda or Ferdinand). This may evoke the anti-corporal proverb of Shakespeare's time, "Do not make the foot the head,"[76] and "foot" could also be homophonous with the obscene French word *foutre,* as in Shakespeare's *Henry V* 3.4.47–52. But in Prospero's use "foot" more probably denotes a scorned body part higher up the leg, for Prospero's immediately following (and indeed enacted) threat to Ferdinand is: "I can . . . make thy weapon drop." This suggests that the "foot" represents a denigrated phallus, in accord with a Freudian observation that anything imagined "'down below' in dreams often relates to the genitals."[77]

Prospero's progression away from his contempt for sexuality begins with his remission of Ferdinand's punishment, and culminates with his "acknowledgment" of Caliban as "mine." A crucial moment in this trajectory is when harvest-celebrating sunburned farm workers and fresh country nymphs dance to please the newly released Ferdinand, and Prospero suddenly says that he has "forgot" Caliban's rebellion (4.1.139). This moment of sudden *remembering* constitutes the solitary unexpected turn of the play, showing a Prospero for once off-guard and out of control. It also makes the play's sole dramatic connection—as opposed to connections through parallel imagery—between the (noble) Ferdinand-Miranda and the (base) Caliban-Stephano subplots.

Prospero's extreme perturbation *"towards the end"* of the nymphs' and reapers' *"gracefull dance,"* is signaled in the Folio's stage direction: "Prospero *starts sodainly and speakes, after which to a strange hollow and confused noyse,* [the dancers] *heauily vanish"* (tln 1807–8). The dancers become suddenly sorrowful ("heavy"), and the music ("noise") strangely confused; an audience also may be sorry and confused by a truncation of the lively performance. Why does Prospero suddenly retract his wedding gift to Ferdinand and Miranda; in what way is this connected with "the beast Caliban"?

One thematic connection may be seen in a converse relation between Prospero's scornful attitude toward laboring and lustful Caliban and the (most unusual) portrayal in his Jacobean masque of sensual rewards for physical labor. Thus, Iris's invitation to the dancers runs:

> You sunburned sicklemen, of August weary,
> Come hither from the furrow and be merry;
> Make holiday, your rye-straw hats put on,
> And these fresh nymphs encounter every one
> In country footing.

> (4.1.134–38)

I would further contend that Prospero viewing the wedding masque, and especially seeing these vigorous couples dance, is in itself the motivation for his sudden recollection of lustful and rebellious Caliban. This response derives from sexual resentment and jealousy, and I believe that its extreme inappropriateness in the context of a celebration of love becomes by degrees apparent to Prospero himself. So Prospero's mid-masque crisis represents the beginning of his uncovering to himself of his repressed possessive and incestuous wishes.

The gift-masque has been an inadequate defensive enclosure for those wishes. It was intended to express a counter-wish for Miranda and Ferdinand to marry. But this gesture was destined to fail because the masque was given half-grudgingly: so Prospero growls "they expect it from me," and ungraciously denigrates it as a mere "vanity" (4.1.41–42). The collision between Prospero's wish to promote the marriage, and his counter-wish, is so explosive that he must break off the masque, and attend the contents of his "beating mind."

Such a dawning realization, and not a suddenly reversed lapse of memory, causes the ending of the masque. Indeed Lee Jacobus has shown that Prospero just after the masque is not really just recalling, but is instead fully conscious of, Caliban's rebellious intentions and Ariel's containment of them.[78] What I think Prospero *is* surprised by is a dawning realization of the "foul" intentions of an internal Caliban.

This hard-to-accept new awareness shunts Prospero from the gratifyingly praised impresario status of Ferdinand's "So rare a wondered father and a wise" (4.1.123), to the status of a pitiable old man. So Ferdinand sees him afflicted by "some passion / That works him strongly," and Miranda comments: "Never till this day / Saw I him touch'd with anger so distemper'd" (4.1.143–45). Strangely, however, this anger or distemper makes Prospero unprecedentedly gentle: he shows an entirely new temper in his succeeding speeches to herself and Ferdinand. He immediately addresses the worried Ferdinand as "my son," for the first time, and then, with counterbalancing respect, addresses him also as "sir." There is no sign here of the asperity with which he had formerly used that salutation "sir" (4.1.147 versus 1.2.445 and 1.2.452).[79] Thus Prospero personally begins to make reparation, without using spirit intermediaries, for his former harshness to Ferdinand, and his boastfulness and demandingness concerning Miranda.

These preliminaries lead on to Prospero's great poetic set speech, "Our revels now are ended. . . ." I have described elsewhere how this conveys several complex feelings in succession, expressing an exceptionally dynamic mental state.[80] For one, it expresses a humility that acknowledges shortcomings without being at one and the same time superior to them; so Prospero describes the insubstantiality of his revels in an elegiac tone that does not share the former defensive scorn with which he had called them a "trick" played by a "rabble," or a "vanity of mine art" (4.1.37–41). He also admits to personal limitations: "Sir, I am vexed. / Bear with my weakness. My old brain is troubled. / Be not disturbed with my infirmity" (4.1.158–60).

Immediately following his "revels" speech, reversing the suspiciousness in his earlier demands on Ferdinand and Miranda for pre-marital sexual abstinence, Prospero invites the young couple to enjoy each other's company privately: "If you be pleased, retire into my cell, / And there repose. A turn or two I'll walk / To still my beating mind" (4.1.161–63). Instead of further displays of omnipotent magic, he offers them his trust.

While Prospero trusts the lovers to moderate their passions, he himself meets his own greatest turmoil. Just as Miranda's has (1.2.177), and Alonso's will (5.1.249), Prospero's mind is now "beating" with his strenuous efforts to enlarge self-knowledge. His "walk" is not a ploy to get Prospero off stage; he continues present for the rest of the play. It signifies instead, with a *physical* gesture, his need to do mental work.

First Prospero summons Ariel, who arrives saying "Thy thoughts I cleave to." As Prospero has already been told ("I told you, sir" [4.1.171]) Caliban's crew actually present no physical threat: they are wallowing in mire, having been misled into the "filthy-mantled pool beyond your cell" (4.1.182). Next they are dredged out, degraded and smelling "all horse-piss," only to be again entrapped by the temptations of what Prospero calls "stale." (This "stale" is thief-bait in the form of flashy clothing, and is perhaps a good deal more.[81]) Then the conspirators are harried with dogs; Prospero participates in an imaginative riot, an anti-masque rout, when his pack terrifies in turn the characters representative of the purportedly low appetites that have terrified him.

At the end of the fourth act Prospero touches the height of his mania: "At this hour / Lies at my mercy all mine enemies" (4.1.260–61). But he resists the worst of psychic splitting, and refrains from using his dogs (two are named "Fury" and "Tyrant" in 4.1.255) actually to tear Caliban, Stephano, and Trinculo—or, Acteon-like, himself—apart. Here, as always, he restricts himself to making frightening impressions through stinks, sounds, wild apparitions, and, most powerfully, imagination. Working his ends through illusion, he does not enforce, but only encourages, new understanding in others. This is in direct contrast to his brother's "perfected" knowledge of "how to grant suits" and "who / To trash" so as to "new form" (reprogram ideologically?) "all hearts i' th' state" (1.2.79–85).[82]

It is interesting to note that, in himself urging on the dogs, Prospero for once does not use Ariel as his only effective arm, but instead participates personally in effecting his arrangements (4.1.254–55). Thus, in undertaking his intention to "meet with Caliban" (4.1.166), he partakes directly of some of the most vigorous actions in the play. The vigor, I would say, arises because in this he also "meets with" his denied impulses.

Following this, Prospero releases (insofar as his art can) the Italian courtiers from "the ignorant fumes that mantle / Their clearer reason" (5.1.67–68). Whether or not his enemies have learned from their experiences, he then forgives them, or at least engages with them humanly and so endorses them as human. He also releases and proposes to "pardon" Caliban. Caliban replies to this proposal with his own first use of a (probably) abstract noun, "grace": he resolves to "be wise hereafter, / And seek for grace" (5.1.297–99).

All of these changes become possible because, as a true spiritual alchemist, Prospero succeeds in working on himself as well as on others.

WHAT DOES PROSPERO "ACKNOWLEDGE MINE"?

Prospero's two partial lines,[83] "This thing of darkness I / Acknowledge mine," have become a touchstone for widely varied readings of The Tempest, and have been used to underpin numerous philological, philosophical, political, or psychological views.[84]

For instance, in a highly influential reading, a "materialist" critic has reduced Prospero's "I acknowledge mine" to an assertion of property relations "when apportioning the plebeians to the masters."[85] But surely "apportioning the plebeians" underplays the point that Prospero ruefully admits to being master of a worse rogue than the rogues of his despised enemies. Moreover, this reading requires the word "acknowledge" to take on a meaning which is not found anywhere else in Shakespeare: all the many Shakespearian instances of this term carry the meaning "own knowledge of," "confess," or "admit to," and most further imply "with individual responsibility."

A range of other critics have indicated, although often without suggesting any specific personal motives, that Prospero's "acknowledge mine" expresses a "realization that he has a bond with Caliban" which is an essential part of the crowning anagnorisis, or discovery, that culminates the play.[86] But a personal motive is of course possible, in terms of the acknowledgment of an incestuous fantasy.[87] How this might work is detailed in a Jungian psychoanalytic reading by R. E. Gajdusek. This specifically links the acknowledgment of Caliban with Prospero's "Every third thought shall be my grave" (5.1.315), holding that for Prospero: "the acknowledgment of his three children—the liberation of daughter, and monster-son, and spirit . . . [is] a profound ritual acceptance of death."[88] This connection suggests that Prospero comes to abjure an unconscious wish to live for ever, and to command the undivided affection of a young daughter, both his and King Lear's initial folly. This at least, if not a meeting with the "third facet of the goddess" suggested by Gajdusek, does seem to me implicit in the play.

But I would add that living with Miranda has been the best part of being alive for Prospero; reacquisition of his dukedom will hardly compensate him for her loss. Only courageous love can motivate his renunciation. And this is a love, I will finally argue, that has a great deal to do with knowledge.

CONCLUSION: THE CONNECTIONS OF "ACKNOWLEDGE" WITH KNOWLEDGE

> A tune upon the blue guitar
> Of things exactly as they are.
>
> . . . .
> That I may reduce the monster to
> Myself, and then be myself . . .
>
> Wallace Stevens, *The Man*
> *with the Blue Guitar*

A "depth psychological" approach to *The Tempest* is hardly new, and neither are readings that stress the importance in the play of learning, work, sex, or Prospero's anger and upheaval. What I am bringing new to the party is a linking of these approaches: my view is that a work of learning, underlying the emotional turmoils dramatized in the play, implies a particular sort of courageous love, involving a love of truth.

Eventually, in *The Tempest*, Prospero's courageous love overcomes his resistance to acquiring self-knowledge. This knowledge was formerly resisted in him by means of tactics of self-blinding (resembling Alonso's). So, when Prospero describes the play's "deceiver" Antonio, he unwittingly describes himself as well:

> like one
> Who having into truth, by telling oft,
> Made such a sinner of his memory
> To credit his own lie.
>
> (1.2.99–102)

Finally, I would question the nature of a love of truth that can over-come such ingrained falsehood.

This must be a love that sustains a quest for knowledge despite both discouraging and frightening obstacles, and which also sus-tains the search when knowledge is clearly only partial, or elusive. Such a love need not be heroic at the outset, yet is still more rare than common. For instance, chapter 1 has connected Ariel's sec-ond song (in terms of images of a newly understood natural proc-ess) with an increment in self-knowledge that transforms Alonso. In Jonathan Bate's understanding of the images of this song "the bodily changes are metaphors for the inner changes that Prospero seeks to work."[89] I agree that Prospero's "work" starts these changes, but would add (on the basis that Antonio does not change) that something on Alonso's part—perhaps curiosity, or honesty, or even nagging despair—is needed to see them through. Chapters 2 and 3 suggest that The Tempest mirrors historical circumstances in which difficult intercultural learning was sadly incomplete. Corre-spondingly, The Tempest, if seen as a drama of seeking understand-ing, is also a drama of incompleteness. Damaged human relations, even between brothers (no less than between nations or cultures), may not be easily susceptible to repair through learning. In conse-quence, unreconciled differences may imply a threat of future trag-edies. The remaining chapters of this book, up to this one, delineate certain technical or intellectual settings for the play, and differentiate styles of confronting knowledge; their aim is especially to clarify the play's oddly limited, yet still central, magian role.

All these notions have application to what has just been argued, namely that The Tempest presents centrally a gain by Prospero of sufficient self-knowledge to allow him freely and completely to re-join humanity, and allow his daughter her own life. To do this he must painfully confront hateful drives which he shares with his im-plicit rival Caliban, accept as worthy his actual rival Ferdinand, and entrust the precious couple and himself to a world where his om-nipotence will not hold sway.

Why would he do that last strange thing? There must be some necessity for it, for Prospero would not needlessly endanger Mi-randa.

The historical discussions of the present book may throw some light on that problem; these discussions have in several ways con-sidered a movement away from magical and omnipotent fantasies that accompanied the early modern acceleration of scientific enter-prise. It is appropriate now to discriminate that particular move-ment from general notions of "Renaissance skepticism." This topic is complex, for in Shakespeare's age, and arguably for Shakespeare himself, "skepticism" had multiple meanings.[90] However, for present purposes, a simple but suggestive distinction made by an older critic is particularly apt: in this, C. L. Barber contrasted Theseus's "proud scepticism" in *A Midsummer Night's Dream* with Prospero's profounder "humble scepticism" in *The Tempest*.[91] Especially today, when slash and burn methods of clearing away human knowledge (especially scientific knowledge) are employed by many who claim epistemological sophistication,[92] it is well to meditate upon what a "humble scepticism" might be.

This, I suggest, is the state of mind prerequisite to the acquisition of a particular kind of knowledge. It is a kind of knowledge that cannot exist at all if it is proposed to be, or sets out to be, totalizing or final. Neither can such knowledge exist as such if it is the product of any automatic method or process granting certainty.[93] Moreover, the quest after such knowledge must be content with the prospects that it may not be forthcoming at all, that by nature it must always be partial, and that it is inevitably bound to be superseded.

These severe limitations, however, do not deny the good of working to seek such knowledge. The operative word is "good": doing such work requires an idealization in the sense of a belief in the existence of something "extremely good" (be it God's order, or truth, or beauty). That something perhaps can never be reached by human striving, but the required faith is that it can be approached. That the approach might be an endless process need not be frustrating, nor a refutation of the validity of the effort.

In Shakespeare's time, strivers after truth having such a faith depended upon an idealization (or the possession of ideals) of an entirely different sort from the glamorizing inflated dreams of the Renaissance "rational artists" described in the last chapter. As has been demonstrated, such strivers did live alongside Renaissance projectors of the impossible. I think they provided a model for the portrayal in *The Tempest* of a limited, but definite, advance of knowledge, such as that underlying Prospero's better accommodation with his world. His advance in this respect, in the phrase of Joseph Westlund, illustrates the value of a partial but "*usable* idealization."[94]

Psychologically, the distinction between having ideals and working toward them, versus magical idealization, is at issue, and this distinction has particular relevance to *The Tempest*. Prospero's anger (to return to that theme for a moment) has been closely linked by Joseph Westlund to idealization. So Westlund claims that

Prospero idealizes his magic, but "undermines this assumption by furious outbursts and threats." Westlund continues:[95]

> Prospero continually tries to idealize himself, to conceive of himself as a standard of perfection—not only as a magician . . . but as an ideal ruler. The play assiduously undermines his attempts . . . Prospero exalts himself as blameless and wronged, but in so doing the text allows us to realize that he is idealizing himself in a defensive maneuver.

Now a defensive maneuver must be to avoid a truth: Westlund cites the truth that Prospero "was partly to blame for the conspiracy against him." I would add that he employs defensive maneuvers also against knowing his desires to possess his daughter. For instance, he makes efforts to provide a wedding masque, intending to prove himself the wholly pure and good father. But he also reveals in his tone of dismissive scorn for the masque (in a way that we and he can sense) that he is not fully committed to these efforts. Prospero thereby presents himself with a paradox, or a problem, yielding material with which he can proceed toward understanding.

But also, thanks to his talents for illusion and deception, Prospero has the power to disguise his own self-revealing contradictions. Even if he is taken to be only a thrasonical magician or a technological showman (resembling Barbara Mowat's Hocus Pocus, or my semi-charlatan engineer Cornelius Drebbel), Prospero is able to convince many others to overlook contradictory impossibles. For instance, his island visitors emerge from salt water with their clothing fresh and glossy (or else not), see both a "tawny" and a "lush and lusty" landscape in the self-same place, and accept that a "monster," as well as a "goddesses," can speak their own "language" (2.1.57–59, 1.2.424–31, 2.2.65–67). If he can achieve this, and moreover can with music alone hypnotize and work his "end upon their senses" (5.1.53), how can he fail to convince himself that all is well with his self-idealizations?

The answer to this must be that an impulse to seek truth exists in Prospero; self-deception has not seized all of him. Notably, however, his freely inquiring impulse is not directly fed by the magical spirit Ariel, who does not inform Prospero that he is a "man of sin," but only that Gonzalo weakly weeps. It is up to Prospero himself to work out that he is caught in what may be termed "Prospero's paradox." This paradox, which Prospero (unlike Gonzalo with his own paradox) himself works out, arises because giving and taking the same thing cannot be coincident, and so there cannot be both vengeance and reconciliation, nor exogamy and paternal possessiveness.

Logic (responding to paradoxes), and close accurate observation, are two of the three things required by Prospero to make much-needed gains in knowledge. He may be helped in his observation by what has been described as a typically Renaissance-pastoral "process of *analysis*—by seeing his situation reflected in those of other people around him, and then coming face to face with his own divided mind."[96] But a third ingredient is also required in order for Prospero to proceed toward the knowledge he needs. This is the peculiar courage, mentioned above, which sustains the work of seeking knowledge in a relatively new mode of his time.

Models for such courage existed, as I have argued, in Shakespeare's world: this courage was implicit in the challenging and often very hard work done by those using careful observation, unbiased reasoning, and unflinching candor in quests for new scientific knowledge. It is in this sense that Shakespeare's creation of Prospero drew its inspiration from a rising scientific enterprise, and not at all in the sense that Prospero's illusory omnipotence and magic-tricks bore any resemblance to science then or now.

Finally, I would like to allegorize the epilogue of *The Tempest*, while being well aware that this will be a biased procedure. This epilogue is a touchstone passage that has exceeded all others in dividing critics. Elsewhere, I have suggested before that primarily it implicates the audience in the positive emotional currents of the play, working in partial homology with the "taking out" of the Jacobean masque.[97] I still believe this, but in terms of the questions about new worlds of knowledge raised here, the epilogue may also be seen to convey a salutary warning.

The speaker of the epilogue, by appealing directly to the audience, suggests that the agreement of a culture makes a cultural work acceptable: that we, as readers or hearers, in effect give Shakespeare, or any artisan, scholar, or scientist, a license to produce meaning. We also may refuse this license, or withdraw it, and thus prohibit meaning no matter how compelling or how modest its claims may be. Also, if we reductively appropriate a cultural work (or the name of a work), we may strip it "bare." The epilogue to *The Tempest* explicitly empowers audiences, making them magicians with "art to enchant": so the actor begs acceptance, and fears the audience's power: "Let me not, / . . . / dwell / In this bare island by your spell."

Also, according to the final lines of *The Tempest*, even in a godlike way (as they may forgive its sins), an audience can grant "indulgence" to a cultural effort. I would add that, conversely, we, as a culture, possess a wizard's power to paralyze vigor, a Virgilian Harpy's power to spoil sustenance, and a scurrilous lackey-courtier's power to mock or sneer. But, I wonder, if we use such powers, who will have to say "my ending is despair"?

This is, of course, a partial reading of the passage. I would no more deny the succession of "despair" by "prayer . . . crimes . . . indulgence" in the epilogue[98] than deny the divergence from their original contexts of the out-of-context (and even out-of-*The-Tempest*) allusions made in the sentence before. My aim, as stated from the outset of this book, has been to trace a theme of knowledge in *The Tempest*, without denying any of the many other themes undoubtedly there. All readings of the play must, I think, be partial and provisional. The argument here has been that, at least in many important areas, so must be all efforts made in the pursuit of interesting and usable knowledge.

Afterword

THIS BOOK HAS EXPOSED A NUMBER OF THEMES CONCERNING *THE TEM-pest* and early modern knowledge that may be summarized in a way that helps explain its long arc from a study of the concrete referent relevant to Ariel's song (in the form of a pearl in an oyster) to the consideration of a psychological "family romance" involving Prospero, Miranda, and Ferdinand.

One such theme has been the denial of knowledge, or to put it in Stanley Cavell's better terms, the "disowning" of knowledge, that besets the lives of many of the characters of *The Tempest*. The play shows that, given an opportunity, many will indulge in a kind of self-induced ignorance or presumption that all is allowable, prompted by fantasies of an easy road to the acquisition of great wealth, eminent power, or even magical omnipotence. At its conclusion the play shows only a few of its characters having recovered from that affliction: arguably, these include Prospero, Alonso, and Caliban. This fewness may be seen as pessimistic, but some limited optimism concerning humanity is implicit in the play's demonstration that some, if not all, may recover from self-generated delusions of grandiosity and dominion. Consequently, the new generation of Miranda and Ferdinand may stand a chance.

Another main theme of this book, which links with the above, concerns the differences between the superficially similar pursuits of a rational or scientific knowledge of nature and human nature and a program of magical domination over nature and the human self. The first type of pursuit has been shown to be characterized by an acceptance of the constraints of limited goals, of logic, and of conformity with evidence; the second type of pursuit characteristically chases unlimited or grandiose goals, discounts illogic or paradox, and overlooks counterevidence. In the world that inspired *The Tempest* the dreams and schemes of a Rudolf II or a Cornelius Drebbel, or the ideals of "the rational artist" replete with *virtu*, instanced the temper of mind present in the second kind of pursuit. The same trend is instanced in the play itself in the fantasies of various usurpers, utopians, and perhaps (until near the play's end) the mage Prospero himself.

195

However, it has been demonstrated that at the time of *The Tempest* the realm of the supernatural was not simply converse to the realm of the natural, but instead there were several kinds of continuities between them. It has been argued that Prospero progressively transfers his primary reliance for effectiveness between these realms in the course of the play, abandoning his magical studies and methods.

It is arguable that the outlook regarding knowledge and power not just of the play's main character, but also of its whole surrounding culture, was in transition. One major cause, which is reflected in *The Tempest*, was the effect of knowing the realities of current English transatlantic expansion. It has been argued that at 1610, if well-regarded, the putative wonders of the English New World were far more sobering and less fabulous than the promoters of quick and easy Virginian wealth and glory had proposed. Indeed the new knowledge derived from a clearheaded analysis of the ethnological and political data returning from the English settlement lay somewhere between humbling and crushing to any inflated hopes of a glorious or quickly profitable plantation.

The specifics of a contemporary North American context have been linked here to particular scientific investigations and also to a range of symbolisms in *The Tempest*. Such specifics are indicative of ongoing changes in the pursuit of knowledge, but are by no means their only indicator. To show this, finally I want to introduce a last voice into this study, that of Sir Epicure Mammon, who will help explain the particular perspective that I have taken on *The Tempest*.

Sir Epicure, a character in Ben Jonson's 1610 *The Alchemist*, is convinced by propaganda about great profits to be made from the New World, as befits an English would-be sophisticate of his time. Expecting a colossal return on his investments with them, Mammon enters inviting the skeptical Surley into the purloined house of a team of alchemical confidence tricksters: "Come on, sir. Now, you set your foot on shore / In *nouo orbe*; Here's the rich *Peru*." He then gestures towards their offstage laboratory: "And there within, sir, are the golden mines" (2.1.1–3).[1] Mammon also plans to use his wealth to "purchase *Deuonshire*, and *Cornwaile*, / And make them perfect *Indies*!" (2.1.35–36), but this reference is no more central to his concerns than is his belief that the sham alchemist Subtle was "A man, the Emp'rour / Has courted, aboue Kelly" (4.1.89–90). This reference to Rudolf II's patronage of alchemists, and particularly to the sorry farce that culminated in the death of John Dee's roguish medium Kelly,[2] again reflects the interests of the age, as does Mammon's reference to a supposedly "Egyptian" practice of time acceleration as seen in the incubation of hens' eggs in furnaces (2.3.124–40). The latter is usually glossed as an echo of Pliny, but since, as has been seen, Jonson was interested in him, this last allusion is likely to one of the genuine achievements of the inventor Cornelius Drebbel, another alchemical servant of Rudolf.

These allusions pale, however, beside the tremendous symphonic crescendo of Epicure Mammon's grand fantasies of how he will use the unlimited wealth and power that the any-minute-expected alchemical "projection" will bring him. He will seize all imaginable luxuries, reign like a tyrant—making men eunuchs and claiming all wives—and possess the key to eternal youth and vigor. His sexual fantasies are based on the exploits depicted by the Roman writer Elephantis which "dull Aretine / But coldly imitated" (2.2.43–45; favorite allusion of the age[3]). But, thanks to Doll Common's part in the confidence trickster team, he is induced into off-stage unchastity with her alone. This unchastity, expressing the "importune, and carnall appetite" he is warned against (2.3.8), is enough to cause the "projection" to fail. To the sound of "A great crack and noise within" (Jonson's stage direction to 4.5.56), all the vessels and furnaces then explode.

The Tempest contains considerable amounts of alchemical terminology and imagery. When Prospero's "project" "gather[s] to a head" and his "charms crack not" (5.1.1–2), this outcome may have been a calculated reply to the greed- and lust-driven debacle seen in *The Alchemist* of the previous year. Successful projection in *The Tempest* is achieved while, concurrently, Ferdinand and Miranda show their voluntary exemplary chastity, and while Prospero (it has been argued) allows this chastity because he practices a purification of his (as Mammon puts it) "owne base affections" (*Alchemist*, 4.5.76).

However, greater virtue is only a part of what is acquired in the course of *The Tempest*; the image of Prospero's spiritual alchemy may be understood as symbolically underlying the penultimate, but not the ultimate, new means to effectiveness portrayed in the play. Success in spiritual alchemy, leading to spiritually re-balancing or healing "projection," required: the operator's long and arduous preparation (Prospero's); a rare combination of auspicious stars (his "zenith"); a proper mixture of earthy substance or manure (Caliban) with subtler fiery substance (Ariel); a surrounding ambience of chastity (Ferdinand's and Miranda's); and the continuing good spiritual condition and non-greediness of the mage. Especially because of the last of these requirements, no alchemical "project" is certain not to fail or "crack." My claim has been that Prospero's "charms crack not" and "time / Goes upright" (5.1.2–3) only because he pulls himself upright. But finally, I have argued, magical control and magical omniscience themselves must be discarded by him, to allow room for other modes of learning and other means of living that would be occluded or spoiled by magical grandiosity or presumption.

And so at last Prospero willingly renounces magic, while the arts of Jonson's alchemist Subtle and his crew are exposed as never having been other than sham. In *The Alchemist* Mammon too is exposed as having wrought his own downfall by believing all that suited his fancy. Mammon even convinces himself that he knows Doll Common's noble brother well; on witnessing this Surley exclaims over Mammon's connivance "To gull himselfe" (2.3.266–82). Likewise, Mammon is at last legally stymied because he is too ashamed to admit publicly that he "did cosen [him] selfe" (5.5.70).

The chief difference between Shakespeare's and Jonson's comedies, played by the King's Men in two successive seasons, is that Jonson wildly satirizes, while Shakespeare subtly analyzes, contemporary matters concerning delusive and genuine modes of knowledge and knowledge use, and the kinds of confusion or effectiveness that these bestow.

Notes

Unless otherwise noted I will cite Shakespeare texts from the electronic version of the Oxford Shakespeare, edited by Wells and Taylor, 1989. This edition supplies the title abbreviations used in the notes, and the lineation used in the notes and running text. I append a table of the Oxford edition Shakespeare title abbreviations.

1H4	*Henry IV, Part 1*
1H6	*Henry VI, Part 1*
2H4	*Henry IV, Part 2*
ADO	*Much Ado About Nothing*
AIT	*All Is True (Henry VIII)*
ANT	*Antony and Cleopatra*
AWW	*All's Well That Ends Well*
AYL	*As You Like It*
COR	*Coriolanus*
CYL	*The First Part of the Contention (Henry VI, Part 2)*
CYM	*Cymbeline*
ERR	*The Comedy of Errors*
H5	*Henry V*
HAM	*Hamlet*
JC	*Julius Caesar*
JN	*King John*
LLL	*Love's Labour's Lost*
LRF	*The Tragedy of King Lear* (Folio)
LRQ	*The History of King Lear* (Quarto)
LUC	*The Rape of Lucrece*
MAC	*Macbeth*
MM	*Measure for Measure*
MND	*Midsummer Night's Dream*
MV	*The Merchant of Venice*
OTH	*Othello*
PER	*Pericles, Prince of Tyre*
R2	*Richard II*
R3	*Richard III*
RDY	*Richard, Duke of York (Henry VI, Part 3)*
ROM	*Romeo and Juliet*
SHR	*The Taming of the Shrew*
SON	*Sonnets*
STM	*Sir Thomas More*
TGV	*The Two Gentlemen of Verona*
TIM	*Timon of Athens*

TIT	*Titus Andronicus*
TMP	*The Tempest*
TN	*Twelfth Night, or What You Will*
TNK	*Two Noble Kinsmen*
TRO	*Troilus and Cressida*
VEN	*Venus and Adonis*
WIV	*The Merry Wives of Windsor*
WT	*The Winter's Tale*

INTRODUCTION

Epigraph from McMullan 1990, 76 and McKeon 1966, 3.

1. Jardine 1988, 711.

2. The wide variety of differing concepts of science that were implicitly or explicitly expressed by the likes of Bacon, Kepler, Descartes, Boyle, Galileo, Newton, and Locke, and an equally wide range of modern assessments of these positions, are fascinatingly reviewed in McMullan 1990. Crombie 1996c even describes the numerous and contradictory philosophical assessments of Galileo as mutually self-canceling. (Yet Osler 1982 does make a good case for the later Galileo as an example of a departure from the search for "real essences.")

3. See Shapin 1996 and the extensive bibliography there.

4. For a philosophical discussion of this, see Richard W. Miller, 1987.

5. See Kepler 1981, 1997.

6. See Gouk 1999.

7. See Panofsky, 1962, 138–39.

8. See respectively: Ibid., 139 (Fracastro will be met again in chapter 2); Grafton 1991; and Sokol 1991a.

9. This often concerned chronology. See Grafton 1991; Wilcox 1987; and chapter 5.

10. On Burtt's influential 1942 thesis see Lindberg 1990, 15–19, and for objections to it see Hatfield 1990. Johnson 1937, 289, also held that "the philosophical background of the chief [English Renaissance] scientists was predominantly Platonic, and . . . they emphasised the Pythagorean element in Platonism."

11. See: Yates 1975; Gatti 1989; or Mebane 1989.

12. Gatti 1989, 114–88, does make a substantial case for *HAM* bearing some generic relations to Bruno's dialogues in terms of types of social and intellectual satire and (less probably) in relation to skeptical epistemological and cosmological thinking. This however does not make a convincing case that Brunonian Neoplatonic doctrines or "heroic" aesthetics had parallels in, or inspired, Shakespeare's play.

13. Some historians, applying the "only exact science, hindsight," have tended to isolate (from our perspective) Kepler's "lasting" achievements from his intellectual origins. Not so Caspar 1959, 382, which comments on how Kepler's outlook—derived from Plato, Proclus, and Pythagoras—saw mathematics as divinely granted to give the human mind a sample of divine thinking, yet comments, (383), "is there any scholar who would have followed up the given facts more diligently and more open-mindedly?" See similarly Hatfield 1990, 108–10.

14. Although in a celebrated pioneering herbal of 1530 the illustrator Hans Weiditz did show "the withering of a leaf . . . damages due to insect depredation,"

as it is put by George Lawrence as quoted in Ritterbush 1985, 162. One such drawing of Weiditz is reproduced in Hoeniger 1985, 134.

15. See: Panofsky 1962, 153–58; Edgerton 1980, 194–97; Ackerman 1985, 107–22; and Hoeniger 1985, 142.

16. See: Ackerman 1985, 110; Hoeniger 1985, 142, which also describes (130) "remarkable realism and beauty . . . astonishing lifelikeness"; Ritterbush 1985, 160, which cites Susanne Langer and E. H. Gombrich on the "dynamic" process of *representing* rather than merely *indicating* objects; ibid., 162.

17. According to Panofsky 1962 and Edgerton 1980 the development by Western visual art of subtle means to represent the dimensions and functions of objects in space helped to establish (or was equivalent to) scientific thinking. Ackerman 1985 offers further evidence of the influence, but qualifies this conclusion, (124–25). On synergy see: Crombie 1996b and Crombie 1985 (these essays will be discussed at length in chapter 6); Hoeniger 1985; and Ritterbush 1985.

18. Objections were sometimes made in the Renaissance to distractions from the scientific text caused by illustrations: see Hoeniger 1985, 130–31 Kusukawa 2000, especially 105–8; and Reeds 1976, 530–31. Reeds shows that the humanists were divided about this because Pliny condemned but Discorides praised the use of illustrations. Mahoney 1985 opposes the views of Panofsky and Edgerton that developments in Renaissance visual art aided the advancement of science, arguing on a technical basis (concerning effectively the vectorial diagrams of dynamics) with which I do not agree.

19. In Eddington 1931, xi–xii, a modern physicist identifies with Kepler's "sense of mathematical form, an aesthetic instinct for the fitness of things. In these later days it seems to us less incongruous that a planet should be guided by the condition of keeping the Action a minimum than that it should be pulled and pushed by concrete agencies . . . It is only in the latest years that we have gone back to something like Kepler's outlook, so that the music of the spheres is no longer drowned by the roar of machinery."

20. These of course include other dramatic and literary works of Shakespeare and his contemporaries. All quotations from Shakespeare and lineation will be taken from Wells, and Taylor 1989, and the notes will use the title abbreviations from that electronic edition (listed above), exceptions for citations of the First Folio from Shakespeare, 1968, which will use through-line-numbers (tln).

21. This method has often been followed recently in order to serve present-day agendas. Such criticism typically adopts an assumption that the events and ideas of pre-industrial or early modern Europe express a set of easily characterized ideologies, thus constituting, in effect, a nearly unitary "olden times." On the contrary, here Shakespeare's age will be seen to have been mercurial, dynamic, layered, confused, and generally hard to know. No presumptions will be made, either, that the generality of the people of that era were unwashed, or unsubtle, or unsophisticated, or inclined to naivete, or incurious, or monological, or morally transparent.

22. In Henry James 1991, 67.

23. All empirically led historical studies must—in proposing patterns to give meaning to data—form hypotheses incapable of confirmation beyond relative corroboration. This limitation need not, however, entail certain disabling doubts that any study of the past can produce only "his" story, "her" story, or "their" story. Of course, evidence is not always available to answer historical questions, and when it is available historical evidence may give rise to alternative interpretations. Honest attempts at explanation also may be colored by distorting attitudes or opinions (al-

though it seems impossible that these could be so invisible as to be uncorrectable, or how would we know of them?). Nonetheless, historical evidence may still be used with measured confidence to corroborate hypotheses or strengthen the relative probabilities of alternative descriptive and explanatory schemes. "Freeing" history from factuality would merely enslave knowledge to wishful, or self-declared-correct thinking. For the view that history should be freed from an "epistemology of authority" see Waller 1989.

24. Mincoff 1992, 102. These are unusually moderate words, but they were written a decade before their posthumous publication in some isolation from heated Western academic differences.

25. Bishop 1996, 13, while excusing the author's resistance in his book on Shakespeare and Wonder to pursuing a master theory of a "culture of wonder," offers an eloquent reply to such sorts of responses. This explains: "A deeper reason for resisting such an historicist path has been my strong sense that complex verbal artifacts such as plays demand and deserve treatment of an answering patience and complexity, one that is not always easy to achieve, least of all where one eye must be kept on the pursuit of a large historical thesis." See, similarly, McDonald 1991, 26, which complains that "most recent political readings" of TMP cannot admit "The sophisticated effects of form and style" and the "self-awareness" in the play itself of larger issues. Willis 1989, 278, complains that in such readings "the play vanishes," while Hamlin 1994, 20–21, argues against the "exclusive" quality of some "colonialist readings of The Tempest [which] tend to condemn all other readings as ahistorical."

26. Bate 1994, 6.

27. Ibid., 7.

28. Ibid., 6, which also gives credit to Bakhtin and Kristeva and to Barker and Hulme respectively for the formulations "intertextuality" and "discursive contexts."

29. Ibid., 6.

30. In Barker and Hulme 1985, further discussed below.

31. Bate 1994, 10.

32. The Folio's "Names of the Actors" is found in Shakespeare 1968, 37. The Folio's attribution to Miranda of the passage beginning "Abhorred Slaue" (ibid. tln 491) is debatable; Proudfoot 2002, 138–39 makes an extremely cogent and interesting argument to the contrary.

33. Yet Jacobus 1992, 143, thinks he does. Hunt 1995, 182–84, correctly notices that while Caliban is enslaved, "Prospero's enslavement of [Ariel]" is only in "Ariel's report"; however, this discrimination is not related to the dramatic text, but instead to a dubiously historical discussion of employment practices versus enslavement.

34. In other words, Prospero employs a method of sarcasm by inversion: he mocks the claims of enslavement made by his aide-de-camp spirit by concatenating a recollection of Ariel's "report" that he has been enslaved by Prospero with the mock-bland misreckoning that Ariel had been only a mere "servant" to the abhorred Sycorax.

35. Or is the misremembering Ariel called "Dull thing" by Prospero in 1.2.286? Again the syntax is ambiguous.

36. Aside from in the treatment of the witty twin Dromios in the classically inspired ERR, and a few places indicating the lover's Petrarchan service to the mistress, almost all Shakespearian references to a "slave" appear in contexts of verbal abuse. An exception occurs in warrior Othello's account of his wild adven-

tures, including "being taken by the insolent foe / And sold to slavery, of my redemption thence" (*OTH* 1.3.136–37); as Slights 1997, 383, points out, Othello's slavery is not seen as any disgrace (although Cheadle 1994 thinks that Brabantio, in questioning the Moor's exotic adventures, indicates a prejudice against him). In short, "slave" is used generally as a term of vilification in Shakespeare's plays, while the immorality of slave-owning is expressed in *MV* 4.1.89–92, as discussed in Sokol 1998.

37. However, Bate, unlike less subtle critics, is still able to diverge from a favored "master-discourse," and so finds near the play's end a "movement away from secular wisdom and power," which are the goals of humanism, and "towards Christian humility and mortification" (Bate 1994, 19).

38. Or, in some cases, these aspects have been denied. See: D. G. James, 1965, 28, which, after contrasting Prospero with Francis Bacon, finds in "the work of Shakespeare as a whole . . . neither a manifest faith nor any concern with the understanding of the physical world"; or Mincoff 1992, 114, which claims that "There is no justification for identifying Prospero . . . with modern science harnessing the forces of nature, for then the breaking of his magic staff becomes inexplicable."

39. Yates 1975, 86–87.

40. See Feldhay 1995, 240–55.

41. Because no stellar parallax was detectable in Shakespeare's age, heliocentrism had nothing to do with the existence of "deep" or "infinite" space. This latter was implied by the trajectories of comets, and by novas, and it was speculated upon by Giodorno Bruno and others. Empson 1993, 216–19, counts Thomas Digges, John Dee's pupil, as first among these others, and emphasizes that the discovery that stars lie at varied and very great distances from the earth made more likely the earth's daily rotation on its axis, if not its annual revolution around the sun. Thomas Digges's widow Anne married Shakespeare's friend Thomas Russell, and Hotson 1937, 118–24, proposes that Shakespeare knew the first husband also. On Thomas Digges's astronomy and its impact see also: Johnson 1937, 144 and 160; McLean 1972, 146–47; and Empson 1994, 203–6. Deep or infinite space is perhaps alluded to in *HAM* 2.2.256–58: "I could be bounded in a nutshell and count myself a king of infinite space, were it not that I have bad dreams"—on this see Gatti 1989, 145–50.

42. Ibid., 132–33 and 140–41 pursues the cosmological implications of the purloined love letter read in *HAM* 2.2.116–19, " 'Doubt thou the stars are fire, / Doubt that the sun doth move / Doubt truth to be a liar, / But never doubt I love," but this avowal refers to only skepticism, not heliocentrism.

43. See Nicolson, 1976. Flynn 1987 locates the stress in *Ignatius* mainly in Donne's attack on the relationship of Robert Cecil with King James, although, ibid., 170, connects the poem with the scientific contacts of Thomas Harriot, Kepler, and the imprisoned Earl of Northumberland.

44. See Nicolson 1960.

45. Since E. M. W. Tillyard's brief pedagogical rendering of it, it has become the favorite straw man of Shakespeare's politicized detractors.

46. Earth must be what is meant by "this centre," since that is distinguished from "The heavens," "the planets" and by extension "the glorious planet Sol."

47. Sig. B4r-B4v, in Smith 1986, 1:48–49. A later account by Smith of this same incident (containing different spellings of Native American names) will be discussed in chapter 5.

48. Empson carried forward into his Shakespearian studies his ideas about

Donne's responses to the New Philosophy and about a supposedly widespread yet covert Elizabethan Copernicanism; see Empson 1993, 197–98, 200–206, and 207–19. Empson relied on Johnson 1937, which includes, aside from his citations, the following statements: 144, "the intemperate and sweeping assault on all ancient authorities which was characteristic of some of the Ramists was not in harmony with the more reasonable and judicious attitude typical of the leading English scientists of the sixteenth century . . . Men like Recorde, Dee, and the latter's pupil, Thomas Digges, were all far abler and more learned in the mathematical sciences than Ramus"; 288, "The English scientists . . . were . . . actively associated with a large circle of persons famous for the parts they played in the history and literature of the Elizabethan age. Their books, furthermore, were widely read in England, often going through several editions"; and 292, "Among scientists of recognized standing in England, the old Ptolemaic system was completely discredited from the end of the first decade of the seventeenth century onward."

49. Empson 1994, 194–222.

50. Ibid., 218, presents the Newtonian equations governing the dynamics of satellites as demonstrable by simple geometrical means. However, this supposed reconstruction of a "likely discovery" by Harriot involves using a differential vectorial diagram and a gravitational law not known until between decades and centuries after Shakespeare's death in 1616.

51. Empson 1993, 207–8.

52. Hall 1999, especially 124–34.

53. Hassel 1980, 221–22.

54. See Hassel 1971, especially 335, which alleges that the Copernican "revolutions frightened Donne and his thoughtful contemporaries."

55. Wagner 1933, 23.

56. Ibid., 28–33.

CHAPTER 1. THE NATURAL HISTORY OF PEARLS

1. Frye 1986, 180.

2. Charles E. Ravan, lecturing in 1951, quoted in Hoeniger 1985, 147 n. 11.

3. Hoeniger 1985, 132.

4. Ashworth 1990, 303. This argues that modern scholarship has overlooked the natural historians of the period 1560–1660 because it insufficiently appreciates their dominantly "emblematic world view." It will be argued here that overcoming such a view was a significant achievement of early modern natural history.

5. Chapter 2 will provide examples from theoretical demographics. Thomas 1971, 647–56, explains further that the life and human sciences became more rational and more mathematical within Shakespeare's century in parallel with the emergence of statistics and probability theory, and attributes to the rise of these theories (and with them an insurance industry) the decline in the uncertainty that may have inspired magical thinking in pre-modern Europe. See also Jacob and Raylor 1991.

6. See the article on Rondelet (1507–1566) by A. G. Keller in Gillispie 1971, 11:527–28.

7. See Bylebyl 1985, especially 38–39, on how the initial purely philological and philosophical humanism of the medical profession mutated during the Re-

naissance toward a new model of the philosopher-physician as an experimenter, practitioner, and anatomist (a model based on Galen).

8. Renaissance questioning of and debate over of Pliny's accuracy began very early, as explained in Reeds 1976 523–24. Ritterbush 1985, 158, claims that Ermolao Barbaro's *Castigationes plinanae* of 1492–1493 examined Pliny's use of textual sources, but "did not seek evidence from contemporary scientific observation." Hoeniger 1985, 137, also notes Renaissance doubts about Pliny, citing (147n) Nicolo Leoniceno in 1492. A critique of *"Plinies* judgement" had become a commonplace, according to Montaigne's "It is Follie to Referre Truth or Falsehood to our Sufficiencie," in Montaigne 1942, 1:190–5, 193.

9. Hoeniger 1985, 135 and 138–39. This evidence, and what will be seen below regarding Rondelet's studies of pearls and his critique of Pliny on pearls, overrides the view in Copenhaver 1990, 278, which includes Rondelet with others whose "humanist natural history was so loaded with philological baggage" that they "recertified the intellectual value of Greco-Roman sources" and depended very "little on contemporary experience." On Rondelet also see Thorndike 1941, 6:212, 268, 271, 290, and on his empiricism especially, 268 and 282.

10. See Thomas 1971, passim, and especially 643–47. For a claim that analogical or emblematic thinking persisted see Ashworth 1990. For a claim that it was being superseded by a use of "symbols" that "are capable of conveying a wide range of meaning, of engaging the imagination of the viewer and enabling him to transcend prior experience" see Ritterbush 1985, 159–60.

11. Hoeniger 1985, 132.

12. Holden 1991, 192.

13. Rondelet's ideas are however reflected in successive editions of Conrad Gesner's *Historiae Animalium Liber IV. Qui est de Piscium & Aquatium animantium natura*. Both Gesner 1558, 620–21, and Gesner 1560, 233–34, name and paraphrase Rondelet on pearl formation, while Gesner 1604, 269 quotes him verbatim, and adds beside this quotation a marginal pointer indicating: "Unio in Conchis quimodo concreseat."

14. Pliny 1601, 254–55 (in chapter 35, 254–58).

15. Ibid., 255.

16. See: Kunz and Stevenson 1993, 57–8; and George Frederick Herbert Smith 1972, 480–81.

17. See: George Frederick Herbert Smith 1972, 483–84; and Bauer 1968, 2:588–89.

18. McLean 1972, 173. Pages 210–24 survey the study of natural history in Tudor England. Reeds 1976, 523 indicates that Pliny was a favorite humanist text, and indicates its (limited) use in universities (536). Kay 1999, 166–67, indicates the continuing importance of Pliny for "early modern scientists."

19. Baldwin 1935.

20. See: Muir 1953; Muir 1957, 127–28; Seaman 1968; Bullough 1975, 7:211; Simmons 1976; and Gutierrez 1985.

21. In *ANT* 2.5.45–46.

22. Pliny 1601, 257.

23. *HAM* 5.2.234–78; on the pearl in *HAM* representing either medicine or poison see Nardo 1985 and West 1991.

24. This was the Jamestown colony, the first that was destined to survive following the failure at Roanoke.

25. New world economic and social themes will be closely considered in the next two chapters.

26. See: Captain Arthur Barlowe's account of his 1584 Virginia reconnaissance, Barlowe 1955, 1:91–116 and 110; the more sober Harriot 1955, 1:333–34; and a manuscript of c. 1609–1612 (which collates several sources, untangled in Culliford, 1950 332–64) presented to the Earl of Northumberland by William Strachey, Strachey 1953, 132. Also see Kunz and Stevenson 1993, 487–89 and 256–57.

27. See: Kunz and Stevenson 1993, 23 and 225–33; and Kunz 1916, 19.

28. *ERR* 3.2.116 and 136–41. Pearls and female noses will be discussed in the next section of this chapter.

29. Conlan 1999, 169 and 184–85 n. 35, claims that much of the plot of *TMP*, and also Caliban's name, come from Peter Martyr. It is often noted that the English translation by Richard Eden, Anglerie 1555, included a report of the voyage of Magellan from which the name of Sycorax's god "Setebos," twice invoked by Caliban in *TMP*, is apparently taken. This god is named in *TMP* 1.2.375 and 5.1.264, and is twice said to have been named by Native Patagonian "giantes" in Anglerie 1555, leaves 219v and 220v.

30. Ibid., leaf 142v.

31. Ibid., leaf 141r.

32. Ibid., leaf 142r.

33. Ibid.

34. From the twelfth century according to Holden 1991, 193; from the thirteenth century according to George Frederick Herbert Smith 1972, 485; from "about" the fourteenth century according to Kunz and Stevenson 1993, 285.

35. Reprinted as Kunz and Stevenson 1993.

36. Teixeira 1902, *Appendix A*, 179–80. This is translated from Teixeira 1610, 32–33, in a separately paginated appendix beginning with a "Breve Relacion del Principo del Reyno Harmvz," occupying 1–45.

37. An unchallenging tone is shared by many of the pioneers of these ideas, but perhaps is especially Teixeira's because, although nominally converted, he was born (and seemingly died) a Jew, and so wanted to avoid seeming heterodox. His book did obtain the requisite Church "certificate of orthodoxy and license to print," printed after 215 in Teixeira 1610, and translated in Teixeira 1902, cviii.

38. Hawkins 1622, 88–89.

39. But note that Strachey 1625, although it was published even later than Hawkins's narrative, was probably read by Shakespeare before *TMP* was written (possibly by the means described in Hotson 1937, 219–26; see also Hantman 1992, 72–73).

40. According to W. H. Smith, editor of Benzoni 1862, ii.

41. Benzoni 1579. Many may have been drawn to read this on account of its striking account of Spanish cruelties in the New World.

42. Ibid., 161–62, my translation.

43. An attempt to trace this by using book provenance studies will be delineated in the forthcoming Sokol, 2004.

44. Boodt 1609, 84, which has an accurate French rendition in Boot and Till 1654, 2:211–12. Thorndike 1941, 6:318–24, emphasizes de Boodt's credulity, not noting his ideas about pearls (and implying beozar stones were not real, although they are). Bolton 1904, 99, mockingly identifies de Boodt as "the favorite physician of Rudolph [II] in his later years . . . being an advocate of the verity of transmutation." It will be argued in chapter 4 that Rudolf may have had a significant importance in the conception of *TMP*.

45. Rondeletius 1554, in an attached second part dated 1555, 33–34, 55–61.

This (34) and a French edition, Rondelet, 1558 2:24–25, make the medical comparisons.

46. Many of these instances were found in computerized searches for the wild-card string "pe*rl*" (used to accommodate alternative spellings) on the Chadwyck–Healey databases of English Poetry (ver. 4.0), English Verse Drama (ver. 2.0), and English Prose Drama (ver. 2.0). Wherever possible the electronic texts were checked against original or early editions.

47. Kunz 1916, 44.

48. The Geneva "Bible," 1587.

49. *TRO* 2.2.80–82.

50. *OTH* 5.2.356–57; this echoes Matt. 7, yet Seaman 1968 finds the parable in Matt. 13 basic to *OTH*.

51. *LLL* 4.2.87–88.

52. Sweat in *LUC* 396; this comparison was common in verse and drama, as in: John Donne's Elegy VIII, "The Comparison," ll. 1–14, in Donne 1960, 81; Christopher Middleton 1596, l. 258; the anonymous play *Dick of Devonshire* in "Dick of Devonshire," 1955, 55, l. 1330; Dekker's 1600 *Old Fortunatus*, in Dekker 1953, 1:176 (4.2.11–14); Tasso 1600, Book 9, verse 81, line 6, and Book 16, verse 18, line 4; and F[letcher], 1633a, 46, Eclogue Seven: "The Prize," verse 10, line 5.

53. A causative connection, accepted by Camden, remained current until 1684, as shown in Kunz and Stevenson 1993, 37 and 39.

54. Marvell 1971, 1:12.

55. *MND* 1.1.209–11.

56. Norden 1614, ll. 431–32.

57. *Midas* (London, 1592), in Lyly 1902, 3:142 (4.9.109–10).

58. *Satiro-mastix* (London, 1602), in Dekker 1953, 1:360 (4.3.46).

59. See George Chapman, *The Memorable Maske of the Middle Temple and Lyncolns Innne* (London, 1613), ed. G. Blakemore Evans in Chapman 1970, 1:557–86. This and a converse treatment of greedy settlers in the suppressed 1605 play *Eastward Ho!* are discussed in Sokol and Sokol 1996 and in Gillies 1986.

60. Reprinted in "True Declaration . . ." 1844, 9.

61. B[astard] 1598, *Liber Quartus*, 85–86.

62. *The Steele Glas* (London, 1576), in Gascoigne 1907, 2:153.

63. Such as Kendall 1577, 97v, "To a certayne Draper": "Thy Nose is precious, full of pearles," or Drummond of Hawthornden 1913, 1:102, "Alcons Kisse": "*What others at their Eare / Two Pearles* Camilla *at her Nose did weare.*"

64. Suckling 1971, 1:33.

65. Davies of Hereford 1609, 203–4.

66. Sylvester 1621, 443 (The second book of the Fourth Day of the Second Week). On page 449, Sylvester actually questions the old theory of pearl formation: "Whether the Heav'ns sweet-sweating Kisse appear / To be Pearls parent, and the Oysters Pheer." "Pheer" means "frere" or mate.

67. The song is part of Lyly's "The Entertainment . . . at Cowdray, 1591," in Lyly 1902, 1:429, l. 10. The proverb is listed as P166.1 in Dent 1981, 190.

68. F[letcher] 1633b, 125.

69. As in Boodt 1609, 84.

70. First published in *Two New Plays* (London, 1657), performed 1613–27, in Thomas Middleton 1981, 52 (2.2.105–6).

71. Thomas Heywood, *Loves Mistress or The Queens Masque* (London, 1636), ll. 4.1.52–55, in Heywood 1792, sig. I4v.

72. Transliterated in James VI of Scotland 1947, 1:150 (ll. 682–84).

73. "Bible," 1587. Shakespeare often responded to Genevan marginalia, as illustrated in Sokol 1998 and Stritmatter 2000.

74. See *TGV* 5.2.11–14. *TIT* 5.1.42 echoes the same proverb, M79 in Tilley 1950, 408: "A black man is a pearl (jewel) in a fair woman's eye."

75. As this law states only that historical contexts may be overridden, not that they are insignificant, it does not fall foul of the "autonomous fallacy" mentioned in Weimann 1974, 166.

76. In chapters 5 and 7.

77. Torrens 1971, 96.

78. Eliot 1934, 49–50.

79. Ferdinand's seeming loss, however, also encourages his accelerated maturing without condemning him as an ingrate like Prince Florizel of *WT*. Ferdinand in relation to his new "father" Prospero will be considered in the last chapter of this study.

80. "Air" is used to mean wordless music or melody alone in *TMP* 5.1.58 (and probably 3.2.139), in accord with *OED* IV.18.

81. *The Duchess of Malfi* (London, 1623), in Webster 1995, 1:545, 4.2.203–5.

82. *WT* 5.3.37, 5.3.24, and 5.3.99.

Chapter 2. Scientific Theory

1. This paralleled developments in early modern English common law which often pressed older procedures or forms to new uses, or radically reinterpreted the meaning of older forms to suit current needs.

2. Crombie 1996c, 261.

3. The advance in knowledge discussed in chapter 1 falls ludicrously short of the "paradigm shifts" posited in some recent views of scientific progression. Yet Krige 1994 argues that certain stages of scientific development must be destructive of past certainties, and so science may be discontinuous or revolutionary, as is typified in Galileo's anti-Aristotelianism. Krige thus sides with Kuhn but not with Lâkatos and certainly not with the radical Feyerabend against Popper's model of scientific rationality. Westman 1982 offers a fascinating alternative to both sides of this debate in its account of Rheticus, an early Copernican realist. In this account neither rationality nor irrationality causes shifts between scientific paradigms or research programs; instead, personal unconscious desires motivate either a mixture or a separation of views that have been only subsequently labeled conceptually incompatible.

4. Jardine 1986; Grafton 1991. For an older view holding that Kepler was mainly devoted to occultism and animistic thinking, see Thorndike 1941, 7:11–31.

5. On Kepler's resistance to prognostication see Caspar 1959, 154–56 and 302–3, and on his methods of evasion see ibid., 339–42.

6. See ibid., 181–85 on Kepler on astrology and a psychological constitution; Keplers's views will be further discussed in chapter 6.

7. Quoted as translated in ibid., 279.

8. For the fuller context and a more prolix translation of the above see Kepler 1997, 375–79.

9. Grafton 1991, 38. Thus Kepler found it is not caused, for instance, by conjunctions or novas; see ibid., 37–39.

10. See: North 1974; and Westfall 1982, 120n.

11. See Van Helden 1982.

12. See Westfall 1982, which argues that Galileo delayed publication until he had arranged to get a chance of patronage well in place. Also, *Sidereus nuncius* enjoyed its immediate fame partly thanks to the response of Kepler who published his generous admiration of the work in 1610 in Kepler 1965.

13. Even Krige 1994, 218, admits: "Revolutionary transformations of the human understanding are neither cataclysmic nor do they demolish an existing structure in one blinding flash. They develop unevenly."

14. Kepler 1992, 1997.

15. Yet Kepler did suffer some personal problems resulting from his religious convictions, and (quite independently of that) his own elderly mother was accused of witchcraft.

16. This was his abandonment of circular planetary orbits, as described in 1609 in Kepler 1992.

17. This is surprising, for literature has some affinities with theoretical science. Similar features of extending received forms or traditions, of playfulness, and of curiosity are equally characteristic in works of speculative scientific theory as they are in some instances of literary brilliance. Influences and traditions may not always cause "anxiety" or be straitjacketing for literature or for science; rather, they have often been the starting points for, and the pointers toward, works in which they are surpassed. A few poets have expressed awareness of the game-like and dramatic-plot-like qualities of speculative science (especially Robert Frost, on whom see Sokol 1996).

18. Sir Charles Cavendish (1591–1662) was a pivotal figure in contemporary intellectual life; see Jacquot 1952a and 1949. He was Margaret Cavendish's close companion, especially when she was stranded in England and writing her first book; see Grant 1957 and Jones 1988, 94.

19. For details see Sokol 2002.

20. For embarrassed excuses see: Bowerbank 1984, 402; Sarasohn 1984, 290–93; and Sherman 1994, 189–90.

21. These include: C. H. Firth, the editor of Cavendish 1906, xxviii; Reynolds 1920, 49; and Mendelson 1987, 37–38.

22. Especially Clucas 1994, 259–64; also Nicolson 1965, 103–14, and Hilda L. Smith 1982, 75–95.

23. C. H. Firth, the editor of Cavendish 1906, xxix. Reynolds 1920, 49, contrasts Cavendish's supposed dogmatism with the "experimental method [which] was having its triumph."

24. Bowerbank 1984, 398. Meyer 1955, 2, wishes that Cavendish had "been a follower of the empirical school of Bacon," and (3) blames her faults on "Cartesian rationalism, the principles of which warped permanently her scientific outlook." Mendelson 1987, 37, laments that "the concept of science as an experimental discipline was not fully established until late in the seventeenth century," thus making space for Cavendish's grotesque propensity for theories.

25. Mintz 1952, 176.

26. Quoted disparagingly from Cavendish's *Observations upon Experimental Philosophy* in Meyer 1955, 4. Bowerbank 1984, 400, similarly finds the elevation of speculative philosophy in this book whimsically "curious."

27. It is, however, possible that Harriot as a mathematician (and a poet!) was distinctly on Shakespeare's mind at the opposite end of his career, when he wrote *LLL*; see Sokol 1991.

28. See Mancosu 1996.

29. The method of starting with simplifying hypotheses and correcting these only when needed is still used in science to good effect. This is clearly described and exemplified, for instance, in Leader and Predazzi 1996, 1:352 and 1:353.

30. See Grafton 1991, 32–39, on Kepler and the study of chronology in which "philology and science intersected."

31. Harriot's population calculations are scattered throughout many folios of his mathematical papers in British Library *Add.* 6782 and 6788. The quotations here derive from British Library *Add.* 6782, fol. 31 recto and verso. The other folios contain rough work, and Harriot's calculations of population for many intervals up to 340 years. These papers are described in detail in Sokol 1974a.

32. For more examples and more technical detail see ibid., which analyzes into a mathematical formula the rules that these calculations follow (212).

33. See ibid., 205 and 212.

34. His English departure and arrival dates were 9 April 1585 and early July 1586: he left from Roanoke with Drake in June 1586. I have consulted the British Library copy (G.7132) of Harriot 1588, but unless otherwise noted I will cite Harriot 1955.

35. Published as: Greenblatt 1981, Greenblatt 1985a, Greenblatt 1985b, and Greenblatt 1988. Unless otherwise noted it will be cited from Greenblatt 1988.

36. McAlindon 1995 and Vickers 1993, 248–71, have powerfully critiqued the methodology of this essay; I am more concerned with the content in Sokol 1994 and (with revisions) here.

37. The description "friend-companion-advisor" was offered to me in private correspondence in 1975 by John W. Shirley, later Harriot's biographer.

38. See Sokol 1974b.

39. Shirley 1983, 364.

40. See Batho 1992, 5–7.

41. Shirley 1983 further details that in about 1595 "Harriot changed his primary allegiance from Ralegh's household to that of the 9th Earl" but that "his interest and friendship remained centered in both," adding that Harriot was a friend and factotum to Raleigh but "With Northumberland . . . he was a pensioned gentleman" (223). This states also, that Northumberland supplied Harriot with "a lavish pension (equal that he gave his younger brothers) from the early 1580s until his death" (365).

42. See Shirley 1974; King James's superstitious questions for the investigation of Harriot are on p. 28.

43. See Shirley and Quinn 1969.

44. Harriot 1955, 368.

45. There are some tantalizing clues about lost or scattered Harriot papers. Shirley 1974, 19, mentions John Pell's 1684 report to Aubrey of Harriot's special alphabet for the Algonkian language: this may be the rediscovered material revealed by Salmon 1993.

46. On the loss of Harriot's American materials see Quinn 1955, 1:54–55 and 1:389; on Harriot's promised but undelivered chronicle of earlier Virginian voyages see ibid., 387.

47. Many of the detractors and defenders of the second Virginia settlement are reviewed in Sokol and Sokol 1996.

48. Quoted in Shirley 1983, 95.

49. Jacquot 1952b, 183. A similar assessment appears in McLean 1972, 150–55.

50. James 1967, 79. Ibid., 79–82 and 114–16, also suggest Harriot's direct influence on Shakespeare.

51. "Learning to Curse: Aspects of Linguistic Colonialism in the Sixteenth Century," 1976, reprinted in Greenblatt 1990, 16–39.

52. Records of Harriot's linguishtic efforts are revealed in Salmon 1993. Vaughan 2002 discusses Harriot's and Raleigh's relations with these and others of their interpreters.

53. All citations will be from the the British Library copy (G.6837) of the English version of de Bry 1590. This edition paginates the initial portion reprinting Harriot's *A briefe and true report* up to 33. Thereafter, following a second title page reading "The True Pictures and Fashions of the People in that Parte of America now called Virginia," it consists of unpaginated captioned illustrations.

54. Quinn 1955, 1:399–400.

55. Although Barlowe's narrative was first printed in Richard Hakluyt's 1589 *Principall navigations* (which contained also a second edition of *A brief and true report*), the authoritative Quinn 1955, 1:16–17, asserts that it was very probably known to Harriot by 1585 and was possibly prepared for publication by Harriot himself. It will be cited from Quinn 1955, 1:91–115.

56. The last phrase, implying Barlowe's knowledge of other regions, is found in ibid., 105, and has variants in ibid., 95, 103, and 106.

57. Ibid., 98–99; for a moving account of the hospitality shown to Barlowe's party by the women of Roanoke Island see ibid., 107–10.

58. Ibid., 110n; this adds that Barlowe's claim that the Native Americans made wine was "almost certainly mistaken."

59. Ibid., 113.

60. Ibid., 108.

61. De Bry's plates 13 and 15; the captions are in Quinn 1955, 1:435 and 1:437.

62. De Bry plates 16 and 15; the captions are in Quinn 1955, 1:430 and 1:438.

63. The John White watercolor drawings are in the British Museum, P. & D. 1906-5-9-1. They and the de Bry engravings related to them are analyzed and reproduced in Quinn and Hulton 1964.

64. White's drawing titles and Harriot's corresponding captions are printed in Quinn and Hulton 1964, and also together with an analysis of the relation of the White drawings and de Bry's engravings in Quinn 1955, 1:390–464.

65. These expert opinions are in the first case paraphrased and in the second directly quoted in Quinn and Hulton 1964, 1:40.

66. This is because in the engraving they are only letters keyed to a caption, a device needed for de Bry's multilingual edition.

67. Edgerton 1980, 202, points out that Christian typology allowed Renaissance views to "suspend their sense of time unity," and that the special techniques of scientific illustration (as for instance simultaneous multiple views as seen here, on which see Introduction above) depended on a corresponding suspension of spatial unity.

68. Harriot 1955, 338.

69. Ibid., 343.

70. However, Kupperman 1980, 5–6, 115, 129, posits that so many died of diseases brought by the first European visitors that the earlier population is hard to estimate.

71. On Harriot's pioneering work in mathematical inequalities, the basis of the idea of limits, see Tanner 1961, 165–67.

72. Harriot 1955, 369 and 343.

73. Moreover, as kindly conveyed to me by D. B. Quinn at the 1994 Thomas

Harriot seminar, Harriot's and White's explorations could well have been focused on the area of the Great Dismal Swamp, which was an unpopulous yet very fertile region of Raleigh's Virginia.

74. See Sokol 1974a, 205.

75. More 1909, 110–18.

76. Harriot 1955, 337–39.

77. Ibid., 343.

78. Based on the ratio of 25 square yards per person in Virginia to the figure of $5^{8}/_{11}$ acres per person in England discussed previously.

79. On the remarks of Nashe, Greene, and Bruno see Jacquot 1952b, 170–74; this does not note that Harriot had a far better reason than they did for wondering about Genesis. Jacquot rather remarks that "Whatever else [Harriot] may have rejected of the Old Testament, he certainly preserved the ethical teachings of universal character."

80. Here it is important to note that, unlike the speculations of Giodorno Bruno, its temper was not in any sense mystical. According to Henry 1982, Harriot was not influenced in his atomism by Bruno's infinitism because he (Harriot) was too mathematically sophisticated and therefore aware of paradoxes.

81. Jacquot 1974, 108.

82. Greenblatt 1988, 24.

83. Ibid., 31. The invisible "subversiveness" is of course attributed to a social, not a personal, unconscious.

84. Ibid., 21.

85. Ibid., 33.

86. This same passage is considered in terms of American university textbooks and a putative "Elizabethan telescope" in chapter 4 herein.

87. A similar understanding to mine is expressed in Jehlen 1994, 62–65. Although I am not convinced by Jehlen's view that in multiple ways Harriot's "report is not balanced but dualistic," I agree that the text of *A briefe and true report* shows Harriot "impressed" when observing the "Indians" he himself set out to impress with European technology. Jehlen's further proposal that in the encounter Harriot "without personal arrogance, nonetheless finds his own and his fellows' powers of mind and making just a little amazing" (63–64) lacks textual support, but in any case Jehlen (unlike Greenblatt) detects in Harriot's account of his encounter mutual responses.

88. Greenblatt 1988, 31–32.

89. In Greenblatt 1981, 41, and Greenblatt 1985b, 277–78.

90. Rosen 1974, 2–4, reviews Harriot's optical interests, and shows that he derived, in advance of Snell and Descartes, Snell's important "sine law" of refraction.

91. Harriot's own copy of Alhazan's and Vitelo's *Optics*, ed. F. Risner, Basle, 1572, was found in Oslo University library by Johannes Lohne and reported upon in Lohne 1959; ibid., 114, transcribes Harriot's note on p. 453 of Risner's edition as dated "158(?) august 29." The last digit of the year is indistinct, but in the photographic facsimile included with Lohne's article it seems like a "4" to me. It does so also in Pepper 1974, 87n.

92. For details of Vitelo or Witelo and Ibn al-Haitham (965–c. 1039) see Rosen 1974, 2–3.

93. Translated from Latin in Kargon 1966, 131.

94. See Kargon 1966, 131. Sokol 2002 shows that her atomism and not, as often alleged, her zaniness worried Margaret Cavendish's friends.

95. Translated from Latin in Kargon 1966, 131. Kepler's reluctance to appear excessively heterodox must be put in the context of his courage in not changing his Protestant religion despite its disadvantages, and of a world in which accusations of witchcraft against his own mother began in 1615 and culminated with threats of torture in 1621 (see Caspar 1959, 240–56 and passim).

96. Greenblatt 1988, 35.

97. Harriot 1955, 380.

98. Ibid., 384–85.

99. Kargon 1966, 130–31. Harriot needed atomism to account for phenomena that were occult in the sense of insensible; on the term "occult" in that technical sense, and on its seventeenth-century history, see Hutchison 1982.

100. This would not have been wholly unprecedented, as Girolomo Fracastro (1478–1553), in his *De Contagione et Contagiosis Morbis et Curatione* of 1546 proposed *semia* of contagion; Bruno Zanobio in his article on Fracastro in Gillispie 1971, 5:104–7, proposes this idea "derived from Democritean atomism."

101. This hard-to-prove claim is made in Jehlen 1994, 65.

102. Harriot 1955, 381.

103. Ibid., 372, but see ibid., n. 1, on how unusual this was in itself.

104. Chapman 1957, 1:15–16.

105. Chapman 1941, 381–84.

CHAPTER 3. *THE TEMPEST* AND NEW WORLD CULTURAL ENCOUNTER

Epigraph from Strachey 1953, 19.

1. For a classical discussion with a survey of earlier critics see Kermode 1962, xxv–xxxiv. See also: Kelsey 1914; Marx 1974; Levin 1970; Knight 1980; Marienstras 1981; Hulme 1986; Orgel 1987a; Vaughan 1988; Greenblatt 1990; Roberts 1991; Vaughan and Vaughan 1991; Knapp 1992; Jowett 1993; Hamlin 1994, 1995; Albanese 1996; and Salingar 1996. Hantman 1992 is unusual, as it attempts to judge the perceptions by Native Americans of the Europeans at Jamestown around 1607.

2. See Introduction.

3. Barker and Hulme 1985, 204.

4. Knapp 1992, 331. This complains of readings of colonialism that "transform Jacobean expansion into a monolithic 'discourse' abstract enough to escape the restrictions of practical counterevidence." For an incisive critique of reductive approaches to *TMP* see Righter 1968, 7–51, especially 21–25. Although all-inclusive theories of "discourses of power" are still often posited, for a decade many have questioned the appropriateness of these to *TMP*, including: Skura 1989; Willis 1989; McDonald 1991; Robin Headlam Wells 1994; and Hamlin 1994.

5. For instance, Burnett 1991, 237, says in relation to racial bigotry in an English encyclopedia 1923 "One might be forgiven for thinking that these imperial views have little to do with the English Renaissance," but demurs that they do, and traces them to *TMP* and other writings of the English Renaissance. Hattaway 1996, 183, holds that Shakespeare in *TMP* "may even be considered the prototype of the post-colonial writer."

6. Lim 1998, 19. Hamlin 1995, 102–3 and 107, similarly critiques limitations.

7. Sokol and Sokol 1996.

8. Barker and Hulme 1985, 200.

9. A wholly opposite view (without reference to Barker's and Hulme's) is expressed in the very recent but unreliable Lee Miller 2001, 217–19, which claims that after 1609 there was a home-front (it seems like an anti-Vietnam-war-style) peace movement against the English oppression of the Powhattan people: "England erupts in massive protest." This is an exaggeration based on selective readings of some of the contexts treated below. Conlan 1999, which is based more firmly on documentary evidence, but which also employs selection, finds Shakespeare in *TMP* to be the covert vanguard of a protest against the English colony, and King James his highly attentive understander.

10. Hulme 1986, 166. For similar views see Brown 1985.

11. This phrase is borrowed from Hamlin 1995, 107, which claims that "colonialist readings [of *TMP*] tend to fail through narrowness of focus . . . moral and sociopolitical agendas often predetermine their conclusions," and is not directed at literary appropriations.

12. This is the conclusion of Jowett 1993, which contains a subtle analysis of the concepts, genres, structures, and literary sources of *TMP*. Edwards 1974, 103–9, comes to a similar conclusion: "*The Tempest* is in many respects a New World play, but it is not a colonial play."

13. Two recent critics concerned with the salvation of the Gates and Summers party and of Jamestown itself have suggested a strong contemporary reaction to the knowledge of shameful English behavior. Bond 1997, 477–78, thinks Jamestown's last-ditch salvation in 1610 may have been seen as a national "hinge point in time" signifying providential approval of the colony. Yet ibid., 478–79, points out that in 1610: "No Spanish vessels carrying an invasion force had entered the James River. No Catholic tyrant ruled the colony. No Roman faction attempted to overthrow the settlement from within. Virginia tottered on the verge of collapse because of the poor government and the colonists' own idleness." Conlan 1999 contrarily holds that English attempts to colonize at Jamestown what was rightfully Spanish territory were for that reason shameful, and this led Shakespeare to introduce a strongly anti-colonialist bias in *TMP*. Conlan further claims that Prospero is implicitly condemned as a black magician, and that this and the geopolitical message of the play was directed at King James, who would have understood its many oblique references to Peter Martyr and to Italian history. Although both Bond and Conlan consider the impact of news from Virginia on Shakespeare's contemporaries, neither writer considers the disordered English behavior in the Bermudas or at Jamestown in its contrast with the successful Algonkian boycott.

14. Reporting general acceptance of an American theme in *TMP*, Skura 1989, 44, concludes "E. E. Stoll and Northrup Frye are the only exceptions I have seen cited." Frey 1979 finds the same exceptions from the consensus, and argues in favor of critics pursuing the American theme. In a later addition to these exceptions, Vaughan 1988 concludes that "intentionalist" theories of Caliban's American identity "*should* be discarded . . . because . . . Shakespeare's contemporaries and their descendants for nearly three centuries did not associate *The Tempest*'s savage with American Indians." Chapter 5 of Vaughan and Vaughan 1991 attenuates this conclusion. Hantman 1992 argues against it.

15. Muir 1972, 280.

16. Bullough 1975, 8:240.

17. Ibid., 239. See also: Hotson 1937, 219–26; Hantman 1992, 72–73; and the sources cited in Edwards 1974, 250 n. 50.

18. See Sokol and Sokol 1996, 354, 358–69, 375, and 377–78.

19. See: ibid., 364–6, 377–78; Crashawe 1610; and Wallis 1960, 29.

20. A good brief account is found in Edwards 1974, 97–103, which relates it to the scandal over *Eastward Ho!*, as does Sokol and Sokol 1996.

21. Strachey's letter was probably excerpted and toned down when it was published as "A True Reportory of the Wracke and Redemption of Sir Thomas Gates, Knight" in Purchas 1625, part 4, book 9, chap. 6, 1734–58. On the likelihood of Shakespeare's knowledge of the letter see: Kermode 1962, xxvii–xxx; Muir 1972, 280; and Bullough 1975, 8:239.

22. Purchas 1625, 1737–38; see also "A True Declaration of the Estate of the Colony of Virginia," London 1610, reprinted in "True Declaration . . .," 1844, 10.

23. As reported in John Smith 1986, 2:233–35, and Percy 1922, 269–70. The survivors were justified in their fears; the colony was saved just as it was being abandoned by the arrival of a relief expedition led by Lord de la Ware.

24. Barbour 1969, 1:68.

25. "True Declaration . . .," 1844, 15–16.

26. For an account of such detraction see Sokol and Sokol 1996, 365–69, 377–78. On the English response to this see Bond 1997, 490–94.

27. Percy 1922, 266–68, 271–73. This manuscript, written in response to John Smith's version of events, is analyzed in Barbour 1971. In it Percy admits his part in punitive beating and killing of some Algonkians (although he did attempt to save one "quene"). The revenges of the English seemingly are countenanced, even the mutilation of an Algonkian "spye," but the Algonkians' counterrevenges are seen as unexpected "Subtellties" (273–74). Although great pity is expressed about the starving times, particular barbaric acts are countenced, as when, under the leadership of Sir Thomas Dale, a group of recaptured English renegades were tortured to death "To terrefy the reste for Attempteinge the Lyke" (280).

28. Barbour 1969, 1:243.

29. Straube and Mallios 2000, 30, describes features of the archaeological record eloquent of a deterioration of Algonkian-English economic relations at Jamestown, from reciprocal, to unilateral, to nonexistent.

30. The geography of *TMP* most confusedly includes North Africa, for Claribel's Tunis is presumed strangely remote from Naples (2.1.115–16, 2.1.251–62). Also in 1.2.262 Ariel says Sycorax was born in Algiers, yet her son Caliban twice names the Patagonian deity Setebos, in 1.2.375 calling this idol "my dam's god." On the symbolic geography of Africa and America in the play, see Fiedler 1974, 167–200.

31. Bond 1997, 487–88. Ibid., 488–90, continues very interestingly with an examination of Jacobean beliefs in the effectiveness of education, and this corresponds with Prospero's policy until he decided that Caliban is "a born devil, on whose nature / Nurture can never stick" (4.1.188–89); education is also treated in Bate 1994, discussed in the Introduction below. On a "discourse of prayer" in *TMP,* in which paradoxically "curses" become "blessings," see McAlindon 2001.

32. Purchas 1625, 1751–52 and 1756.

33. The phrase of Quinn 1971, xlvi.

34. Montaigne 1942, 1:215–29.

35. Levin 1970, 125–26 and 187–88.

36. See Sokol and Sokol 1996, 366.

37. *Pace* Stephen Orgel, Shakespeare did not take "everything from Montaigne except the point" as claimed in Orgel 1987b, 36, but rather deployed Montaigne-like irony in having Gonzalo miss the point.

38. Jourdan 1610, for instance, which is often placed among "sources" of

TMP, resembles at large a *Good Food Guide.* See: Kermode 1962, xxxv; Levin 1970, 74–81; and Marx 1974, 49–50 and 55.

39. As in: Kermode 1962, xxxiv; Fiedler 1974, 193–94 and 201; and Ryan 1989, 102.

40. Kupperman 1984, 67, which adds that "As a propagandist for the later Jamestown colony put it, 'trust is the mother of deceit,' " and further alleges that although the Roanoke promoters "sincerely believed that the Indians would be won over by a pacific approach," yet the colonists themselves "could not place their trust in that belief because of . . . contemporary ideas."

41. Shirley 1949, 227–28, outlines the wretched dissension between the early leaders of the colony. For more detail see Barbour 1964, passim, and especially 109–20, and Barbour 1969, 1:68, 1:125–29. For a graphic if partisan contemporary account of the conflicts see Edward Maria Wingfield's post–1608 manuscript "Discourse of Virginia" printed in Barbour 1969, 1:213–34. For other sides of the argument see Percy 1946, 22, and the bitter remarks in John Smith 1986, 2:188–90 and 2:234–35 and passim.

42. Barlowe 1955, 108 and 113–14.

43. Quinn 1971, 185.

44. Kupperman 1984, 67, finds it significant that Humphrey Gilbert and many of those who settled Virginia had soldiered in Ireland, where they may have acquired unchristian attitudes to native inhabitants, combined with a hunger for their land.

45. Knapp 1992, 231, which locates these calls in specific pamphlets and sermons preceding *TMP.*

46. In Barbour 1969, 1:241–45.

47. Native Americans were rarely portrayed by Englishmen as spiritual beings, except by Harriot, who, as has been seen, admired both their abstemiousness and their religion. Despite clear evidence of their skill and intelligence, they were generally poorly esteemed by Shakespeare's countrymen. Quinn 1977, 101, contrasts English attitudes with French ones:

> Champlain from 1603 onward showed an immense capacity for making friends with many Indian chiefs and producing a continuing atmosphere of mutual trust . . . in closer intercourse, Englishmen came easily to despise Indian socio-political arrangements . . . and tended to equip themselves, as the French rarely did, with a built-in attitude of superiority.

The claim made in Jehlen 1994, 65, that Harriot made friends among the Algonkians could indicate an exception.

48. Harriot 1955, 381.

49. On Roanoke's laws see Kupperman 1984, 66, and for Jamestown's see Strachey 1844, especially 11, 13, 27.

50. Bullough 1975, 8:295–99.

51. "True and Sincere Declaration," 1610, 2–4.

52. "True Declaration . . .," 1844, 6–7.

53. "True Declaration . . .," 1844, 24–25. Similar Elizabethan ideas were expressed, for example, in Peckham 1600. With typical exaggeration, Lee Miller 2001, 219–20, says Virginian settlement was motivated by England's "massive overpopulation," not distinguishing propaganda from fact.

54. Purchas 1625, 1753.

55. The nice euphemism "snatching up" leaps from the page. Also ibid., 1751, "and to take any thing from the Indian by force, we neuer vsed, nor willingly euer

will: and though they had well deserued it, yet it was not now time" stands in strange contrast to Strachey 1844, Strachey's edition of the "Lawes Divine, Morall and Martiall" of Jamestown, which specify severe punishments for theft from or maltreatment of the "Indians" (13, 16, 27, 44).

56. Strachey 1953, reprinting a manuscript of Strachey written c. 1609–1612, contains detailed praise of Algonkian material culture and technology (72–88).

57. Ibid., 84.

58. Sanders 1949, 129.

59. If not assumed of the Golden Age, then these people were typically seen as allied to either the devil or to animals, as noted in relation to *TMP* in Mariens-tras 1981, 161–64. However, Roberts 1991, especially 110–17, most interestingly disrupts this familiar view of the pattern in the play by suggesting that *TMP* elides the single hierarchy between man and beast. Also deviating from the familiar criti-cal perspective, Hantman 1992 concludes that vice-versa "American Indian per-ceptions of the European other were equally contradictory and dynamic" (81).

60. Caliban uses excellent blank verse, as opposed to the demotic of his con-federates, a conventional sign of elevated standing. Yet, according to Nuttall 1967, 140, Caliban's "world is near-sighted, tactile, downward-looking, lacking in distant prospects."

61. Anglerie 1555. This was republished in 1577, 1587, and 1612; the impor-tance of the book and its reissues for *TMP* is speculated upon in Conlan 1999, 178, 187–88n, and passim.

62. Montaigne 1942, 3:128–51.

63. Benzoni 1862 gives striking accounts of Spanish cruelties to native Ameri-cans (even leading to mass suicide), and to African slaves.

64. See Sokol and Sokol 1996.

65. Prosser 1965, 261–64.

66. Montaigne 1942, 2:108–24.

67. Quint 1990, 473, contrasts these two essays, finding "as many dystopian as utopian features" in Montaigne's stoical "cannibal culture." In general, the im-plicit contrasts between these two essays reflect the "perpetual oscillation of the *Essays*," to borrow a phrase of Spires 1999, 223.

68. Montaigne 1942, 1:227 and 1:223.

69. Montaigne 1942, 2:108.

70. Servile status alone was not an index of ethical unworthiness in Shake-speare's late work. A "peasant" servant in *King Lear* (*LRQ* S.14.77, *LRF* 3.7.77) avenges the blinding of Gloucester; Timon of Athens's loyal steward is the one thoroughly good man of the play; in *TMP* princely Ferdinand takes over Caliban's "wooden slavery" (3.1.62). See Sokol and Sokol 2000 under "Slave."

71. Montaigne 1942, 1:227.

72. In *AIT* 5.3.32–33 a Porter bawdily asks: "Or have we some strange Indian with the great tool come to court, the women so besiege us?."

73. "True and Sincere Declaration," 1610, 6.

74. Barlowe 1955, 107–9.

75. See, for instance, John Smith's account of his 1608 explorations of Chesa-peake Bay, in Quinn 1971, 306: "their men, women, and children, with dances, songs, fruits, fish, furres, & what they had kindly entertained us . . . stretching their best abilities to expresse their loves." Algonkian fish traps are described in great detail in Strachey 1953.

76. Straube and Mallios 2000, 38.

77. This is proposed in ibid., which cites a 1609 letter which disapproves of a

"somewhat a puritane" minister to the colony, possibly because he had preached against such fraternization, and John Smith's 1623 *The general History of Virginia* (in Barbour 1969, 2:257), which quotes a comment on the practice of "diverse" colonists keeping "Salvages" as their armed servants: "we lived together as if wee had beene one people." However, marginalia in the Smith text reading "A Bad president" clearly disapprove. Knapp 1992, 237–41 and 336–38 (notes), adduces (rather weak) evidence that intermarriage was taboo and Pocahontas a sole exception.

78. Hulme 1986, 147–52, supposes that a system of gift-giving like that described in Marcel Mauss's 1925 *The Gift*, a classic study of other non-European societies, pertained also to the Virginia Powhattan Algonkians. But these people were familiar with an economy based on trade (rather than gift-giving); they traded for copper with Great Lakes Native Americans, and probably had traded with the Spanish before the English arrived. Making general assumptions concerning tribal economic systems is not supportable.

79. On the terrible consequences and sequence of that breakdown of relations up to 1611 see Straube and Luccketti 1996, 51–52. On the Algonkians' own side of the story see Hantman 1992.

Chapter 4. *The Tempest,* Atmospheric Science, Prague Magi

1. Electronic digital computers can do nothing at all (for instance, they cannot "read" a keyboard or a hard disk, or "load" a program into memory and then run it) except by running a software program, and yet when they are first turned on they have no programs in their "volatile" memories to enable them to load any other program, and so on. Special bootstrapping methods (involving "non-volatile" memory containing programs in so-called 'firmware') are employed to overcome this problem; a tiny program stored in firmware is executed and it allows the computer to do rudimentary versions of basic functions such as "read" a hard disk. These functions are used to "load" bigger programs into memory; these bigger programs in turn replace the rudimentary functions with more complex ones; further programs including an "operating system" are then loaded in successive layers; and finally full communications are established and useful "application" programs can be used.

2. For instance, on the two-way traffic in Renaissance England between scientific understanding and practical advances in navigation see Shirley 1985.

3. On connections of English instrument-making and instrument-makers with advances in science see: E. G. R. Taylor 1967, passim; and McLean 1972, 164.

4. See Grafton 1991, 37–38, on Kepler's remarks on this. How this affected intellectual life in general and Kepler, Fludd and Galileo in particular is discussed in Nummedal and Finden 2000, especially 167–85.

5. Tottel's *Miscellany*, which Tottel like Slender called *Songs and Sonettes*, was multiply reprinted with great profit to this publisher between 1557 and 1597.

6. Especially in *ROM*.

7. See: *LLL*, 1.1.73–93, 1.2.104–11, 4.2.24–27, and passim; *TGV*, 1.1.19; *SHR* 1.1.82 and passim; *ROM* 3.2.83; *MND* 3.1.48–50, 4.1.211; *1H4* 2.2.44–45; *2H4* 4.2.44–48; *H5* 5.2.159; *WIV* 1.1.181–88; *AYL* 5.4.88–89; *HAM* 1.5.99–100; *AWW* 2.1.172; *OTH* 1.1.23; *COR* 4.5.225; *ANT* 5.2.211–17; *PER* S.1.58; *CYM* 5.5.227–29; *WT* 4.4 passim.

8. *CYL* 4.2 and 4.7.

9. Morever, Gombrich 1990 suggests that Prospero Visconti of Milan, who in an obscure poem published in 1576 was connected with the "idea that the noble service of the Muses is equivalent in dignity to the exercise of ducal power," may have been a model for Shakespeare's Prospero.

10. *MM* 1.3.8.

11. *CYL* 1.1.259.

12. Shakespeare's would-be philosophers in *LLL*, King Ferdinand of Navarre and his followers, may have been satirized as intending to become Hermetic adepts. (Notably, Giodorno Bruno was an admirer of the real Henri of Navarre as seen in Yates 1936, 1964; and Bossy 1991.) But in Shakespeare's play the young men of Navarre fail to proceed beyond their initial fashionable intentions to study high philosophy. And indeed, although taking cognizance of the overthrow of the "School of Night" theory as found in for instance Bradbrook 1936, Sokol 1991, argues that Thomas Harriot himself may be satirized in *LLL*. In the real world, Rudolf II was an Hermetic adept, as will be discussed presently.

13. Books, from here onward in this chapter, will be left behind; none of the users of instruments to be considered here are memorable for having written them.

14. See especially Nicolson 1960.

15. For technical details see North 1974, especially 158–60. Van Helden 1982, 134, allows that an Italian telescope may possibly have existed from 1600, but it "remained practically unknown until, because of a patent application in 1608 [in Holland], its usefulness became common knowledge."

16. Ibid., 135–36, explains that Galileo probably did this without much understanding of optical theory. But, as has been seen in chapter 2, from as early as 1584 Thomas Harriot's manuscripts showed work on the question of refraction, which provides the science behind the operation of lenses. Also, Kepler 1980, first published in 1604, applied geometrical reasoning to optics and arrived at the first rational understanding of the optics of the human eye (and the camera obscura). It is not certain if mathematical optics played a part in the first phases of telescope development out of the artisan craft of spectacle making, but after Kepler's revolutionary *Dioptrice* of 1610–1611, it probably did.

17. See Van Helden 1982, 146–47.

18. Westfall 1982, 122; this article treats Galileo's management of his career in a time when noble patronage, not University advancement, supported many scientists.

19. Rufus 1931, 24.

20. This was Kepler 1965.

21. On this newness see also North 1974 on Thomas Harriot's careful telescopic observations of sunspots just before Galileo's, offering another instance of simultaneous independent scientific discovery.

22. Kepler 1965, 21.

23. An experts' debate on whether or not there was an Elizabethan telescope runs through Ronan 1993, Turner 1993, and Darius 1993, with by far the better technical and historical points made by Turner, proving *contra*.

24. Turner 1993 also shows that optical glass was of such poor quality that the claims of inventors of the earlier ages were absurd.

25. Ronan 1993 acccepts such claims; views expressed by Ronan on another occasion that Thomas Digges had an Elizabethan telescope are endorsed in the editor's introduction of Empson 1993, 34.

26. Turner 1993.

27. Harriot 1955, 375.

28. Turner 1993.

29. Harriot 1955, 375–76.

30. McLean 1972, 148–50, and Ronan 1993 argue "pro," but McLean hedges and Turner 1993 refutes Ronan.

31. Greenblatt and Abrahms 2000, 1:901 and 1:904n.

32. Mebane 1989, 180, being his translation from *Theologica Platonica*, 2:229.

33. See Yates 1984a for a survey of much of the literature.

34. Aubrey 1983, 95. See Hotine 1987.

35. Clulee 1988, 39. Ibid., 67–68, says there is no documentary evidence that Dee tried to connect planetary causes to weather, although that would have accorded with his "programme." In Kepler 1997 (first published in 1618), 359–63, Kepler explains why for twenty years he had observed the weather in relation to the "aspects."

36. Drake-Brockman 1994, 125, cites a letter of John Speed suggesting he was in England from 1604. Others suggest a year or two later; Drebbel was certainly there from 1607.

37. These included Robert Boyle, Henry Briggs, Kenelm Digby, Robert Hooke, Constantyn Huygens, Gottfried Leibniz, Denis Papin, Marin Mersenne, Henry Oldenberg, and Christopher Wren. On these see: Tierie 1932, 25–8 and passim; Harris 1961, 170, 175–76, and 178–81. On Francis Bacon's allusions to Drebbel, c. 1611–1619, see Bacon 1996, xxvii–xxviii and 60–81. Professor Graham Rees, the editor of Bacon 1996, has kindly informed me of several other "Drebbelian things" that will appear and be indexed in the new Oxford Francis Bacon.

38. Harris 1957 presents a robust, but not seemingly wholly self-convinced, argument that Drebbel was no charlatan. See also Thorndike 1941, 7:492–97.

39. This often-cited passage was translated from the Dutch chronicle *Kronycke van Alcmaer*, 1645, in Dousa 1850, 7.

40. See note to Bacon 1872, 1:628, and 4:417. Colie 1954, 250, speculates that Bacon was present on the occasion.

41. See Drake-Brockman 1994.

42. Claims for Drebbel's priority in making a thermometer are examined in: F. Sherwood Taylor 1942, 154–56; Thorndike 1941, 7:495; and W. E. Knowles Middleton 1966, 19–21. The complexity here is due to problems of definition as well as of evidence.

43. W. E. Knowles Middleton 1966, 12 and 22.

44. Gillispie 1971, 12:102.

45. On this see: Chaldecott 1952; and W. E. Knowles Middleton 1966, 11–12.

46. F. Sherwood Taylor 1942, 156. Chaldecott 1952, 201, similarly wonders about independent inventions in Italy at the same time as Telioux's.

47. W. E. Knowles Middleton 1966, 18.

48. Bacon 1872, 2:267.

49. J[ohn] B[ate] 1977, 28–39; also (the rather different) John Bate 1635, 34–44.

50. John Bate 1635, 34.

51. Ibid., 44, which continues: "The sudden falling of the water is an evident token of rayne . . . The continuance of the water at any one degree, is a certain token that the weather will continue at that stay it is on then at, whether it be fayr or foule, frost or snow. But when the water either riseth or falleth, the weather will then presently change."

52. See Copenhaver 1990, 282–86, on the debates in which Kepler distinguished his own "philosophical" quest and methods from Fludd's pejoratively named "hermetic" ones. Copenhaver's article warns against overly simple uses of the term "Hermetic."

53. See: Godwin 1979, 60–61; W. E. Knowles Middleton 1966, 14–19; and F. Sherwood Taylor 1942.

54. Godwin 1979, 60.

55. Ibid., 60 and 61.

56. Tymme 1612, 60–3.

57. Ibid., 63.

58. Of course a machine driven by climate changes does not meet a reasonable definition of an inherent perpetual motion.

59. On these uses and the Eltham exhibition see the editors' comments in Jonson 1925, 10:43–44.

60. Farley 1621, sig. E4r-E4v: the other attractions are the spectacles of mad Tom singing, a dancing woman aerialist, and "Bull-baiting also at the *Hope*." This extraordinary poem is partly excerpted in Tierie 1932, 38.

61. W. E. Knowles Middleton 1971, 98–99.

62. For instance, W. E. Knowles Middleton 1966, 4, defines a "thermometer" as any kind of thermoscope provided with a numerical scale, a "thermoscope" being any device giving a visible indication of temperature, while he later notes that in 1617 Giuseppi Biancani called his uncalibrated weather glass a *"thermos-copium"* (10–11).

63. The principle of this was fully explained in 1638 by Galileo, in Galilei 1952, 161.

64. Harriot 1955, 384–85.

65. False assumptions about the North American climate in accord with the latitude were still found in: Captain John Smith's 1624 *A Generall Historie of Virginia, New-England and the Summers Isles*, in John Smith 1986, 2:410–11; and in Smith's 1631 *Advertisements*, in John Smith 1986, 3:259–302, 3:291. A more realistic account of the American climate (although still not cognizant of the effect of the Gulf Stream on England) is found in a manuscript c. 1606–1612, edited in Strachey 1953, 37–38.

66. Members of the Jamestown Rediscovery project had been excavating the rediscovered Jamestown Fort from 1994. They could not have been kinder to us, then and since.

67. Straube and Luccketti 1996, 41–42.

68. Thus Straube and Luccketti 1996 identifies the Jamestown figurines as "fragments of what is believed to be" a thermoscope, citing Henkes 1995 which illustrates a range of glass thermoscope weights. I must, however, add that a personal communication to myself from Professor G. L'E. Turner dated 23 February 1996 expressed doubt that the American settlement "had such a device."

69. Straube and Luccketti 1996, 42.

70. A survey of the libraries of slightly later Virginian planters in Wright 1940 indicates scant evidence of scientific interests.

71. Luxury items were sent there, as seen from the letters quoted in Shirley 1949a. Among the items excavated at Jamestown were a silver bodkin. Yet the Jamestown statute in Strachey 1844, 3, specifies "to have a bodkin thrust through his tongue" as punishment for a second offense of blasphemy—this possible use for the object was suggested to Beverly Straube by my wife and myself after we saw it at the Jamestown excavations, and was published with her report on bodkins in

Straube and Luccketti 1996, 44–45 and 53n. On the other hand, probably nothing but aesthetics or luxury explains the elaborate silver ear picker excavated at James Fort, which exceeds in "complexity of design" all the many similar items found in England according to Straube and Luccketti 1999, 17–19.

72. These are listed in Barbour 1969, 1:xxv–xxvii.

73. George was the youngest of a crowd of younger brothers to the Earl, on whom see Nicholls 1992. One of these, William Percy, was an amateur poet and playwright, and was imprisoned for debt. Details of George Percy's health problems and financial affairs are found in Nicholls 1992, 311–12.

74. Purchas 1625, 4:1685–90, also reprinted in: Percy 1946; Barbour 1969, 1:129–46; and Quinn 1967. A copy of Percy's 1607–1608 journals may well have been sent back to England in June 1607; this is proposed on the basis of internal evidence in Quinn 1967. A later journal seems to be the basis of Percy's grim manuscript account, Percy 1922, of the fate of the colony between the "starving time" 1609–1610 and his departure in 1612.

75. This inference is drawn in Barbour 1971, 11–12, on the basis of differing readings in alternative editions, despite the lack of Percy's manuscript.

76. Percy 1946, 8, 22. Barbour 1964, 118, notes that "Brookes's death is the first recorded in the long inventory of the human cost of colonizing Virginia" [as opposed to Raleigh's North Carolina, then called Virginia].

77. Shirley 1949a, 235–42. There are no further relevant details in the extracts published in Batho 1962, 88–92, nor in Historical Manuscripts Commission 1877, 221–33. George Percy's debts for expenses were paid by his brother in lieu of his pension, as explained in Nicholls 1992.

78. Shirley 1949a, 240, which lists twelve "Sondrie other persons" thus paid.

79. Quinn 1974, 49–50.

80. Shirley 1949a, 239.

81. Quinn 1992, 4, claims that Harriot misunderstood the Virginian climate because "the only winter he spent in North America seems to have been a very mild one," and adds that Harriot also thought subtropical fruits could grow in Virginia on account of a "failure to understand the climatic zones of the western Atlantic" (14).

82. The phrase "persistent and accurate . . . observer" is from Quinn 1992, 9, but the fact is proved by all we know of Harriot's nearly one thousand pages of scientific manuscripts. Clucas 1995, 20–36, gives astonishing details of Harriot's experimental and instrumental ingenuity and rigor (and also shows that he lavished these upon alchemical experiments as well as on many now-accepted areas of research).

83. *PRO* SP14/28, fol. 57v, in the postscript to a letter from Dudley Carleton to Mr [John] Chamberlaine.

84. Batho 1992, 4, which adds that Northumberland's library concentrated on "Mathematics, Medicine, Chemistry, Witchcraft, Optics, Astronomy, Architecture, and, above all, the Art of War and Fortification" (14). On Warner see Jacquot 1974, 116–25.

85. Indeed E. G. R. Taylor, 1967, 210, suggests that the John Bate quoted above as a writer on the weather glass may have been the same as the John Bates (fl. 1626) who was an instrument-maker on Tower Hill, and whose wares were recommended by Captain John Smith of Virginia. However this recommendation, unreferenced in Taylor 1967, is from Smith's late work of 1626, *An Accidence or the Path-way to Experience*, in John Smith 1986, 3:9–29, 3:26. It will be seen in chapter 5 that John Smith brought at least one scientific instrument with him to pre–1610 Virginia.

86. Grassl 1996 explains that the English New World explorers Frobisher and Gilbert took German mineral experts to America even earlier, in 1577, 1578, and 1583. This adds that Joachim Gans's brother was the astronomer and mathematician David Gans (1541–1613), and that another German mineral expert, Daniel Hochstetter Jr., may also have been at Roanoke in 1585.

87. Straube and Kelso 1997, 19–22.

88. See Straube and Luccketti 1996, 49–51, on the documentary and archaeological evidence. See also Straube, Kelso, and Luccketti 1994, 27, 32, and Straube and Kelso 1997, 14. Straube and Luccketti 1998, 23, writing in relation to the discovery of a crucifix, suggest that the German glassmakers who arrived in 1608 may have been Roman Catholics.

89. The additional material is a fragment of another scientific instrument, a compass dial. The presence of these instruments at Jamestown, if it was known to Shakespeare, could raise the intriguing possibility that Prospero's "brave utensils, for so he calls them" (3.2.97) are treasured scientific research instruments, not, it may be noted, to be drowned or buried like his book and staff (5.1.54–57).

90. See: Sokol and Sokol 1996; Hantman 1992, 72–73; and Hotson 1937, 219–26.

91. Many readings cast Dr. John Dee, or even as wild an enthusiast as Giodorno Bruno, as a model for the magician Prospero. Indeed Gatti 1989, 79, connects Bruno's dialogues with Virginia, and connects Shakespeare with Bruno (114–88). However, Gatti concentrates on *HAM*, and it is doubtful if these claimed connections could be extended to *TMP*.

92. The quotations is from Harris 1961, 194. Very similar remarks are found in: the long note on Drebbel in Rye 1865, 232–42, 240; Tierie 1932, 10; and Grudin 1991, 196.

93. Nichols 1828, 3:1042.

94. Westfall 1982, 120–21.

95. For a brief account see Edelstein 1971.

96. de Peiresc 1624, ms. 1774, fol. 407, also quoted in de Peiresc 1992, 104–5n.

97. See ibid., which surveys Drebbel's claimed achievements in order to gloss a comment in a letter of 22 May 1634, that great use could be made of a microscope, or "lunettes" of Drebbel. See also: Dousa 1850, 7; and Tierie 1932, 49–52.

98. de Peiresc 1624, ms. 1776, fol. 408v.

99. Ibid., fols. 409v and 412v.

100. See Harris 1961, 137–40.

101. A lively if not wholly accurate account is found in Bolton 1904.

102. Yates 1984c, 216–17, claims that Evans 1973 proves Rudolf's "mental world" was not "mad" but typical, rather, of that of "members of the great noble families of Bohemia" of his time. Yates 1984c, 212 does, however, admit that Rudolf suffered a "near-breakdown" around 1600.

103. Logan Pearsall Smith 1907, 1:417 (letter from Venice to the Earl of Salisbury 28 March 1608) and 477 (letter from Venice to the Earl of Salisbury 14 November 1609).

104. Grudin 1991, 184–85 and 187–88; Mowat 1981, 285 and n. 10. After the suggestion (noted above) is made in Gombrich 1990 that Prospero Visconti of Milan may have been a model for Shakespeare's Prospero, this essay notes a closer parallel of Prospero's story in *TMP* with the deposing of Rudolf II by his younger brother.

105. Grudin 1991, 183.

106. See de Peiresc 1624, ms. 1776, fol. 409r.

107. Evans 1973, 189.

108. de Peiresc 1624, ms. 1776, fol. 409v, my translation. Harris 1961, 144, translates this, but apparently in an effort to avoid the image of Drebbel practicing alchemy suppresses the mention of "fourneaux" and makes other changes.

109. On Drebbel's later shabbiness see Tierie 1932, 18.

110. Translated in Harris 1961, 145–48.

111. Tierie 1932, 26.

112. Tierie 1932, 72, attributes to Drebbel and others the contrivance of a display of "rare fireworks" on 4 January 1608. Drake-Brockman 1994, 130, finds it "tempting to surmise" that two payments of twenty pounds from Prince Henry to "Cornelis the Dutchman" made by 18 December 1609 and 29 March 1610 were for his efforts toward the scenic effects of the Prince's *Barriers* of twelfth night 1609, and the masque *Tethy's Festival* of June 1610. Evans 1973, 189, claims that Drebbel was entrusted with preparing spectacular effects for James's court masques. Grudin 1991, 195–96, admits that the "only hard evidence" of Drebbel's theater involvement is both slender and post-Shakespearian, yet still suggests that Shakespeare knew Drebbel and used him as well as Rudolf as "archetypes" for Prospero (and Rudolf for Vincentio of *MM* as well). A main flaw in Grudin's article is not its belief that Drebbel had theatrical tendencies, but its assumption that Drebbel was really able to perform his promises thanks to "astonishing initiative and technical precision," and that his work presented "a classic example of the almost seamless transition from magic to science in the Renaissance" (194). In my view, if *TMP* reflected an interest in a Drebbel-type magus, this was because Drebbel's inflated claims were often false and nonscientific.

113. de Peiresc 1624, ms. 1776, fol. 407v.

114. See Tierie 1932, 38–41.

115. Shirley 1949b, 55, which does not notice this confusion but shows this report to be in some other ways confused.

116. de Peiresc 1624, ms. 1776, fol. 413r.

117. See above on Drebbel; on the fame of Hocus Pocus and his ilk see Mowat 1981, 298–301.

118. Gombrich 1990, in a long note supplied by Edward Chaney, 189n.

119. Sokol 1989.

120. Traister 1984, 146. Although denying all "neo-Platonic thurgist" connections with Prospero, Mincoff 1992, 114, makes a partly similar point by claiming that "There is no justification for identifying Prospero . . . with modern science harnessing the forces of nature, for then the breaking of his magic staff becomes inexplicable."

CHAPTER 5: "THE STRONG NECESSITY OF TIME"

Epigraph in this chapter from Thomas 1971, 333.

1. So, in 1638, Galilei 1952, 208, described Galileo using his own pulses and a water clock to determine gravitational acceleration on an inclined plane. A perennial question for physical science is whether time can or should be "factored out" of the study of nature; at the start of G. J. Whitrow's authoritative *The Natural Philosophy of Time*, Whitrow 1980, 1, distinguishes "two opposing points of view which may be conveniently associated with the names of Archimedes and Aristotle," in which "Archimedes is the prototype of those whose philosophy of

physics presupposes the 'elimination' of time, i. e. of those who believe that temporal flux is not an intrinsic feature of the ultimate basis of things," while Aristotle "is the forerunner of those who regard time as fundamental." A footnote to this adds the names of Parmenides and Heraclitus as "earlier" and "shadowy" predecessors holding a pair of parallel positions. Renaissance scientists also argued whether statics or kinematics should be the key to physics, but after Galileo and Kepler kinematics won the race for supremacy "hands-down" (that lovely kinesthetic metaphor).

2. See especially *1H5* 1.2.1–12. This would have been a particularly apt parody of a "puritan work ethic," if it was one, because Falstaff has been connected by several critics (for instance, Poole 1995 and Tiffany 1998) with spoofs of puritanism.

3. The first is proverb T329 in Tilley 1950, 670, of which the earliest instance is from Ben Franklin in 1748; Tilley lists part-parallels without the same thrust in T329, 670 (from Bacon's *Essays*, 1612), and in T295, 667 (from 1616 and 1640). The second proverb does not appear at all in Tilley (it would be in 336–37).

4. Smith's letter is printed in Barbour 1969, 1:241–45. However, physical work is imaged as a punishment in *TMP*, while it is not in *PER*; this difference will be explored in chapter 7.

5. See the excellent discussion in Whitrow 1990, 7–8.

6. Gurr 1996.

7. Seaver 1995, 160–61, provides evidence that London apprentices were required to carry out all sorts of lowly duties shows that they were required to work at unusual hours (162, 164).

8. See Barton 1994, 201, on "cunning" disruptions of dramatic convention in *TMP*, and also Ewbank 1980 on Shakespeare's mixture of fantastic plots with highly realistic characterization in his late plays.

9. Frederick Turner 1971, 3–5, lists them.

10. The various critics neither share nor debate their notions of which, or of how many, types of Shakespearian time are to be distinguished. Quinones 1965 finds "augmentative," "contracted," and "extended" ideas of time emerging successively in Shakespeare's work (and finds at least two of these in *TMP*); Peterson 1973, 18ff., argues for a new "twofold conception" of time in Shakespeare's age, on which see below.

11. Frederick Turner 1971, 2, even argues for the valid application of distinctly twentieth-century notions of time in the criticism of Shakespearian "thoughts, feelings and attitudes."

12. For Quinones 1972 there is actually a "Renaissance discovery of time" reflected in Rabelais, Montaigne, Spenser, Shakespeare, and Milton; Peterson 1973, 18, calls the Shakespearian notion of time being either duration or occasion a "twofold conception of time that is new in the Renaissance;" G. F. Waller 1976, 38–41, identifies especially with Giodorno Bruno new Renaissance doctrines of time having a bearing on Shakespeare's views of nature, fate, providence, and human striving; for Kastan 1982, 5–6, time in the Renaissance becomes newly "a source of anxiety."

13. Peterson 1973, 18.

14. Kastan 1982, 5–6. Mutual disparities are often seen in this area of study.

15. The development of the concept of a universal time scale for history is treated with great care but with a very odd emphasis in Wilcox 1987, which demonstrates that many chronologers and historians in the period immediately before

Newton's sought universal time scales. Yet this study has a bizarre aspect: it does not consider Galileo's or Kepler's or Newton's needs for a time substratum for kinematics, nor the Renaissance pursuit of a more accurate biblical and ancient chronology (which bridged history, philology, and the rising sciences, as is very well argued in Grafton 1991). Wilcox, seemingly led by a preference for post-modern rejections of "linearity," alleges instead that Newton's insights were a temporary aberration now happily discarded together with Newton's few errors in historical detail. For a briefer but less strange account of similar developments, see Whitrow 1988, 130–38.

16. Frye 1983, 86. The second part of Frye's claim, alleging the creative possibilities of time in *TMP*, will be considered shortly.

17. Whitrow, 1990, 11–15, explains with admirable clarity that Galileo, Harriot, and Newton's predecessor Barrow had ideas of a temporal substratum prior to motion. See also Wilcox 1987. Moreover, Whitrow 1988, 128, finds similar concepts in the fourteenth century in the thought of Nicole Oresme.

18. See: Whitrow 1990, 15; Whitrow 1988, 128–30; and Whitrow 1980, 36–38, 41–44. Nor do I see any reflection in *TMP* of the concepts embodied in Thomas Harriot's sophisticated discussions of paradoxes (proposed in Aristotle and earlier by Zeno) concerning continuous time; these are discussed in Sokol 2002.

19. Mowat 1976, 87–88. I disagree, however, with her suggestion that simultaneity is a symptom of the unique narrative-involving dramaturgy of the Shakespearian Romances; perceived simultaneity is also a leading feature elsewhere in Shakespeare, for instance in *MM*, in which the Isabella bed trick and the Claudio head trick exactly coincide in time.

20. Dated from 1561.

21. Frederick Turner 1971, 4–5 and passim, sees this aspect of time as linked to determinism, or fate, or providence.

22. The matter of science needing to judge its own limitations will be discussed later in this chapter and in other ways in each of the following ones.

23. So Whitrow 1980, 19, reports: "The scientific revolution which reached its climax in the seventeenth century is generally believed to have owed its success to the fact that natural philosophers like Galileo ceased to speculate about the world as a whole and confined their attention to definite limited problems in which specific objects and processes were regarded in isolation from their environment."

24. Dean 1989 discusses causality and Shakespeare's tragedies and histories, but largely excludes consideration of the comedies and Romances. This alleges (25) that Shakespeare "stands, as so often, between these two poles of thought; his plays inhabit both the medieval world where causes are supernatural and magical, and the new world of natural science where they are subject to rationally deducible laws . . . The improbabilities, coincidences, theophanies and visionary moments in his comedies and romances point us to controlling causal agencies who can be comfortably seen benignly directing what we do."

25. Whitrow 1988, 132–36. See also Saxl 1936.

26. Religious ideas about intersections of time with eternity were relevant to medieval and Renaissance notions of timelessness.

27. On this see especially: Saxl 1936; Wind 1961; Ewbank 1968; Peterson 1973; McAlindon 1973; Tayler 1979; and Garner 1985.

28. See Sokol 1994a, 36–41, 162, 181.

29. Jacobus 1992, 145, holds that "time is kairotic in the hands of Prospero,"

and Peterson 1973, 42 and 219–23, implies the same, but I will argue that it may not be in his hands at all.

30. Whitrow 1980, 1.

31. Frederick Turner 1971, 171, which adds that "a person can grow and contradict the law of time that rules that all things must decay."

32. *1H4* 1.2.2–12.

33. *H5* 2.3.13–17.

34. Quoted in G. F. Waller 1976, 61.

35. Linton 1998, 156.

36. Ibid., 104–7.

37. Landes 1983, 212–15.

38. Evans 1973, 188 and 81n.

39. Ibid., 80–81, which calls Rudolf the "sanest madman" in Christendom.

40. To measure shorter intervals the human pulse and the weight of water dripped into a pan are used in the context of Galilei 1952, 208, as noted above.

41. See Whitrow 1990, 13, and Whitrow 1988, 22–27.

42. *1H4* 1.2.8–9.

43. *LLL* 3.1.184–88.

44. *ROM* 2.3.104–5.

45. *TMP* shares with *OTH* and *R2* an obsessively frequent use of the word "hour."

46. *JC* 2.1.192 and 2.2.114; *CYM* 2.2.51 and 5.6.153–54; and *TNK* 2.2.42.

47. In addition to *AYL* 2.7.20 and 2.7.33, see: *ERR* 5.1.119; *RDY* 2.5.24; *ROM* 2.3.104–5; (ambiguously) *R2* 5.5.53; *1H4* 1.2.8 and 5.2.83; (possibly) *H5* 1.2.210; (probably) *AWW* 2.5.5; *OTH* 3.4.172; and sonnets 77 and 104.

48. As described in Joseph Moxom, *Mathematical Science*, London 1703, quoted in Straube and Luccketti 1999, 30n.

49. Straube and Luccketti 1999, 23, reports the discovery and speculates on this.

50. *A True Relation*, 1608, sig. B4r-B4v, in John Smith 1986, 1:48–49.

51. John Smith 1986, 2:147.

52. Gouk 1988, 24; ibid., 7–24 and 87–94, describes the basis of their complex features and functions.

53. Straube and Luccketti 1999, 23–25. Whitrow 1990, 11, describes a late medieval "tremendous craze" for clockwork used as "mechanical models of the cosmos."

54. Straube and Luccketti 1999, 25.

55. Gouk 1988, 111–12.

56. As has been noted in chapter 4, Kepler undertook this investigation seriously and John Dee at least made gestures at it. Yet, part of Pico della Mirandola's famous 1495 attack on astrology was based on an observation that less than eight out of his sample of 130 astrological weather predictions came to be true, as is pointed out in the handy Shumaker 1972, 20. (Shumaker 1972 is highly criticized in Yates 1984b, 57–59, but even this crushing review admits that Shumaker's book is useful in some ways.)

57. As noted in chapter 4, Colie 1954, 250, proposes that Bacon was present on the occasion of Drebbel's supposed refrigeration of Westminster Hall. Colie further conjectures that an acquaintance between Bacon and Drebbel which might have gone back to 1608 or earlier helped inspire Salomon's House in the *New Atlantis* (249). This article generally credits Drebbel and his "scientific colleague" Salomon de Caus with technological achievements claimed for them that were unlikely or impossible.

58. Quoted from *Magnalia naturae praecipue quoad usus humanos* in Rossi 1968, 21.

59. Ibid.

60. Ibid., 91, which finds this belief in della Porta, Campanella, Cardano, and Paracelsus.

61. Ibid., 18–19, quoted from Agrippa's *On the Vanity and Uncertainty of Arts and Sciences*, 1527.

62. Conlan 1999, 171.

63. Ibid., 170–71; this also claims that the literary source for Prospero's storm is Anglerie 1555, sig. 219v–224v.

64. *Poetics* 1460a 27–28, with particular reference to epic poetry, holds that "A likely impossibility is always preferable to an unconvincing possibility," in Aristotle 1941, 1482.

65. See ibid., 1565, *Poetics* 1452a 2–11, on how to increase the marvelous in drama for aesthetic purposes. There is a long and distinguished critical literature of both theatrical uses of wonder, and the aesthetic of the marvelous in the early modern art generally. See, for instance: Weinberg 1961; Cunningham 1964; Bishop 1996; Platt 1997; Mirollo 1999. For heavily ideological treatments of wonder and the New World see Greenblatt 1991 and Albanese 1996. The epistemological dangers of succumbing to wonder were particularly recognized in Shakespeare's age by Francis Bacon, Ben Jonson, and especially Fulke Greville; see Sokol 1980.

66. This is no new vision of the play; it is presented, for instance, in D. G. James 1967, 44–71, which states that in *TMP* we see "the farewell of the human imagination to magic and all its ways" (68). What I hope to add is a sense of a greater context and significance for this.

67. Prospero continues: "whose influence / If now I court not, but omit, my fortunes / Will ever after droop" (1.2.182–85). "Omit" is here used with the sense of "fail or forbear to use" (OED 2), as in *JC* 4.2.270–73: "There is a tide in the affairs of men / Which . . . / Omitted, all the voyage of their life / Is bound in shallows and in miseries."

68. It could be objected that Miranda refers only to the raising of the magic storm and Prospero to the gathering up of his old enemies, but that would be a superfine distinction.

69. See Thomas 1971, 114–16, 125.

70. These views hold that human choices are a strong but partial determinant of outcomes in time. This accords with the meaning of "contingency" mentioned above, in *OED* II.3.c.

71. Poppi 1988.

72. Writing about Shakespeare and time, G. F. Waller 1976, 21, remarks that Aquinas held "that the dignity of causality is imputed even to creatures," but Calvin and his followers objected that this would be to make "God ruler 'onelye in name and not in deede' ." Waller continues, 22–23, that the Calvinist doctrine of "panergism" or "continued grace" continued to be influential through the seventeenth century (not just in Calvinism), but this adds that a vital importance of acting for salvation in every moment, of "the seizing of a personal *kairos*," was also emphasized by some Protestants, for instance Hooker and Launcelot Andrewes, making personal action in time crucial (24–25).

73. Machiavelli 1961, 130–33; see also 53–61. Poppi 1988, 660, connects this famous passage with the complex theories on free will of Pomponazzi, which it describes 653–60. Machiavelli's secularization of the idea of fortune would seem,

however, to accord not so much with the neo-Stoicism of Pomponazzi as with the tendency seen in the historical works of Bodin and Bacon toward a "more pragmatic, metaphysically uncommitted approach to history" (as it is put in G. F. Waller 1976, 61).

74. As said sarcastically by Hamlet and bombastically by the Player King in *HAM* 2.2.237–38 and *HAM* 2.2.496, and described bitterly in *MAC* 1.2.14–15 respectively.

75. See G. F. Waller 1976, 57–64, on Raleigh's importance. Yet Waller (34–40) and Poppi 1988, 641–43, trace Christian objections to the classical concept of fortune.

76. On the tradition of magi animating statues see Sokol 1994a, 158 and 238n.

77. See: Spenser, *The Faerie Queene* 2.4.4; Wittkower 1937; Peterson 1973, 18–70 (especially 37 on *tempus commodum* and the "difference between occasion and opportunity"); Tayler 1990, 123–47; McAlindon 1973, 87–8; and McAlindon 1991, 148 and 189.

78. The words "occasion" or "opportunity" are actually used in *TMP* in this way in 2.1.178, 2.1.212, and 4.1.26, but many more instances arise unnamed.

79. An essay on music and *TMP*, Auden 1963, 327, further remarks that in the play's conclusion "justice has triumphed over injustice, not because it is more harmonious, but because it commands superior force; one might even say because it is louder." Thus this is one of the disillusioned readings of the play, but one in which no advantage is seen in the shedding of illusions.

80. Kastan 1982, 442.

81. McAlindon 2001.

82. Frye 1986, 180.

83. Ibid. Frye's somewhat gnomic comment seems to me correct: as grown and married away from their parents, both children are not living in the same way as before, and may truly be accounted partly lost to them.

84. Paulina's parallel deceptions in *WT*, where the audience is denied similar insight, seem more genuinely necromancer-like, as explained in Sokol 1994a, 151–66. But this is not necessarily thanks only to dramatic construction allowing surprise. Oddly, as it seems to me, Vincentio's deceptive maneuvers using pretended deaths in *MM* are even more sinister than Paulina's, although in *MM* the audience is party to them. Perhaps this is because Vincentio is disguised as a death-promoting Friar, who says "Be absolute for death" (3.1.5–42), and "O death's a great disguiser" (4.2.175). There is much that is morbid in Vincentio's dealings in executions, corpses, and parts of human bodies.

85. Conlan 1999, 172–73, argues that the storm was arranged by Shakespeare to be seen as diabolical, especially by King James.

86. Gifford 1931, sig. K2v-K3r.

CHAPTER 6. THE NATURAL AND THE SUPERNATURAL

1. Studies of Shakespeare's own "pneumatology," or of its contemporary background, include: Robert Hunter West 1939; Butler 1948; Walker 1958; Briggs 1962; Yates 1964, 1975; Reed 1965; Rossi 1968; Wind 1968; Thomas 1971; Lemmi 1972; Shumaker 1972; Woodman 1973; Harris, Anthony 1980; Charles Webster 1982; Traister 1984; Corfield 1985; Mebane 1989; Copenhaver 1990; Empson 1993, 1994; Gouk 1999.

2. A breezy assurance of this is expressed, for instance, in Sinfield 1992, 103: "For many members of Jacobean audiences, witches were a social and spiritual reality: they were as real as Edward the Confessor, perhaps more so." This is followed by an unfounded assumption that the apparition of witches in *MAC* was simply like "phenomena one might encounter on a heath." But in the real withchcraft experiences reported in Shakespeare's age witches were hardly ever so met, as is shown in Larner 1984, 73 (also see Sokol 1995).

3. See Lewis 1954, 6–7 and 12.

4. An appendix on Ariel in Kermode 1962, 142–45, distinguishes the classical from the native forms of genii, but then finds these merged in both *TMP* and its sources.

5. Empson 1994, 170. Empson leads from detailed considerations of the Hermetic Corpus, Agrippa, Paracelsus, and Pomponazzi, and on to the fairies in *MND* (170–248). See also a reprint of Empson's review of Frances Yates's 1979 *The Occult Philosophy in the Elizabethan Age* (155–69), which argues that the importance of the middle spirits goes wrongly unmentioned in Yates's book.

6. Ibid., 192–96.

7. Ibid., 171.

8. See: Woodman 1973, 23–27; and Robert Hunter West 1939, 39–48.

9. See Kay 1999 which notes a tendency in the Geneva Bible glosses derived from Calvin to diminish the miraculous in biblical passages (170). On one of Shakespeare's pointed use of these glosses, see Sokol 1998.

10. See Kay 1999, 165, on the Shakespearian commentary, and passim on the concept.

11. An analysis of an instance of these tendencies of Lafeau will be found in the forthcoming Sokol and Sokol, 2003.

12. Rossi 1968, 91.

13. See: Porta 1658, translated from the 1598 second edition; Guazzo 1929, published 1608; and chapter 5 of this book.

14. This is argued at length with regard to *MAC* in Sokol 1995.

15. See Copenhaver 1990, 282–86, on Kepler's objections to Fludd's "theosophical," "hermetic" uses of picture drawing, and 278–80, which conclude that "no single feature of the Scientific Revolution . . . convinced educated Europeans to end their fascination with magical objects."

16. See: Lemmi 1972; Rees 1977a, b.

17. This phrase, used in relation to two of Montaigne's essays, and which continues to name as other permeable boundaries "the knowable and the occult, the self and the other," is taken from Spires 1999, 205.

18. Freud 1975, 300–308.

19. Ibid., 323–25.

20. Ibid., 324.

21. Montaigne 1942, 3:282.

22. Lewis 1954, 11–12; see 4–14 for an important survey of the background.

23. These arguments are analyzed in Kristeller 1972, 1–21. This shows that for Ficino man's rational soul "comes to occupy the place in the center, below God and the angels and above qualities and bodies" (10), while for the neo-Aristotelian Pomponazzi man's nature is ambiguously placed also "in the middle between mortal and immortal things" (18).

24. Ibid., 11–17. Rattansi 1985, 51–53, explains that, although he rejected the Aristotelian elements and hierarchies, Paracelsus also believed that mankind spanned ontological orders.

25. *LLL* 1.1.7 and *SHR* 1.1.23.

26. Sokol 1991a.

27. So Daston 1999, 81, writes of an "early modern vogue for the preternatural"; this is verified by a welter of recent studies of early modern interests in malformation and monstrosity.

28. Daston 1999, 81, claims this was so "until the late seventeenth century."

29. Ibid., 80.

30. Ibid. Yet Daston also describes as consistent with Aristotle's, Galileo's, and Descartes' ideals of science a rejection of considerations of the singular, and *a fortiori* of the preternatural (87).

31. See Rossi 1968, 31, which continues by remarking on the attack in Bacon's (early, unpublished) *Temporis partus masculus* on vulgar ambition and ostentation in Paracelsus and clownish levity in Agrippa.

32. Thorndike 1941, throughout vols. 5–8. See also Charles Webster 1982. A linking of alchemy with practical mineralogy and chemistry is taken for granted in Snelling 1994, which mixes unlikely alchemical readings of many details of *TMP* with anachronistic uses of the technical vocabulary of nineteenth- and twentieth-century chemistry ("valence," "catalyst"). This hard-to-find article, replete with misspellings and solecisms, also associates Prospero with Rudolf II, but takes no cognizance of others who earlier did the same more persuasively.

33. Rossi 1968, 21. With regard to particulars, Shumaker 1972, 161, rejects a view, which it finds to be commonly "taken for granted," that "alchemists were the first precursors of modern chemists," while Westman 1977, 70, sums up that in relation to sixteenth- and seventeenth-century astronomical reform, "Hermeticism may perhaps be credited [at most] with a modest supporting role." Although the matter falls outside the period of Shakespearian concern, it is interesting that a companion essay, McGuire 1977, argues that Hermeticism had even less importance for Newton's thinking.

34. Daston 1999, 88, continuing that Bacon's "grounds for studying the preternatural were metaphysical as well as epistemological."

35. Daston 1994, 56, which describes the strangeness of "Baconian facts" which "were neither public nor indubitable."

36. On the twentieth century see: Popper 1968; Lâkatos 1976, 1978. On the importance of paradox in the Renaissance see Colie 1966.

37. See Pérez-Ramos 1988, 237–85, on that error regarding Bacon.

38. Bacon, n.d., 29.

39. Ibid., 70.

40. See Pérez-Ramos 1988. There is an excellent review of this and other new work on Bacon in Vickers 1992, especially pages 507–17. Vickers 1991 and 1992 also discuss the persistence of the typical older views of Bacon (such as those expressed in Bacon, n.d., vii–viii). The still very important Rossi 1968, 219–23, presents some of these older views, suggesting that Bacon's "*Sylva silvarum* is no different from the magical texts of Della Porta and Cardano or . . . John Dee and Robert Fludd" (219), and that Bacon "total[ly] neglected mathematics as a scientific instrument" (220). But the later-written Rossi 1996 gives a vigorous defense against both "no scientist," and also later-heard "typical scientist" denigrations of Bacon.

41. Rees 1996, 136–37. Also see Rees 1977b, 115, which sees in qualification of Bacon's typical arguments using antitheses an equally typical Baconian "assumption that an *intermediate* state, substance or entity often resides between extremes and that the intermediate either embodies the contrary qualities of an

antithesis or represents a transitional state between them. Bacon shared this belief with other philosophers of the period—notably of course with Paracelsians."

42. Rees 1977b, 119, offers: "The *Sylva*, a complex work, is both natural history and a 'high kind of natural magic' . . . Bacon was trying the strength of the
theory by trying to 'pneumatize' the phenomena in much the same way as some
of his younger contemporaries and successors were trying systematically to mech-
anize the phenomena—phenomena often just as 'literary,' untested and fabulous
as *some* of those to which Bacon himself gave *provisional* credence." Here, however, we move well beyond the time of the composition of *TMP,* for as Rees points
out: "In the final stage (1620–26), the [Baconian] cosmology underwent further
refinement and *for the first time* Bacon began to elaborate and apply in detail his
ideas about the attached spirits and other terrestrial intermediates of the matter
theory" (121).

43. Private communication. A further objection also arises to the application
of Bacon's cosmology in the connection I am seeking: the intermediates identified
by Rees in Bacon's bi-quaternion cosmology all lie on the horizontal axis between
antitheses and not on the vertical axis between levels or orders of being.

44. Rees 1977a.

45. On a 1597 Scottish Privy Council order to revoke all commissions to per-
secute witchcraft see Larner 1984, 24–25. On a theory that the Elizabethan Anglican Church's struggles for dominance were behind official and intellectual
opposition to witchcraft-persecution in England see MacDonald 1991, ix–lv. This
may not fully explain the mild English witchcraft legislation and high rate of ac-
quittal discovered in many studies and discussed in Sokol 1995. Continental authorities also restrained excesses of witchcraft-persecution, as detailed in:
Henningsen 1980, on the Basque region, which adds that in Spain and Denmark
as well "it was not unusual for the 'witch' to be acquitted" (17); Tedeschi 1987,
on Italy, which describes Inquisition "moderation" (104); and Martin 1989, 26–
32, which finds the Inquisition in Venice responsible for careful investigation,
moderate interrogation, mild punishments, and for saving Venice "from the true
horrors of the great European witch hunt" (251). Even in socially and religiously
torn counter-Reformation France, where Muchembled 1985, 241, argues witch-
mongering was used to impose absolutism on recalcitrant outlying regions, this
"politico-religious" motive did not prevent central legal bodies from restraining
the excessive persecutory zeal of provincial ones.

46. These few include: Weyer 1991; Scot 1973; and, in a qualified way, "Of
the Lame or Crippel" in Montaigne 1942, 3:284–86. Although Scot is attacked in
King James's 1597 *Daemonologie*, Robert Hunter West 1984, 106–7, claims that
James did not really understand him.

47. See Sokol and Sokol 2000 under "Witch/Witchcraft," which also explains
the differences between malefic, demonic, and other varieties of witchcraft.

48. See ibid. and Sokol 1995.

49. James VI of Scotland 1924, 29–30.

50. MacDonald 1991, xlvii–liv.

51. This was noted in Kittridge 1972, 267–328 (first published in 1929).
Notestein 1968, 137–45 (first published in 1911), claimed a reduction in James's
witch-mongering and his attacks on impostures began even earlier, alleging a religio-political motive. Larner 1973, 81 and 88, comments on Kittridge and more
fully explores James's changing attitudes (75–76).

52. Clark 1984, 358.

53. Montaigne 1942, 3:282–83, presents a splendid example of a prank or

spoof succeeding too well and getting out of hand, with perhaps fatal consequences.

54. See Debus 1987.

55. Thomas 1971, 350–56.

56. See Shumaker 1972, 16–27.

57. See Thomas 1971, 358–85, especially 361.

58. See Montaigne 1942, 3:277–89, "Of the Lame or Crippel," especially 277–78 and 282. On fantasy underlying the power of enchantments see Montaigne 1942, 1:92–104, "Of the Force of the Imagination." However, an opposite position allowing the possibility of witchcraft, enchantments, and the like is expressed in Montaigne 1942, 1:191, in "It is Follie to Referre Truth or Falsehood to our Sufficiencie." Spires 1999, 222–23, points out that Montaigne vacillated on many such points, in accord with "the perpetual oscillation of the *Essays*." Spines generally stresses the contrasts between and within the adjacent Essays 25 and 26 in Book One (as they are numbered in the Florio translation, Montaigne 1942, 1:148–95), claiming the first rejects the supernatural and the second reasserts a belief in its possibility.

59. On the principles, practitioners, flourishing, and decline of early modern astrology see Thomas 1971, 283–385.

60. Patrick Grant 1985 discusses literature and the rise of scientific method with reference to Ben Jonson's plays of 1600 and 1614 and Donne's "Anniversaries" of 1611–12, as well as earlier and later works. This supposes that early modern science implied a "calculus of determinism," and that "poets" felt "a most compelling evidence of how humanly unacceptable is the calculus of determinism, that twofold tyranny of grace and of mechanism with which the discovery of method . . . challenges us" (17). This however is anachronistic, even if applied only to the "theologians" and "scientists" from whom poets were supposedly "constrained" to differentiate themselves.

61. Yet, as has been mentioned, clockwork astronomical models or their makers were exchanged between Rudolf II and James I quite soon before the date of *TMP*. The date of Rudolf's gift was 1609, as noted in chapter 5, whereas Drebbel himself was lent to Rudolf by James in 1610, as noted in chapter 4.

62. Galilei 1952, first published 1638, shows that falling bodies gain velocity in proportion to time elapsed, not distance traveled, giving time the role of what we now call an independent variable or a parameter.

63. Kepler 1992 contains Kepler's first and second mathematical formulations of the trajectory of Mars; the second states that equal radial areas are swept out by planets in equal intervals of time. Kepler's development of his extraordinary first "law" in about 1605, which abandoned circular orbits for elliptical orbits and thereby first established astronomy as a physical science, is described and analyzed in Koyré 1973, 225–64.

64. Johnson 1937 points out that England was especially receptive to Kepler's ideas, and claims that the "English scientists" were "actively associated with a large circle of persons famous for the parts they played in the history and literature of the Elizabethan age" (288). The suggestion that Shakespeare was cognizant of complex planetary dynamics, made in Empson 1994, 215–19, is discussed in the Introduction herein.

65. Grafton 1991, 38, points out that Kepler "was by no means the first humanist to venture such analyses. . . ."

66. There may be a chronological question over this, for according to the Introduction to Kepler 1981, 24–25, differences between the 1596 first and the 1621

second editions of this text show Kepler's evolving ideas about astrology; changes in the later edition show dissatisfaction with his earlier discussion, calling it digressive or even meaningless. Kepler 1997, 358–85, in a late work long planned, shows a qualified distrust of astrology as indicative of or formative of human fate; this chapter has been discussed in chapter 2.

67. Kepler's revealing psychological self-analyses using his horoscope are discussed in Baumgardt 1952.

68. These have been treated in the famous Koestler 1968: Grafton 1991, 22–23, and have given rise even to novelistic adaptations.

69. Reprinted in Crombie 1996b.

70. Ibid., 90. The sources for this include Leon Battista Alberti, Piero della Francesca, Leonardo da Vinci, Albrecht Dürer, Giorgio Valla, Marsilio Ficino, and Daniele Barbaro on Michelangelo (99–103).

71. Ibid., 90. Crombie refers here to medieval as well as early modern science.

72. Ibid., especially 90, attributes the motivation in all these areas to ideas of *virtu*.

73. Ibid., 91.

74. Ibid. Crombie also adduces the example of the mistaken first impressions of those using the microscope or telescope.

75. See Houghton 1942.

76. The Lord of the Induction of *SHR,* clearly a *virtuoso*, is scathingly treated by Shakespeare, as detailed in Sokol 1985. Several characters in Ben Jonson's plays are similarly ridiculed as would-be sophisticates and *virtuosi*; these include Sir Pol, Sir Jack Daw, Sir Epicure Mammon, and Sir Moth Interest.

77. The phrase is from Crombie 1985, 23, an essay that gives an abbreviated version of the argument of Crombie 1996b, but in addition historically "stages" the processes described and also, especially page 23, gives greater emphasis to the epistemological implications of the "successes of the mathematical and technical arts in solving limited and clearly defined problems."

78. Kepler 1980; on this achievement and how it typified Kepler see Crombie 1996a, 344–45.

79. In the words of Rufus 1931, 23.

80. See Rossi 1968, 219–23, which holds that although Bacon was "incapable of appreciating the works of Copernicus, Galileo and Gilbert," yet his "modernity [lies] in his courageous rejection of pre-established limitations to scientific enquiry, and in his disdain for an 'Atlas of thoughts' to hold up his heaven."

81. From a 1968 review of Rossi 1968, reprinted in Yates 1984a, 61.

82. Rossi 1996, 31.

83. D. G. James 1967, 68, concluding chapter 3, 44–71, on magic. Ibid. adds that as the play progresses "our sense of [Prospero] as merely human, in spite of all his magic powers, grows steadily stronger" (163). Quinones 1972, 443, concludes: "In his most airy and imaginative work, Shakespeare bids farewell to Ariel and to his imaginative, cosmos-invoking art. Reasonableness brings with it reduced dimensions. Unlike Spenser or Donne, Shakespeare does not turn his back on the new age of reason. Like Montaigne, although with greater dramatic struggle, he proceeded from the world where man was everything, through the necessary break-up of *chorismos* [separation], toward a more integrated experience of aspiration and reality." For a similar but more pessimistic view on disenchantment with magic in *TMP* see Corfield 1985. In Fitz 1975 the contrasting imagery in the magical and physically descriptive parts of the play is related to a great gap between the "harsh physical reality" of Prospero's island and the magic that is

abandoned. But Barton 1994, 201, more convincingly finds in the island's ambiguously "balmy" or "barren" quality a "cunning" dramatic use of deliberate inconsistency with purposes independent of the question of magic.

84. Mincoff 1992, 97–98.

85. Ibid., 112, which cites the "nasty and malevolent punishments" of Caliban; see also ibid., 113, on Prospero's speech from Ovid smacking of black magic.

86. Ibid., 114.

87. See Vickers 1992, 513–14.

88. Pérez-Ramos 1988. For a summary of earlier arguments for "what might be called the operational explanation of the genesis of 'modern' science," that is its derivation from "engineers, instrument-makers and artists rather than professors," see Panofsky 1962, 136n.

89. Bacon, n.d., 29.

90. Ibid., 100–101.

91. Nuttall 1967, 159.

92. Kermode 1962, 143.

93. An enlargement in the understanding of the "Suggestive range" of the role of Ariel is promoted in Berry 1979.

94. Empson 1994, 170–248.

95. Ibid., 167.

96. Woodman 1973, 44–49; and Robert Hunter West 1939, 136. The same sorts of contests recur notably in Spenser's *Faerie Queene* also, of course.

97. The practice of witchcraft in early modern English villages and towns was so complexly situated between the realms of the everyday and acceptable (or even useful) and the reprehensible (although not necessarily demonic) that studies of the topic required the preliminary development of multi-axis definitional matrices in the classic study Macfarlane 1970, 3–4.

98. Kermode 1962, 143–44.

99. For a bibliography and discussions of this see: Sokol 1995; Sokol 1994a, especially 152–63; and Sokol and Sokol, 2000 under "Wise Woman/Wise Man" and under "Witch/Witchcraft."

100. Black 1986, 147, interestingly points out that by hesitating to act—in effect by doing nothing at all—Prospero would destroy his foes, because they murder one another. Revenge would follow unless a definite choice were made to forestall it.

101. See Fowler 1970. For lengthy charts of the symbolism of the number twelve see also Agrippa 1987, 216–21. Hall 1999, 158–59, offers an implausible interpretation of the symbolism of the number twelve in *TMP* in terms of Church history, and a somewhat more plausible one in terms of the twelve-day feast of fools (32 and 85–91).

102. The duration of indentures for apprentices was fixed at a standard of seven years by the 1563 Statute of Artificers. But that period could be varied or even "bated"; see Gurr 1996. As for waged employment, an analysis of the applicable statutes in Holdsworth 1922, 4:331, shows that "in a large number of specified employments, the hiring must be for one year," but there were allowed exceptions for shorter terms.

103. See the discussion of the Elizabethan Statute of Artificers in Cornish and Clark 1989, 289–95, especially 291–92: "There is considerable evidence that, in line with human relationships generally, in-servants and wage-labourers treated their employers argumentatively, aggressively, truculently." See also Bernthal 1991, 51–52 and references there. As seen in Shakespeare's own *STM* and *CYL,*

London apprentices were also often at odds with their masters, sometimes violently. As detailed in Seaver 1995, they were frequently tried for offenses of dishonesty, immorality, violence, or extreme idleness in the Courts of Assistants of livery companies, before the City Chamberlain, or at Bridewell.

104. See Cornish and Clark 1989, 287 n. 10, which refers to underage servants (but Grumio, for instance, in *SHR* is not such). This adds that only justices could imprison runaway servants, and that if death resulted from a master's beating, it would be considered to be death by misadventure unless "so barbarous as to exceed all bounds."

105. This was, however, the unusually long term of a London goldsmith's apprenticeship.

106. Flegg 1983, 276. This traces the superstition to "the time of the Book of Esther onward (from the second century B.C.)," but not earlier.

107. Agrippa 1987, 222.

Chapter 7. Why Prospero Abjures "Rough Magic"

Epigraphs in this chapter are from Hunt 1982, 289 and from Stevens 1965, 165 and 175.

1. Montaigne 1942, 3:282.
2. Freud 1975, 324.
3. Montaigne 1942, 3:282.
4. The rejection in Montaigne 1942, 1:91, of Montaigne's own former doubtfulness regarding "Ghosts walking, of foretelling future things, of enchantments, of witchcrafts" on the basis that "it is rather custom, than science that removeth the strangenesse of [most things] from us," makes his essay "It is Follie to Referre Truth or Falsehood to our Sufficiencie" a surpassing statement of that proposition.
5. Hunt 1982, 285.
6. Ibid., p, 289; this interprets especially *CYM* 5.3.53–58.
7. See Pérez-Ramos 1988.
8. Because, as has been argued in chapter 6, true science requires a proper awareness of the limits of knowledge, self-knowledge must also involve realizing limits. It will be argued in the following that *TMP* demonstrates how omnipotence may block knowledge, and so be ineffective.
9. Sidney 1961, 12–28.
10. Ibid., 13. Here Sidney is not, I think, suggesting otherworldly aims, as Hunt 1988, seems to suggest when it argues (mentioning Sidney) that Shakespeare's last plays produced a new genre of the "romance of knowing" based on a Protestant paradigm of spiritual salvation through suffering.
11. See Auden 1945, 349–404, especially Antonio's interjections, 361–73.
12. Berger 1969, 273–74.
13. Hunt 1988, 154.
14. The usual basis for this is a presumption of Prospero's great wisdom, as in Cantor 1980, which proposes that Prospero's anger is often only feigned (65–66). Black 1986, 143, shows the inadequacy of an attempt in Kermode 1962, lxiii, to ascribe Prospero's short temper to folklore motifs.
15. Woodman 1973, 40–43.
16. Ibid., 77 and 78.
17. The punctuation of 4.1.145 adopted by the Oxford editors eliminates a comma after "anger" that is found in the First Folio text, tln 1816. But that

comma, if retained, still would not indicate that Miranda never before saw Prospero angry; on this see Lindenbaum 1984, 161–62, and passim.

18. Lindenbaum 1984.

19. Woodman 1973, 77.

20. Knight 1932, 247. Readings of the play as affirmative as Knight's are found in the criticism of Tillyard, Traversi, Frye, and many others. This was seen as the "general interpretation of *The Tempest* now current" in 1961, when Frank Kermode revised his preface to his 1954 Arden edition, Kermode 1962, lxxxiii.

21. Although I agree with the conclusion of Cantor 1980 that "The very dramatic structure of *The Tempest* . . . stresses the difference between knowledge and the lack of it," it seems to me that much must be ignored in the play to allow the view expressed that Prospero "is relatively free of passion to begin with, and remarkably in control of those passions he is subjected to" (65).

22. These need not be post-modern; see the approval of Renan's play *Caliban* in Wyndham Lewis 1927, 282.

23. Such critics have often been very helpful in other respects, but miss a great deal in the play. See: Wagner 1933; Briggs 1962, 83 and 116; Traversi 1969, 322; Woodman 1973; Cantor 1980; Traister 1984; Mebane 1989, 180–83; and Jacobus 1992, 137–60 (despite this chapter's title "The Renunciation of Certainty; *The Tempest*").

24. Marienstras 1981, 171–72, provides an updated version of the indefinite island, connecting it with a putatively disoriented reception of travel narratives.

25. As in Richard Levin 1988, which generally disapproves of making excuses for "bad" Shakespeare.

26. Jacobean audiences highly sensitive to diction would no doubt have been inclined to wonder why Prospero communicates so badly. This would seem to signify inner turmoil, as do the parallel instances of turgidly euphemistic rhetoric in *WT* 1.2.1–9 and 1.2.69–77 having violent undertones (on these see Sokol 1994a, 24–26). Moreover, the setting of *TMP* 1.2 is intimate rather than the semi-public as in *WT* 1.2, making the anomaly even more peculiar.

27. See chapter 5 on Renaissance doubts about wonder, or its aesthetic uses.

28. This indicates that Miranda is not portrayed as a bland or mindlessly serene heroine, no more than are the distinctively voiced Imogen, the anxiety-filled Perdita, or the persuasive and talented Marina. Yet Sundelson 1980, 36, claims that Miranda lacks all "critical faculty of her own, and her responses are just what her father wants" and that she "has neither Perdita's liveliness nor Imogen's dignity." Sundelson continues that she is merely the passive recipient of the lessons of an overweening patriarch who congratulates himself as her excellent "schoolmaster" or "tutor" (1.2.173–75). Westlund 1995, 242, more convincingly claims that "the text prevents us from imagining Miranda as a pallid idealized creature."

29. See the Introduction in which a similar pattern of disproportionate illtemper has been described with regard to Prospero's harshness to Ariel in the course of instructing him about the past. Most thoughts of his past, and any imagining of ingratitude, seem to ignite Prospero's wrath.

30. See: Klein 1986a, b, c. For Kleinian readings of *TMP* see Westlund 1989 and Sokol 1993.

31. Summers 1984, 143. This is from a chapter (135–58) which extends Summers 1973.

32. Summers 1984, 141.

33. Ibid., 145.

34. Ibid., 140.

35. For instance, Hunt 1995, 163–92, explores a number of aspects of labor in *TMP*; this contrasts "easy, vicious" rhetorical efforts in the play with the labor of childbirth, of study, of magic, of toilsome log-bearing, of the lover, of agricultural husbandry, or of weary sicklemen, and questions if Prospero as magus really does do "work."

36. Ronald B. Bond 1978, 336–38, which illustrates this from the Elizabethan homilie "Against Idlenesse" and other contemporary sources. See Bond (339) on Sebastian's quip on his "Hereditary sloth" in 2.1.228. Yet Hunt 1995, 178–81, maintains that Prospero's art is in more than one sense contrary to work. So Hunt (185) insists that the "utensils" of aristocratic Prospero convey "overtones of aesthetic uselessness," and claims that *TMP* devalues or "parodies" his magical labors (186–88). Nonetheless, Hunt finally acknowledges a possibility of significant mental work performed by Prospero and others in the play (189–91).

37. See the lively but wayward Berger 1969.

38. Partridge 1947, 54 and 53; see also Colman 1974, 155.

39. See: Williams 1994, 2:790; Colman 1974, 155; and Partridge 1947, 139–40. Colman finds another instance in *TIM* (221), which I doubt. There may be non-misogynist menstrual implications in Olivia's remark in *TN*, " 'Tis not that time of moon with me to make one in so skipping a dialogue" (1.5.192–93).

40. The provocation of the mariner to insubordination, and his initial restraint, are delineated in Summers 1984, 145–46.

41. Shakespeare's depiction of voices heard in the storm is more lifelike than William Strachey's in his account of his actual experience of shipwreck, printed as a source in Bullough 1975, 8:135: "panting bosoms . . . Prayers . . . in the heart and lips, but drowned in the outcries of the Officers."

42. Edwards 1974, 99.

43. Ronald B. Bond, 1978, 334.

44. But, *pace* Hunt 1995, 163, it is not suggested that this "causes the ship to sink."

45. Strachey 1625.

46. Even his courtier's clothes are kept clean (2.1.66–69). Filthiness, such as that of the renegades at the end of *TMP*, or Falstff's at the end of *2H4*, is degrading. No unwashed audience is implied.

47. No more than Antigonus of *WT* or Leonine of *PER* could; but Pisano of *CYM* does manage to avoid this.

48. Ronald B. Bond 1978, 341, describes how that sin came in Shakespeare's time to be extended to include failure to perform worldly as well as in spiritual duties.

49. Ford 1998, 52, uses the last of these pairs, "id" and "superego," but acceptably in a kind of shorthand, in an argument that the epilogue of *TMP* contains "a statement of guilt over incest wishes and fantasies, and the acceptance of the resolution of that guilt."

50. Henry James 1991, 88.

51. *OED* 2.b and 2.c, and numerous uses by Shakespeare, all show that Kermode 1962, 95n, is incorrect in claiming that the word "rabble" was "not at this stage of development contemptuous."

52. So are some critics' ideas that Ariel is "too dainty" for "Prospero's tasks," as in Hunt 1982, 300.

53. Dobreé 1952, 21.

54. See Sokol 1993, 211.

55. English "matter" also connects with timber. See *OED* "matter" and "hyle."

56. Cleft trees are inimical to Ariel, but matter itself is not to this middle spirit who happily transacts Prospero's four-element-involving "business."

57. Mark Taylor 1982, 141–47, argues that the supposed rape is Prospero's false assessment of Caliban's actually courteous wooing, paralleling Brabantio's false accusation of Othello's witchcraft. This adds, "Rather than indict the daughter for disloyalty in choosing a man other than himself, the father castigates the suitor's dishonorable methods—a classic displacement . . ." (143). But, although the image of a courteous suitor fits Othello, it cannot be made to fit Caliban; his assumption that Miranda is to be taken and not asked for is made wholly explicit in *TMP* 3.2.99–106.

58. Mark Taylor 1982, 159, connects wood-gathering with a task imposed on a suitor, in folklore, of clearing a forest to prepare new fertile land (see also Taylor, 175–82, for Ovidian and mythological analogues). Somewhat similarly, Hamilton 1990, 97–103, compares Ferdinand's log-carrying with the physical labor of Aeneas in building Carthage. These ingenious suggestions fall foul of the fact that Caliban is ordered by Prospero to the same task. Prospero certainly does not want to assess Caliban's fertility (!); neither does the play make Caliban comparable with an empire-founder.

59. See Nevo 1987, 147, and Hunt 1989. Jonathan Bate 1993, 260, supposes "it is only in reading that we stop to think about the business about the threat of Venus and Cupid." But a Renaissance audience would have been far more attentive to emblematic meanings than that.

60. Adelman 1992, 193.

61. Might this explain Ariel's abhorrence of certain earthy "hests," the danger to him/her in trees?

62. Prospero's hate-filled initial description of the "freckled whelp" (1.2.284) Caliban does not indicate any sort of synthesis in an image of dappling, *pace* Gajdusek 1974, 155, but rather serves as an initial benchmark of disgust.

63. See Jonathan Bate 1993, 249–55, and Mincoff 1992, 113. Kermode 1962, 149, tries to reassure worried readers that "only those elements which are consistent with 'white' magic are taken over [from Ovid] for Prospero."

64. It is interesting that in a survey of images of pregnancy in Shakespeare, Sacks 1980, 90, cites only one instance of a direct verbal reference in *TMP*, which is in an image of a *man* giving birth (2.1.234–36). However Sacks finds many indirect allusions to natural procreation in the play (87–104).

65. Fiedler 1974, 167–71, is pioneering.

66. Jowett 1993, 47.

67. That her illicit love affair with Aeneas (as reported by Virgil, Ovid, and Dante) was only a literary concoction is stressed in Boccaccio 1964, 86–92. On Shakespeare on "lustful" widows see Sokol and Sokol 2000 under "Dowager/Widow."

68. See Pittock 1986. See also Orgel 1987b, 40–43 (repeating Orgel 1987a, 58–62), and Mebane 1989, 188–89. Paster 1984 finds several thematic links between accounts of Dido and *TMP* generally.

69. See Hunt, 1988, 145–50.

70. Although some discussions, such as Williamson 1986, 113, find the "terrifying spectre" of incest arising in only the first three Romances, others, such as Ford 1998, 47–53, make a strong case for its pervasive presence in *TMP*. On relevant historical, definitional, and other complexities concerning incest see: Marienstras 1981, 186–92; Thomas 1983, 39; Neely 1985, 166–209; Forker 1990, 141–68; and McCabe 1993, 3–63.

71. Cited and discussed in McCabe 1993, 47; see McCabe on problems of definition of and the history of "incest" (3–63).

72. See ibid., and Sokol and Sokol 2000 under "Divorce" and "Impediments."

73. See Rank 1926, 352n (this book was first published in 1912, and was conceived in 1906). Many footnotes, including that referring to *TMP*, are unhappily removed (as superfluous examples) in the translation Rank 1992. Melchiori 1960, 65–72, explains why, in relation to a repeated father-daughter incest theme in the last plays of Shakespeare, "*The Tempest* goes deeper than the others." Gajdusek 1974, 158, begins a complex psychoanalytic analysis of *TMP* with: "there is an incestuous base to the image of a father alone on an isle with his daughter for many years." There are some partly contrary voices, as in McCabe 1993, 188–89, which suggests that "Prospero and Miranda represent the apparent transcendence of incestuous desire in circumstances which might well have promoted it," and that "The distinctive quality of Shakespeare's use of the incest motif is its restraint and subtlety." Barber and Wheeler 1986, 335, suggest that Prospero's "anxious control over the fate of Miranda's sexuality is the way this play protects its action from the threat of incest." But is it the play, or the self-image of the dramatized father, that protects itself? As mentioned, Ford 1998, 47–53, robustly asserts that the incest theme pervades the play.

74. Melchiori 1960, 71–72.

75. Just as Pericles does in *PER* Scene 9.47–52. A detailed commentary on Prospero's anger in Mark Taylor 1982, 149–57, leads on to the remark that "from Prospero's unconscious perspective, then, Ferdinand entirely deserves the appellation of traitor" (163). This is said to be because in one part of a divided mind Prospero wants "to hold [Miranda] to him forever," but this idea is not closely pursued. There are instead some comments on Prospero's charming of Ferdinand's sword as resembling the encounter of Laius and Oedipus (183–84).

76. F562 in Tilley 1950, 232.

77. Freud 1967, 410.

78. Jacobus 1992, 154, shows that Ariel tells Prospero what he "already knows" when replying to his "Say again: where didst thou leave these varlets?," for Ariel uses the past tense, beginning: "I told you, sir . . ." (4.1.170–71).

79. In 1.2.447 Miranda explicitly says that he speaks "ungently."

80. For an analysis of this speech and its context in Kleinian terms see Sokol 1993.

81. Shakespeare's "stale" is a highly complex word, meaning more than just bait. "Horse urine," an important second meaning, is reflected in Octavius Caesar's praise of Roman Antony in *ANT* 1.4.61–63. Klein 1986c, 183, connects urethral-sadistic impulses with primitive fantasies of projecting "harmful excrements, expelled in hatred, split-off parts of the ego"; Caliban does not want to take up Prospero's worthless stale, so may be understood to resist Prospero's voiding into him of denied parts of himself, Klein's "projective identification."

82. In the language of today's psychology one could say that Antonio uses behaviorist techniques on a mass scale, whereas Prospero grants his countrymen safe psychodynamic freedom (a protected place-apart where fantasies can flourish), although also a possibly punishing freedom, to facilitate autonomous change or growth.

83. Jonathan Bate 1993, 254–55, is among those who emphasize the importance of the line break, and in particular connects this with an allusion to Medea in Ovid. Bate's explanation, 255–57, concerns the loss of the Golden Age.

84. Prospero's full commitment to this acknowledgment has been played

down by some critics. For instance, Adelman 1992, 237, finds that as "the last of Shakespeare's mother's sons . . . Caliban must finally be acknowledged; but he cannot be incorporated into that psyche." Barber and Wheeler 1986, 335–36, argues similarly.

85. Brown 1985, 68. Brown then discusses how this suggests an identification between Prospero and Caliban which points to ideological contradictions in the "colonialist project," but still stresses power relations alone. Greenblatt 1985a, 29, interprets the phrase as instancing "the containment of a subversive force by the authority that has created that force in the first place"; in this Caliban is again property in the sense of a thing or force contained. The later version, Greenblatt 1988 (discussed in chapter 2 above), does not reiterate this. Greenblatt 1976, 570, goes part of the way to inverting it, admitting that Caliban "is claimed as Philoctetes might claim his own festering wound. Perhaps, too, the word 'acknowledge' implies some moral responsibility. . . ." But this concludes that "Prospero has acknowledged a bond; that is all" (571). Vaughan and Vaughan 1999, 281n, suggests a wholly diminished reading in which "Prospero may be merely acknowledging Caliban as his servant," but names critics who disagree.

86. Ronald B. Bond 1978, 338. Among many others who have found similar meanings, a particularly strong statement is made in D. G. James 1967, 121.

87. Strangely, it is only at the very end of a (sometimes stretched) study of Shakespeare and incest, Mark Taylor 1982, 186, that the suggestion is made that the Caliban acknowledged by Prospero may represent an incestuous fantasy.

88. Gajdusek 1974, 156.

89. Jonathan Bate 1993, 245.

90. See Bradshaw 1987 and Cavell 1987.

91. Barber 1963, 161.

92. For instance, in a discussion of the intellectual background to *TMP*, Marienstras 1981, 184, tendentiously assumes the doctrine "that meaning is never fixed unless imposed by violence."

93. Kessler 1995 argues that any correct paradigm of scientific achievement must involve matters about which "we can never be sure"; history shows that the possibility of achievement, even in the absence of certainty, has often been sufficient to motivate a passionate pursuit.

94. Westlund 1995, 246, concluding an article on *TMP* that applies the Kleinian theory of the necessity of desires for the "extremely good." Wholly contrary views of the desires seen in *TMP* have been taken; Westlund argues here, and more theoretically in Westlund, 1989, that such doubts are inevitable.

95. Westlund 1995, 243–44.

96. Hunt 1988, 136, describing a process of analysis seen as typical of sixteenth-century pastoral works by Walter R. Davis. Hunt suggests that Prospero seeing the suffering of Gonzalo prompts his insight. I would add his seeing himself.

97. Sokol 1993, 213.

98. That is, I would not deny in *TMP* the importance of a "discourse of prayer," as so well argued for in McAlindon 2001.

AFTERWORD

1. Citations are from Jonson 1925, 5:282–408.

2. Edward Kelly was twice imprisoned by Rudolf II for failing to make good on his alchemical promises; his attempt to escape led to a broken leg and his death in 1595. Kelly also attempted to dupe Dee into "mystical" adultery.

3. See Sokol 1994a, 99–109.

Bibliography

Ackerman, James. 1985. "The Involvement of Artists in Renaissance Science." In *Science and the Arts in the Renaissance*, edited by John W. Shirley and F. David Hoeniger, 94–129. Washington, D.C.: Folger Library.

Adelman, Janet. 1992. *Suffocating Mothers: Fantasies of Maternal Origin in Shakespeare's Plays, Hamlet to The Tempest*. New York: Routledge.

Agrippa, Henry Cornelius. 1987. *Three Books of Occult Philosophy*. Translated by J[ohn] F[rench] 1651, reprint. London: Chthonios.

Albanese, Denise. 1996. *New Science, New World*. Durham, N.C.: Duke University Press.

Anglerie, Peter Martyr. 1555. *The Decades of the Newe Worlde of East India by Peter Martyr of Anglerie*. Translated by Richard Eden. London.

Aristotle. 1941. *The Basic Works*. Edited by Richard McKeon. New York: Random House.

Ashworth, William B., Jr. 1990. "Natural History and the Emblematic World View." In *Reappraisals of the Scientific Revolution*, edited by David C. Lindberg and Robert S. Westman, 303–32. New York: Cambridge University Press.

Aubrey, John. 1983. *Brief Lives*. Edited by Richard Barber. London: Book Club Associates.

Auden, W. H. 1945. *Collected Poetry*. New York: Random House.

———. 1963. "Music in Shakespeare." In *Shakespeare Criticism, 1935–1960*, edited by Anne Ridler, 306–28. London: Oxford University Press.

Bacon, Francis. 1872. *Works*. Edited by James Spedding, Robert Leslie Ellis, and Douglas Denon Heath. London: Longmans.

———. 1996. *Philosophical Studies c. 1611–c. 1619*. Edited by Graham Rees. The Oxford Francis Bacon vol. VI. Oxford: Clarendon Press.

———. n.d. *Of The Advancement of Learning*. Originally published 1605. Everyman's Library edition, edited by G. W. Kitchen. London: J. M. Dent.

Baldwin, T. W. 1935. "A Note Upon William Shakespeare's use of Pliny." In *The Parrot Presentation Volume: Essays on Dramatic Literature*, edited by Hardin Craig, 157–82. Princeton: Princeton University Press.

Barber, C. L. 1963. *Shakespeare's Festive Comedy: A Study of Dramatic Form in Relation to Social Custom*. Cleveland: World Publishing Company.

Barber, C. L., and Richard P. Wheeler. 1986. *The Whole Journey: Shakespeare's Power of Development*. Berkekey: University of California Press.

Barbour, Philip L. 1964. *The Three Worlds of Captain John Smith*. Boston: Houghton Mifflin and Company.

———, ed. 1969. *The Jamestown Voyages Under the First Charter 1606–1609*. 2 vols. Cambridge: Cambridge University Press, for the Hakluyt Society.

———. 1971. "The Honorable George Percy, Premier Chronicler of the First Virginia Voyage." *Early American Literature* 6: 7–17.

Barker, Francis, and Peter Hulme. 1985. "Nymphs and Reapers Heavily Vanish: The Discursive Con-texts of The Tempest." In *Alternative Shakespeares*, edited by John Drakakis, 191–205. London: Methuen.

Barlowe, Arthur. 1955. "Discourse of the First Voyage." In *The Roanoke Voyages*, edited by David Beers Quinn, 1:91–116. 2 vols. London: The Hakluyt Society.

Barton, Anne. 1994. *Essays, Mainly Shakespearean*. Cambridge: Cambridge University Press.

B[astard], T[homas]. 1598. *Chrestoleros. Seuen bookes of Epigrams written by TB*. London.

Bate, John. 1635. *The Mysteries of Nature and Art*. London, 1635.

B[ate], J[ohn]. 1977. *The Mysteries of Nature and Art*. Facsimile of London, 1634. Amsterdam: Theatrum Orbis.

Bate, Jonathan. 1993. *Shakespeare and Ovid*. Oxford: Clarendon Press.

———. 1994. "The Humanist Tempest." In *Shakespeare: La tempête: Etudes critiques*, edited by Claude Peltrault, 5–20. Besançon: Faculté des Lettres.

Batho, G. R., ed. 1962.*The Household Papers of Henry Percy Ninth Earl of Northumberland (1564–1632)*. Camden Third Series vol. 93. London: Royal Historical Society.

———. 1992. *Thomas Harriot and the Northumberland Household*. The 1991 Oxford Thomas Harriot Lecture. Oxford: Oriel College.

Bauer, Max. 1968. *Precious Stones*. Translated, with additions by L. J. Spenser, from the first edition of 1904. 2 vols. New York: Dover.

Baumgardt, Carola. 1952. *Johannas Kepler: Life and Letters*. Introduction by Albert Einstein. London: Victor Gollancz.

Benzoni, Girolamo. 1579. *Histoire Nouvelle du Nouveau Monde*. Extracted from the Italian and enriched with many discourses by Urbain Chauveton. Geneva.

———. 1862. *History of the New World by Girolamo Benzoni of Milan, Shewing His Travels in America from A. D. 1541 to 1556*. Translated and edited by by W. H. Smith from the 1572 edition. London: Hakluyt Society.

Berger, Harry, Jr. 1969. "Miraculous Harp: A Reading of Shakespeare's *Tempest*." *Shakespeare Studies* 5: 253–83.

Bernthal, Craig A. 1991. "Treason in the Family: The Trial of Thumpe v. Horner." *Shakespeare Quarterly* 42: 44–54.

Berry, Edward I. 1979. "Prospero's 'Brave Spirit.'" *Studies in Philology* 76: 36–48.

The Bible. 1587. Known as the Geneva or Breeches Bible. London: Christopher Barker.

Bishop, T. G. 1996. *Shakespeare and the Theatre of Wonder*. Cambridge: Cambridge University Press.

Black, James. 1986. "Shakespeare and the Comedy of Revenge." In *Comparative Critical Approaches to Renaissance Comedy*, edited by Donald Beecher and Massimo Ciavolella, 137–51. Ottawa, Canada: Dovehouse.

Blake, William. 1914. *The Poetical Works*. Edited by John Sampson. London: Oxford University Press.

Boccaccio, Giovanni. 1964. *Concerning Famous Women. De Claris Mulieribus* c.

1359, translated from the Berne, 1539 edition by Guido A. Guarino. London: George Allen and Unwin.

Bolton, Henry C. 1904. *The Follies of Science at the Court of Rudolph II*. Milwaukee: Pharmaceutical Review Publishing Co..

Bond, Edward L. 1997. "England's Soteriology of Empire and the Roots of Colonial Identity in Early Virginia." *Anglican and Episcopal History* 46: 471–99.

Bond, Ronald B. 1978. "Labour, Ease and *The Tempest* as Pastoral Romance." *Journal of English and Germanic Philology* 77: 330–42.

Boodt, Anselmus Boëtius de. 1609. *Gemmarum et Lapidum Historia*. Hanoviae.

Boot, Anselme Boèce de, and André Toll. 1644. *Le Parfaict Joaillier, ou Histoire des Pierres*. Translated from the 1609 edition "enrichi de belles anntotations, indices & figures" by Toll. Lyon.

Bossy, John. 1991. *Giodorno Bruno and the Embassy Affair*. New Haven: Yale University Press.

Bowerbank, Sylvia. 1984. "The Spider's Delight: Margaret Cavendish and the 'Female' Imagination." *English Literary Renaissance* 14: 392–408.

Bradbrook, Muriel C. 1936. *The School of Night: A Study in the Literary Relationships of Sir Walter Ralegh*. Cambridge: Cambridge University Press.

Bradshaw, Graham. 1987. *Shakespeare's Scepticism*. Brighton, U.K.: Harvester.

Briggs, K. M. 1962. *Pale Hecate's Team: An Examination of the Beliefs on Witchcraft and Magic amongst Shakespeare's Contemporaries and His Immediate Successors*. London: Routledge & Kegan Paul.

Brown, Paul R. 1985. "'This thing of darkness I acknowledge mine': *The Tempest* and the Discourse of Colonialism." In *Political Shakespeare*, edited by J. Dollimore and A. Sinfield, 48–71. Manchester, U.K.: Manchester University Press.

Bullough, Geoffrey, ed. 1975. *Narrative and Dramatic Sources of Shakespeare*. 8 vols. London: Routledge & Kegan Paul.

Burnett, Mark Thornton. 1991. "Colonialist Discourses in the English Renaissance." In *Langues et nations au temps de la Renaissance*, edited by Marie-Thérèse Jones-Davies, 237–53. Paris: Klincksieck.

Butler, E. M. 1948. *The Myth of the Magus*. Cambridge: Cambridge University Press.

Bylebyl, Jerome L. 1985. "Medicine, Philosophy, and Humanism in Renaissance Italy." In *Science and the Arts in the Renaissance*, edited by John W. Shirley and F. David Hoeniger, 27–49. Washington, D.C.: Folger Library.

Cantor, Paul A. 1980. "Shakespeare's *The Tempest*: The Wise Man as Hero." *Shakespeare Quarterly* 31: 64–75.

Caspar, Max. 1959. *Kepler*. London: Abelarad-Schuman.

Cavell, Stanley. 1987. *Disowning Knowledge in Six Plays of Shakespeare*. Cambridge: Cambridge University Press.

Cavendish, Margaret. 1906. *The Life of William Cavendish, Duke of Newcastle*. Edited by C. H. Firth. Second edition. London: George Routledge and Sons Ltd.

Chaldecott, J. A. 1952. "Bartolomeo Telioux and the Early History of the Thermometer." *Annals of Science* 8: 195–201.

Chapman, George. 1941. *Poems*. Edited by Phyllis Brooks Bartlett. London: Oxford University Press.

———. 1957. *Chapman's Homer*. Edited by A. Nicoll. London: Routledge & Kegan Paul.

———. 1970. *The Plays*. Edited by Allan Holiday. Urbana: University of Illinois Press.

Cheadle, Brian. 1994. "The 'Process' of Prejudice: *Othello* I.iii.128–45." *Notes and Queries* 41: 491–93.

Clark, Stuart. 1984. "The Scientific Status of Demonology." In *Occult and Scientific Mentalities in the Renaissance*, edited by Brian Vickers, 351–74. Cambridge: Cambridge University Press.

Clucas, Stephen. 1994. "The Atomism of the Cavendish Circle: A Reappraisal." *The Seventeenth Century* 9: 247–73.

———. 1995.*Thomas Harriot and the Field of Knowledge in the English Renaissance*. Oxford: Oriel College.

Clulee, Nicholas H. 1988. *John Dee's Natural Philosophy*. London: Routledge.

Colie, Rosalie L. 1954. "Cornelis Drebbel and Salomon de Caus: Two Jacobean Models for Salomon's House." *Huntington Library Quarterly* 18: 245–60.

———. 1966. *Paradoxia Epidemica: The Renaissance Tradition of Paradox*. Princeton: Princeton University Press.

Colman, E. A. M. 1974. *The Dramatic Use of Bawdry in Shakespeare*. London: Longman.

Conlan, J. P. 1999. "*The Tempest* and the King's Better Knowledge." *Ben Jonson Journal: Literary Contexts in the Age of Elizabeth, James and Charles* 6: 161–88.

Copenhaver, Brian P. 1990. "Natural Magic, Hermeticism, and Occultism in Early Modern Science." In *Reappraisals of the Scientific Revolution*, edited by David C. Lindberg and Robert S. Westman, 261–301. New York: Cambridge University Press.

Corfield, Cosmo. 1985. "Why Does Prospero Abjure His 'Rough Magic'?" *Shakespeare Quarterly* 36: 31–48.

Cornish, W. R., and G. de N. Clark. 1989. *Law and Society in England, 1750–1950*. London: Sweet and Maxwell.

Crashawe, William. 1610. *A Sermon Preached in London before the Lord Lewarre, Lord Gouernor and Captaine Generall of Virginia . . . Febr 21 1609*. London.

Crombie, Alistair Cameron. 1985. "Science and the Arts in the Renaissance: The Search for Truth and Certainty, Old and New." In *Science and the Arts in the Renaissance*, edited by John W. Shirley and F. David Hoeniger, 15–26. Washington, D.C.: Folger Library.

———. 1996a. "Expectation, Modelling and Assent in the History of Optics." In *Science, Art and Nature in Medieval and Modern Thought*, edited by Alistair Cameron Crombie, 301–56. London: Hambledon.

———. 1996b. "Experimental Science and the Rational Artist in Early Modern Europe." In *Science, Art and Nature in Medieval and Modern Thought*, edited by Alistair Cameron Crombie, 89–114. London: Hambledon.

———. 1996c. "Galileo Galilei: A Philosophical Symbol." In *Science, Art and Nature in Medieval and Modern Thought*, edited by Alistair Cameron Crombie, 257–62. London: Hambledon.

Culliford, S. G. 1950. "William Strachey, 1572–1621." Ph.D. diss., University of London.

Cunningham, J. V. 1964. *Woe or Wonder*. Chicago: Swallow Press.

Darius, John. 1993. "Report of Discussion on Elizabethan Telescopes." *Bulletin of the Scientific Instrument Society* 37: 6.

Daston, Lorraine. 1994. "Baconian Facts, Academic Civility, and the Prehistory of Objectivity." In *Retinking Objectivity*, edited by Allan Megill, 37–64. Durham N.C.: Duke University Press.

―――. 1999. "Marvelous Facts and Miraculous Evidence in Early Modern Europe." In *Wonders, Marvels, and Monsters in Early Modern Culture*, edited by Peter G. Platt, 76–104. Newark: University of Delaware Press.

Davies of Hereford, John. 1609. *Humours Heau'n on Earth: The Picture of the Plague, according to Life, as it was Anno Domini 1603*. London.

Dean, Paul. 1989. "Shakespeare's Causes." *Cahiers Elisabethains: Etudes sur la Pre-Renaissance et la Renaissance Anglaises* 36: 25–36.

de Bry, Theodore, ed. 1590. *America, Part i*. English version of multilingual edition of Thomas Harriot, *A Briefe and True Report*. Frankfort.

Debus, Allen G. 1987. "Key to Two Worlds: Robert Fludd's Weather Glass." In *Chemistry, Alchemy and the New Philosophy, 1550–1700*, Section XIII, reprinted from *Annali dell'Instituto e Museo di Storia della Scienza di Fiorenze* 7, (1982): 109–43. London: Variorum Reprints.

Dekker, Thomas. 1953. *The Dramatic Works*. Edited by Fredson Bowers. 4 vols. Cambridge: Cambridge University Press.

Dent, R. W. 1981. *Shakespeare's Proverbial Language*. Berkeley: University of California Press.

Dick of Devonshire. 1955. Edited by James G. McManaway and Mary R. McManaway. Oxford: Malone Society Reprints, Oxford University Press.

Dobreé, Bonamy. 1952. "*The Tempest*." *Essays and Studies* 5: 26–31.

Donne, John. 1960. *Poems*. Edited by Sir Herbert Grierson. Oxford: Oxford University Press.

Dousa, Janus. 1850. "Query: Cornelis Drebbel." *Notes and Queries* 2,31: 6–7.

Drake-Brockman, Jennifer. 1994. "The *Perpetuum Mobile* of Cornelius Drebbel." In *Learning, Language and Invention: Essays presented to Francis Madison*, edited by W. D. Hackmann and A. J. Turner, 124–47. Aldershot and Paris: Variorum and Societe Internationale de l'Astrolabe.

Drummond of Hawthornden, William. 1913. *The Poetical Works*. Edited by L. E. Kastner. 2 vols. Edinburgh: William Blackwood & Sons.

Eddington, Arthur S. 1931. "Introduction." In *Johann Kepler*, edited by History of Science Society, xi–xii. Baltimore: Williams & Wilkins.

Edelstein, Sidney. 1971. "Drebbel." In *Dictionary of Scientific Biography*, edited by Charles C. Gillispie, 14:82–85. 16 vols. New York: Charles Scribner and Sons.

Edgerton, Samuel Y., Jr. 1980. "The Renaissance Artist as Quantifier." In *The Perception of Pictures*, edited by Margaret A. Hagen, 1:179–212. 2 vols. New York: Academic Press.

Edwards, Philip. 1974. *Threshold of a Nation: A Study in English and Irish Drama*. Cambridge: Cambridge University Press.

Eliot, T. S. 1934. *Elizabethan Essays*. London: Faber & Faber.

Empson, William. 1993. *Essays on Renaissance Literature. Volume 1: Donne and the New Philosophy*. Edited by John Haffenden. Cambridge: Cambridge University Press.

———. 1994. *Essays on Renaissance Literature. Volume 2: The Drama.* Edited by John Haffenden. Cambridge: Cambridge University Press.

Evans, R. J. W. 1973. *Rudolf II and His World: A Study in Intellectual History.* Oxford: Clarendon Press.

Ewbank, Inga-Stina. 1968. "The Triumph of Time." In *The Winter's Tale: A Casebook*, edited by Kenneth Muir, 98–115. London: Macmillan.

———. 1980. "My name is Marina." In *Shakespeare's Styles*, edited by Inga-Stina Ewbank, P. Edwards, and G. K. Hunter, 111–30. London: Cambridge University Press.

Farley, Henry. 1621. *St Paules Church, Her Bill for the Parliament.* n.p.

Feldhay, Rivka. 1995. *Galileo and the Church: Political Inquisition or Critical Dialogue?* Cambridge: Cambridge University Press.

Fiedler, Leslie A. 1974. *The Stranger in Shakespeare.* Frogmore, St. Albans: Paladin.

Fitz, L. T. 1975. "The Vocabulary of the Environment in *The Tempest.*" *Shakespeare Quarterly* 26: 42–47.

Flegg, Graham. 1983. *Numbers.* London: Deutsch.

F[letcher], P[hineas]. 1633a. *Piscatorie Eclogs.* Published together with *The Purple Island*, but separately paginated. Cambridge.

———. 1633b. *The Purple Island or The Isle of Man.* Cambridge.

Flynn, Dennis. 1987. "Donne's *Ignatius His Conclave* and Other Libels on Robert Cecil." *John Donne Journal: Studies in the Age of Donne* 6: 163–83.

Ford, Jane M. 1998. *Patriarchy and Incest from Shakespeare to Joyce.* Gainesville: University of Florida Press.

Forker, Charles R. 1990. *Fancy's Images: Contexts, Settings, and Perspectives in Shakespeare and his Contemporaries.* Carbondale: Southern Illinois University Press.

Fowler, Alastair. 1990. *Triumphal Forms: Structural Patterns in Elizabethan Poetry.* London: Cambridge University Press.

Freud, Sigmund. 1967. *The Interpretation of Dreams.* Translated and edited by James Strachey. London: George Allen & Unwin Ltd.

———. 1975. "The Psychopathology of Everyday Life." In *Pelican Freud Library Vol. 5*, edited by Angela Richards, 35–382. First published 1901. London: Penguin.

Frey, Charles. 1979. "*The Tempest* and the New World." *Shakespeare Quarterly* 30: 29–41.

Frost, Robert. 1967. *The Poetry of Robert Frost.* Edited by Edward Connery Lathem. New York: Holt Rinehart and Winston.

Frye, Northrop. 1983. *The Myth of Deliverance: Reflections on Shakespeare's Problem Comedies.* Brighton, U.K.: Harvester Press.

———. 1986. *Northrop Frye on Shakespeare.* Edited by Robert Sandler. New Haven: Yale University Press.

Gajdusek, R. E. 1974. "Death, Incest and the Triple Bond in the Later Plays of Shakespeare." *American Imago* 31: 109–58.

Galilei, Galileo. 1952. *Dialogues Concerning the Two New Sciences.* Translation of

1638, in Britannia Great Books vol. 28, *Gilbert, Galileo, Harvey* pp. 129–260. Chicago: William Benton.

Garner, Stanton B., Jr. 1985. "Time and Presence in *The Winter's Tale.*" *Modern Language Quarterly* 46: 347–67.

Gascoigne, George. 1907. *The Complete Works.* Edited by John W. Cunliffe. 2 vols. Cambridge: Cambridge University Press.

Gatti, Hilary. 1989. *The Renaissance Drama of Knowledge: Giodorno Bruno in England.* London: Routledge.

Gesner, Conrad. 1558. *Historiae Animalium Liber IV. Qui est de Piscium & Aquatium animantium natura.* Tiguri.

———. 1560. *Historiae Animalium Liber IV. Nomenclator Aquatilium Animantium Icones Animalium Aquatilium.* Bound with incorrect title page in Wellcome Institute EPB 2108/D. Geneva.

———. 1604. *Historiae Animalium Liber IV. Qui est de Piscium & Aquatium animantium natura.* Editio secunda. Francofurti.

Gifford, George. 1931. *A Dialogue Concerning Witches and Witchcraftes, 1593.* Shakespeare Association Facsimiles No. 1, with an introduction by Beatrice White. London: The Shakespeare Association.

Gillies, John. 1986. "Shakespeare's Virginian Masque." *ELH* 53: 673–707.

Gillispie, Charles Coulston, ed. 1971. *Dictionary of Scientific Biography.* 16 vols. New York: Charles Schribner and Sons.

Godwin, Joscelyn. 1979. *Robert Fludd.* London: Thames and Hudson.

Gombrich, E. H. 1990. "'My library was dukedom large enough': Shakespeare's Prospero and Prospero Visconti of Milan." In *England and the Continental Renaissance: Essays in Honour of J. B. Trapp,* edited by Edward Chaney and Peter Mack, 185–90. Woodbridge, Suffolk: Boydell.

Gouk, Penelope. 1988. *The Ivory Sundials of Nuremberg 1500–1700.* Cambridge: Whipple Museum of the History of Science.

———. 1999. *Music, Science and Natural Magic in Seventeenth-Century England.* New Haven: Yale University Press.

Grafton, Anthony. 1991. "Humanism and Science in Rudolphine Prague: Kepler in Context." In *Literary Culture in the Holy Roman Empire, 1555–1720,* edited by James A. Parente Jr., Richard Erich Schade, and George C. Schoolfield, 19–45. Chapel Hill: University of North Carolina Press.

Grant, Douglas. 1957. *Margaret the First: A Biography of Margaret Cavendish, Duchess of Newcastle.* London: Rupert Hart-Davis.

Grant, Patrick. 1985. *Literature and the Discovery of Method in the English Renaissance.* Houndsmill, UK: Macmillan.

Grassl, Gary C. 1996. "German Mineral Specialists in Elizabethan England and Early English America." *Yearbook of German-American Studies* 31: 45–61.

Greenblatt, Stephen. 1976. "Learning to Curse: Aspects of Linguistic Colonialism in the Sixteenth Century." In *First Images of America: The Impact of the Old World on the New,* edited by Fred Chiappelli, 2:561–80. 2 vols. Berkeley: University of California Press.

———. 1981. "Invisible Bullets: Renaissance Authority and its Subversion, *Henry IV* and *Henry V.*" *Glyph* 8: 40–61.

———. 1985a. "Invisible Bullets: Renaissance Authority and its Subversion, *Henry IV* and *Henry V.*" In *Political Shakespeare: New Essays in Cultural Mate-*

rialism, edited by J. Dollimore and A. Sinfield, 18–47. Manchester: Manchester University Press.

———. 1985b. "Invisible Bullets: Renaissance Authority and its Subversion, *Henry IV* and *Henry V*." In *Shakespeare's "Rough Magic": Renaissance Essays in Honor of C. L. Barber*, edited by Peter Erickson and Coppélia Kahn, 276–302. Newark: University of Delaware Press.

———. 1988. "Invisible Bullets." In *Shakespearean Negotiations*, 21–56. Oxford: Clarendon Press.

———. 1990. *Learning to Curse*. London: Routledge.

———. 1991. *Marvelous Possessions*. Chicago: University of Chicago Press.

Greenblatt, Stephen, and M. H. Abrahms, eds. 2000. *The Norton Anthology of English Literature*. 7th edition. 2 vols. New York: W. W. Norton.

Greville, Fulke. 1945. *Poems and Dramas*. Edited by Geoffrey Bullough. 2 vols. New York: Oxford University Press.

Grudin, Robert. 1991. "Rudolf II of Prague and Cornelis Drebbel: Shakespearean Archetypes?" *Huntington Library Quarterly* 54: 181–205.

Guazzo, Francisco Maria. 1929. *Compendium Maleficarum*. Milan, 1608. Edited by Montague Summers. Translated by E. A. Ashwin. London: John Rodker.

Gurr, Andrew. 1996. "Industrious Ariel and Idle Caliban." In *Travel and Drama in Shakespeare's Time*, edited by Jean-Pierre Maquerlot and Michèle Willems, 193–208. Cambridge: Cambridge University Press.

Gutierrez, Nancy A. 1985. "An Allusion to 'India' and Pearls." *Shakespeare Quarterly* 36: 220.

Hall, Grace R. W. 1999. *The Tempest as Mystery Play: Uncovering Religious Sources of Shakespeare's Most Spiritual Work*. Jefferson, N.C.: McFarland & Co.

Hamilton, Donna B. 1990. *Virgil and The Tempest: The Politics of Imitation*. Columbus: Ohio State University Press.

Hamlin, William M. 1994. "Men of Inde: Renaissance Ethnography and *The Tempest*." *Shakespeare Studies* 22: 15–44.

———. 1995. *The Image of America in Montaigne, Spenser, and Shakespeare: Renaissance Ethnography and Literary Reflection*. New York: St. Martin's Press.

Hantman, Jeffrey L. 1992. "Caliban's Own Voice: American Indian Views of the Other in Colonial Virginia." *New Literary History* 23: 69–81.

Harriot, Thomas. 1588. *A Briefe and True Report of the New Found Land of Virginia*. London.

———. 1955. "A Briefe and True Report of the New Found Land of Virginia, 1588." In *The Roanoke Voyages*, edited by David Beers Quinn, 317–87. Vol. 1. 2 vols. London: Hakluyt Society.

Harris, Anthony. 1980. *Night's Black Agents: Witchcraft and Magic in Seventeenth-Century English Drama*. Manchester, U.K.: Manchester University Press.

Harris, L. E. 1957–59. "Cornelis Drebbel: A Neglected Genius of Seventeenth Century Technology." *Transactions of the Newcomen Society* 31: 194–204.

———. 1961. *The Two Netherlanders Humphrey Bradley and Cornelis Drebbel*. Leiden: E. J. Brill.

Hassel, R. Chris. 1971. "Donne's *Ignatius His Conclave* and the New Astronomy." *Modern Philology* 68: 329–37.

———. 1980. *Faith and Folly in Shakespeare's Romantic Comedies*. Athens: University of Georgia Press.

Hatfield, Gary. 1990. "Metaphysics and the New Science." In *Reappraisals of the Scientific Revolution*, edited by David C. Lindberg and Robert S. Westman, 93–166. New York: Cambridge University Press.

Hattaway, Michael. 1996. "'Seeing things': Amazons and Cannibals." In *Travel and Drama in Shakespeare's Time*, edited by Jean-Pierre Maquerlot and Michèle Willems, 179–93. Cambridge: Cambridge University Press.

Hawkins, Sir Richard. 1622. *The Observations of Sir Richard Hawkins Knight, in his Voyage into the South Sea. Anno Domini 1593*. London.

Henkes, H. E. 1995. "Aan de Lamp Geblazen Figuurtjes: de 'Bevokin' van een Souvenirfles." *Westerheem* 44: 111–14.

Henningsen, Gustav. 1980. *The Witches Advocate: Basque Witchcraft and the Spanish Inquisition 1609–1614*. Reno: University of Nevada Press.

Henry, John. 1982. "Thomas Harriot and Atomism: A Reappraisal." *The History of Science* 20: 255–96.

Heywood, Thomas. 1792. *Loves Mistress or The Queens Masque*. London.

Historical Manuscripts Commission. 1877. *Sixth Report*. London: Historical Manuscripts Commission.

Hoeniger, F. David. 1985. "How Plants and Animals Were Studied in the Mid-Sixteenth Century." In *Science and the Arts in the Renaissance*, edited by John W. Shirley and F. David Hoeniger, 130–48. Washington, D.C.: Folger Library.

Holden, Martin. 1991. *Encyclopedia of Gemstones and Minerals*. Philadelphia: Michael Friedman.

Holdsworth, Sir William. 1922–1966. *A History of English Law*. 17 vols. London: Methuen.

Hotine, Margaret. "Contemporary Themes in *The Tempest*." *Notes and Queries* 34: 224–26.

Hotson, Leslie. 1937. *I, William Shakespeare*. London: Jonathan Cape.

Houghton, Walter E., Jr. 1942. "The English Virtuoso in the Seventeenth Century." *The Journal of the History of Ideas* 3: 51–73 and 190–219.

Hulme, Peter. 1986. *Colonial Encounters: Europe and the Native Caribbean 1492–1797*. London: Routledge.

Hunt, Maurice. 1982. "'Stir' and Work in Shakespeare's Last Plays." *SEL: Studies in English Literature, 1500–1900* 22: 285–304.

———. 1988. "Shakespeare's Romance of Knowing." *Journal of the Rocky Mountain Medieval and Renaissance Association* 9: 131–55.

———. 1989. "Controlling Cupid in Shakespeare's Last Romances." *The Upstart Crow* 9: 63–76.

———. 1995. *Shakespeare's Labored Art: Stir, Work, and the Late Plays*. New York: Lang.

Hutchison, Keith. 1982. "What Happened to Occult Qualities in the Scientific Revolution?" In *The Scientific Enterprise in Early Modern Europe*, edited by Peter Dear, 86–106. Chicago: University of Chicago Press.

Jacob, James R., and Timothy Raylor. 1991. "Opera and Obedience: Thomas Hobbes and 'A Proposition for Advancement of Moralitie' by Sir William Davenant." *The Seventeenth Century* 6: 205–50.

Jacobus, Lee A. 1992. *Shakespeare and the Dialectic of Certainty*. New York: St. Martin's Press.

Jacquot, Jean. 1949. "Un Amateur de Science, Ami de Hobbes et de Descartes, Sir Charles Cavendish." *Thales*: 81–88.

———. 1952a. "Sir Charles Cavendish and his Learned Friends." *Annals of Science* 8: 175–91.

———. 1952b. "Thomas Harriot's Reputation for Impiety." *Notes and Records of the Royal Society* 9: 164–87.

———. 1974. "Harriot, Hill, Warner and the New Philosophy." In *Thomas Harriot: Renaissance Scientist*. Edited by John W. Shirley, 107–28. Oxford: Oxford University Press.

James, D. G. 1965. *The Dream of Learning: An Essay on The Advancement of Learning, Hamlet, and King Lear*. Oxford: Clarendon Press.

———. 1967. *The Dream of Prospero*. Oxford: Clarendon Press.

James, Henry. 1991. "Introduction to *The Tempest* (1907)." In *The Tempest: A Casebook*, edited by D. J. Palmer, 67–81. London: Macmillan.

James VI of Scotland. 1924. *Daemonologie*. Edited by G. B. Harrison. Reprint of 1597. London: Bodley Head.

———. 1947–1958. *Poems of James VI of Scotland*. edited by James Craigie. 2 vols. Edinburgh: William Blackwood & Sons.

Jardine, Nicholas. 1986. *The Fortunes of Inquiry*. Oxford: Clarendon Press.

———. 1988. "Epistemology of the Sciences." In *The Cambridge History of Renaissance Philosophy*, edited by Charles B. Schmitt, 685–711. Cambridge: Cambridge University Press.

Jehlen, Myra. 1994. "The Literature of Colonialization." In *The Cambridge History of American Literature*, edited by Sacvan Bercovitch, 1:13–168. 7 vols. Cambridge: Cambridge University Press.

Johnson, Francis B. 1937. *Astronomical Thought in Renaissance England*. Baltimore: Johns Hopkins Press.

Jones, Kathleen. 1988. *A Glorious Fame: The Life of Margaret Cavendish, Duchess of Newcastle*. London: Bloomsbury, 1988.

Jonson, Ben. 1925–1952. *Works*. Edited by C. H. Herford, P. & E. Simpson. 11 vols. Oxford: Oxford University Press.

Jourdan, Silvester. 1610. *A Discovery of the Barmudas*. London.

Jowett, John. 1993. "Plantation of This Isle." *Glasgow Review* 1: 39–51.

Kargon, Robert. 1966. "Thomas Hariot, the Northumberland Circle, and Early Atomism in England." *The Journal of the History of Ideas* 27: 126–36.

Kastan, David Scott. 1982. *Shakespeare and the Shapes of Time*. London: Macmillan.

Kay, Dennis. 1999. "Who Says 'Miracles are Past'?: Some Jacobean Marvels and the Margins of the Known." In *Wonders, Marvels, and Monsters in Early Modern Culture*, edited by Peter G. Platt, 164–86. Newark: University of Delaware Press.

Kelsey, Rachel M. 1914. "Indian Dances in *The Tempest*." *Journal of English and Germanic Philology* 13: 98–103.

Kendall, Timothy. 1577. *Flowers of Epigrammes*. London.

Kepler, Johannes. 1965. *Kepler's Conversation with Galileo's Siderial Messenger*. Translated by Edward Rosen. New York: Johnson Reprint Corporation.

Kepler, Johann. 1980. *Paralipomenes a Vitellion (1604)*. Translated by Catherine Chevalley. Paris: J. Vrin.

Kepler, Johannes. 1981. *Mysterium Cosmographicum: The Secret of the Universe*. Translated by A. M. Duncan, commentary by E. J. Alton. New York: Abaris Books.

———. 1992. *New Astronomy*. Translated by William H. Donahue. Cambridge: Cambridge University Press.

———. 1997. *The Harmony of the World*. Translated with an Introduction and Notes by E. J. Alton, A. M. Duncan, and J. V. Field. Philadephia: American Philosophical Society.

Kermode, Frank, ed. 1962. *The Tempest*. Second Arden Shakespeare edition. First published 1954. London: Methuen & Co.

Kessler, Eckhard. 1995. "On Achievement: A Philosophical Approach." In *Wellsprings of Achievement*. Edited by Penelope Gouk, 77–93. Aldershot: Variorum.

Kittridge, George Lyman. 1972. *Witchcraft in Old and New England*. Reprint of 1929 Harvard University Press edition. New York: Athenaeum.

Klein, Melanie. 1986a. "A Contribution to the Psychogenesis of Manic-depressive States." In *The Selected Melanie Klein*. Edited by Juliet Mitchell, 116–45. First published 1935. Harmondsworth: Penguin.

———. 1986b. "Infantile Anxiety Situations Reflected in a Work of Art and in the Creative Impulse." In *The Selected Melanie Klein*, edited by Juliet Mitchell, 84–94. First published 1929. Harmondsworth: Penguin.

———. 1986c. "Notes on some Schizoid Mechanisms." In *The Selected Melanie Klein*, edited by Juliet Mitchell, 176–200. First published 1946. Harmondsworth: Penguin.

Knapp, Jeffrey. 1992. *An Empire Nowhere: England, America and Literature from Utopia to The Tempest*. Berkeley: University of California Press.

Knight, G. Wilson. 1932. *The Shakespearian Tempest*. London: Oxford University Press.

———. 1980. "Caliban as a Red Man." In *Shakespeare's Styles*, edited by Inga-Stina Ewbank, P. Edwards, and G. K. Hunter, 205–20. London: Cambridge University Press.

Koestler, Arthur. 1968. *The Sleepwalkers*. London: Hutchinson.

Koyré, Alexandre. 1973. *The Astronomical Revolution*. Translated by R. E. W. Maddison. Ithaca: Cornell University Press.

Krige, John. 1994. *Science, Revolution and Discontinuity*. Aldershot: Gregg Revivals.

Kristeller, Paul Oskar. 1972. *Renaissance Concepts of Man*. New York: Harper & Row.

Kunz, George Frederick. 1916. *Shakespeare and Precious Stones*. Philadelphia: J. B. Lippincott Co.

Kunz, George Frederick, and Charles Hugh Stevenson. 1993. *The Book of the Pearl*. Reprint of The Century Co. edition, New York 1908. New York: Dover.

Kupperman, Karen Ordahl. 1980. *Settling with the Indians: The Meeting of English and Indian Cultures in America, 1580–1640*. Totowa, N.J.: Rowman & Littlefield.

———. 1984. *Roanoke: The Abandoned Colony*. Totowa, N.J.: Rowman & Allanheld.

Kusukawa, Sachiko. 2000. "Illustrating Nature." In *Books and the Sciences in History*, edited by Marina Frasca-Spada and Nick Jardine, 90–113. Cambridge: Cambridge University Press.

Lâkatos, Imre. 1976. *Proofs and Refutations*. Edited by John Worrall and Elie Zahar. Cambridge: Cambridge University Press.

———. 1978. *Mathematics, Science and Epistomology: Philosophical Papers Volume 2*. Cambridge: Cambridge University Press.

Landes, David S. 1983. *Revolution in Time*. Cambridge: Harvard University Press.

Larner, Christina. 1973. "James the VI and I and Witchcraft." In *The Reign of James the VI and I*, edited by Alan G. R. Smith, 74–90. London: Macmillan.

———. 1984. *Witchcraft and Religion: The Politics of Popular Belief*. Oxford: Basil Blackwell.

Leader, Elliot, and Enrico Predazzi. 1996. *An Introduction to Gage Theories and Modern Particle Physics*. 2 vols. Cambridge: Cambridge University Press.

Lemmi, C. W. 1972. "Mythology and Alchemy in *The Wisdom of the Ancients*." In *Essential Articles for the Study of Francis Bacon*, edited by Brian Vickers, 51–92. London: Sidgewick & Jackson.

Levin, Harry. 1970. *The Myth of the Golden Age in the Renaissance*. London: Faber and Faber.

Levin, Richard. 1988. "Shakespearean Defects and Shakespeareans' Defenses." In *"Bad" Shakespeare: Revaluations of the Shakespeare Canon*, edited by Maurice Charney, 23–36. Rutherford, N.J.: Fairleigh Dickinson University Press.

Lewis, C. S. 1954. *English Literature in the Sixteenth Century*. New York: Oxford University Press.

Lewis, Wyndham. 1927. *The Lion and the Fox*. London: Grant Richards.

Lim, Walter S. H. 1998. *The Arts of Empire: The Poetics of Colonialism from Ralegh to Milton*. Newark: University of Delaware Press.

Lindberg, David C. 1990. "Conceptions of the Scientific Revolution from Bacon to Butterfield." In *Reappraisals of the Scientific Revolution*, edited by David C. Lindberg and Robert S. Westman, 1–26. New York: Cambridge University Press.

Lindenbaum, Peter. 1984. "Prospero's Anger." *Massachusetts Review* 25: 161–71.

Linton, Joan Pong. 1998. *The Romance of the New World: Gender and the Literary Formation of English Colonialism*. Cambridge: Cambridge University Press.

Lohne, Johannes. 1959. "Thomas Harriot (1560–1621): The Tycho Brahe of Optics." *Centaurus* 6: 113–21.

Lyly, John. 1902. *Works*. Edited by R. Warwick Bond. 3 vols. Oxford: Clarendon Press.

MacDonald, Michael, ed. 1991. *Witchcraft and Hysteria in Elizabethan London: Edward Jordan and the Mary Glover Case*. London: Tavistock Routledge.

Macfarlane, Alan. 1970. *Witchcraft in Tudor and Stuart England*. London: Routledge & Kegan Paul.

Machiavelli, Niccolò. 1961. *The Prince*. Harmondsworth, U.K.: Penguin.

Mahoney, Michael S. 1985. "Diagrams and Dynamics: Mathematical Perspectives on Edgerton's Thesis." In *Science and the Arts in the Renaissance*, edited by

John W. Shirley and F. David Hoeniger, 199–220. Washington, D.C.: Folger Library.

Mancosu, Paolo. 1996. *Philosophy of Mathematics and Mathematical Practice in the Seventeenth Century*. Oxford: Oxford University Press.

Marienstras, Richard. 1981. *New Perspectives on the Shakespearean World*. Cambridge: Cambridge University Press.

Martin, Ruth. 1989. *Witchcraft and the Inquisition in Venice, 1550–1650*. Oxford: Basil Blackwell.

Marvell, Andrew. 1971. *Poems and Letters*. Edited by H. M. Margoliouth. Third edition revised by Pierre Legouis. 2 vols. Oxford: Clarendon Press.

Marx, Leo. 1974. *The Machine in the Garden: Technology and the Pastoral Ideal in America*. Reprint of Oxford, 1964. London: Oxford University Press.

McAlindon, Thomas. 1973. *Shakespeare and Decorum*. London: Macmillan.

———. 1991. *Shakespeare's Tragic Cosmos*. Cambridge: Cambridge University Press.

———. 1995. "Testing the New Historicism: 'Invisible Bullets' Reconsidered." *Studies in Philology* 92: 411–38.

———. 2001. "The Discourse of Prayer in *The Tempest*." *SEL: Studies in English Literature, 1500–1900* 41: 335–55.

McCabe, Richard A. 1993. *Incest, Drama and Nature's Law 1500–1700*. Cambridge: Cambridge University Press.

McDonald, Russ. 1991. "Reading *The Tempest*." *Shakespeare Survey* 43: 15–28.

McGuire, J. E. 1977. "Neoplatonism and Active Principles: Newton and the *Corpus Hermeticum*." In *Hermeticism and the Scientific Revolution*, edited by Robert S. Westman and J. E. McGuire, 93–142. Los Angeles: University of California Press.

McKeon, Richard. 1966. "Philosophy and the Development of Scientific Methods." *The Journal of the History of Ideas* 27: 3–22.

McLean, Antonia. 1972. *Humanism and the Rise of Science in Tudor England*. London: Heinemann.

McMullan, Ernan. 1990. "Conceptions of Science in the Scientific Revolution." In *Reappraisals of the Scientific Revolution*, edited by David C. Lindberg and Robert S. Westman, 27–92. New York: Cambridge University Press.

Mebane, John S. 1989. *Renaissance Magic and the Return of the Golden Age*. Lincoln: University of Nebraska Press.

Melchiori, Barbara. 1960. "'Still Harping on my Daughter.'" *English Miscellany (Rome)* 11: 59–74.

Mendelson, Sara H. 1987. *The Mental Life of Stuart Women: Three Studies*. Brighton, U.K.: Harvester Press.

Meyer, Gerald Dennis. 1955. *The Scientific Lady in England, 1650–1760*. Berkeley: University of California Press.

Middleton, Christopher. 1596. *The Historie of Heauen*. London.

Middleton, Thomas. 1981. *Women Beware Women*. Edited by J. R. Mulryne. Manchester: Manchester University Press.

Middleton, W. E. Knowles. 1966. *A History of the Thermometer and its Use in Meteorology*. Baltimore: Johns Hopkins Press.

————. 1971. *The Experimenters: a Study of the Academia del Cimento*. Baltimore: Johns Hopkins Press.

Miller, Lee. 2001. *Roanoke: Solving the Mystery of England's Lost Colony*. London: Pimlico.

Miller, Richard W. 1987. *Fact and Method: Explanation, Confirmation and Reality in the Natural and Social Sciences*. Princeton: Princeton University Press.

Mincoff, Marco. 1992. *Things Supernatural and Causeless: Shakespearean Romance*. Newark: University of Delaware Press.

Mintz, Samuel I. 1952. "Margaret Cavendish's Visit to the Royal Society." *Journal of English and Germanic Philology* 51: 168–76.

Mirollo, James V. 1999. "The Aesthetics of the Marvelous: The Wonderous Work of Art in a Wonderous World." In *Wonders, Marvels, and Monsters in Early Modern Culture*, edited by Peter G. Platt, 24–44. Newark: University of Delaware Press.

Montaigne, Michel Lord of. 1942. *Essays*. Translated by John Florio. 3 vols. London: J. M. Dent & Sons Ltd.

More, Thomas, Sir. 1909. *More's Millennium*. Translated by V. Paget. London: Alston Rivers.

Mowat, Barbara. 1976. *The Dramaturgy of Shakespeare's Romances*. Athens: University of Georgia Press.

————. 1981. "Prospero, Agrippa, and Hocus Pocus." *English Literary Renaissance* 11: 281–303.

Muchembled, Robert. 1985. *Popular Culture and Elite Culture in France, 1400–1750*. Translated by Linda Cochrane from the 1978 edition. Baton Rouge: Louisiana State University Press.

Muir, Kenneth. 1953. "Holland's Pliny and *Othello*." *Notes and Queries* 198: 513–14.

————. 1957. *The Sources of Shakespeare's Plays*. London: Methuen & Co.

————. 1972. *The Sources of Shakespeare's Plays*. London: Methuen & Co.

Nardo, Anna K. 1985. "'Here's to thy health': The Pearl in Hamlet's Wine." *English Language Notes* 23: 36–42.

Neely, Carol Thomas. 1985. *Broken Nuptials in Shakespeare's Plays*. New Haven: Yale University Press.

Nevo, Ruth. 1987. *Shakespeare's Other Language*. New York: Methuen.

Nicholls, Mark. 1992. "'As Happy a Fortune as I Desire': The Pursuit of Financial Security by the Younger Brothers of Henry Percy, 9th Earl of Northumberland." *Historical Review* 65: 296–314.

Nichols, John. 1828. *The Progresses of King James the First*. 4 vols. London: J. B. Nichols.

Nicolson, Marjorie Hope. 1960. *The Breaking of the Circle*. New York: Columbia University Press.

————. 1965. *Pepys' Diary and the New Science*. Charlottesville: University Press of Virginia.

————. 1976. *Science and the Imagination*. First edition 1956, Cornell University Press. Hamden, Conn.: Archon Books.

Norden, J[ohn]. 1614. *The Labyrinth of Mans Life*. London.

North, John. 1974. "Thomas Harriot and the First Telescopic Observations of

Sunspots." In *Thomas Harriot: Renaissance Scientist*, edited by John W. Shirley, 129–65. Oxford: Oxford University Press.

Notestein, Wallace. 1968. *The History of Witchcraft in England from 1558 to 1718.* Reprint of Washington, 1911. New York: Thomas Y. Crowell.

Nummedal, Tara, and Paula Finden. 2000. "Words of Nature: Scientific Books in the Seventeenth Century." In *Thornton and Tully's Scientific Books, Libraries and Collectors*, edited by Andrew Hunter, 164–215. Aldershot, U.K.: Ashgate.

Nuttall, A. D. 1967. *Two Concepts of Allegory: A Study of Shakespeare's The Tempest and the Logic of Allegorical Expression.* London: Routledge & Kegan Paul.

Orgel, Stephen. 1987a. "Shakespeare and the Cannibals." In *Cannibals, Witches and Divorce: Estranging the Renaissance*, edited by Marjorie Garber, 40–66. Baltimore: Johns Hopkins University Press.

———, ed. 1987b. *The Tempest.* Oxford Shakespeare edition. Oxford: Oxford University Press.

Osler, Margaret J. 1982. "Galileo, Motion, and Essences." In *The Scientific Enterprise in Early Modern Europe*, edited by Peter Dear, 107–11. Chicago: University of Chicago Press.

Panofsky, Erwin. 1962. "Artist, Scientist, Genius: Notes on the 'Renaissance Dämmerung.'" In *The Renaissance: Six Essays*, edited by Wallace K. Ferguson, 123–82. From a paper given in 1952. New York: Harper & Row.

Partridge, Eric. 1947. *Shakespeare's Bawdy.* London: Routledge & Kegan Paul.

Paster, Gail Kern. 1984. "Montaigne, Dido, and *The Tempest*: 'How came that widow in?.'" *Shakespeare Quarterly* 35: 91–94.

Peckham, George. 1600. "A Discourse of the Necessity and Commoditie of Planting English Colonies upon the North Partes of America." In *Principal Navigations Voyages Traffiques & Discoveries of the English Nation*, edited by Richard Hakluyt, 42–78. Vol. 6. Everyman's Library edition, n.d. London: J. M. Dent.

de Peiresc, Nicolas-Claude Fabri. 1624. *Relation de ceque jay appris de la vie et inventions de Cornelius Derbble de la Ville d'Alcmar en Hollande, par Abraham Kuffler son gendre et Gilles Kuffler son frère.* Paris au comencement de Sept 1624. Bibliothèque Inguimbertine, Carpentras, ms. 1774, fols. 407–409, and ms. 1776 fols. 407–413.

———. 1992. *Lettres a Claude Saumise et a son Entourage (1620–1637).* edited by Agnès Bresson. Florence: Leo S. Olschki.

Pepper, John V. 1974. "Harriot's Earlier Works on Mathematical Navigation." In *Thomas Harriot: Renaissance Scientist*, edited by John W. Shirley, 54–90. Oxford: Clarendon Press.

Percy, George. 1922. "A Trewe Relacyon: Virginia from 1609 to 1612." *Tyler's Quarterly Historical and Genealogical Magazine* 3: 259–82.

———. 1946. "Observations by Master George Percy, 1607." In *Narratives of Early Virginia*, edited by Lyon Gardiner Tyler, 5–23. New York: Barnes & Noble.

Pérez-Ramos, Antonio. 1988. *Francis Bacon's Idea of Science and the Maker's Knowledge Tradition.* Oxford: Clarendon Press.

Peterson, Douglas L. 1973. *Time Tide and Tempest, A Study of Shakespeare's Romances.* San Marino, Calif.: Huntington Library.

Pittock, Malcolm. "Widow Dido." *Notes and Queries* 33: 368–69.

Platt, Peter G. 1997. *Reason Diminished: Shakespeare and the Marvelous.* Lincoln: University of Nebraska Press.

Pliny. 1601. *The Historie of the World, Commonly Called The Natvrall Historie of C. Plinivs Secundus, Translated into English by Philemon Holland.* London.

Poole, Kristen. 1995. "Saints Alive! Falstaff, Martin Marprelate, and the Staging of Puritanism." *Shakespeare Quarterly* 46: 47–75.

Popper, Karl. 1968. *The Logic of Scientific Discovery.* Author's trans. of *Logik der Forshung*, 1934. London: Hutchinson.

Poppi, Antonio. 1988. "Fate, Fortune, Providence and Human Freedom." In *The Cambridge History of Renaissance Philosophy*, edited by Charles B. Schmitt, 641–67. Cambridge: Cambridge University Press.

Porta, Giovanni Battista della. 1658. *Natural Magick: In Twenty Bookes.* Translation of *Magica Naturalis* from the second edition, Naples, 1598 (first edition 1538). London.

Prosser, Eleanor. 1965. "Shakespeare, Montaigne, and the Rarer Action." *Shakespeare Studies* 1: 261–64.

Proudfoot, Richard. 2002. "New Conservatism and the Theatrical Text: Editing Shakespeare for the Third Millenium." In *Shakespearean International Yearbook 2: Where Are We Now in Shakespeare Studies?*, edited by John M. Mucciolo and W. R. Elton, 127–42. Burlington, Vt.: Ashgate.

Purchas, Samuel. 1625. *Purchas his Pilgrimes.* London, 1625.

Quinn, David Beers, ed. 1955. *The Roanoke Voyages 1584–1590.* 2 vols. London: Hakluyt Society.

———, ed. 1967. *George Percy, Observations Gathered out of "A Discourse of the Plantation of the Southern Colony in Virginia by the English, 1606".* Charlottesville: University Press of Virginia.

———. 1971. *North American Discovery Circa 1000–1612.* New York: Harper & Row.

———. 1974. "Thomas Harriot and the New World." In *Thomas Harriot, Renaissance Scientist*, edited by John W. Shirley, 36–53. Oxford: Clarendon Press.

———. 1977. *North America from Earliest Discovery to First Settlements.* New York: Harper & Row.

———. 1992. *Thomas Harriot and the Problem of America.* Oxford: Oriel College.

Quinn, David Beers, and Paul Hulton. 1964. *The American Drawings of John White 1577–1590.* 2 vols. London: Trustees of the British Museum and University of North Carolina Press.

Quinones, Ricardo J. 1965. "Time in Shakespeare." *The Journal of the History of Ideas* 26: 327–52.

———. 1972. *The Renaissance Discovery of Time.* Cambridge: Harvard University Press.

Quint, David. 1990. "A Reconsideration of Montaigne's 'Des Cannibales.'" *Modern Language Quarterly* 51: 459–89.

Rank, Otto. 1926. *Das Inzest-Motiv in Dichtung und Sage.* First published 1912. Leipzig and Vienna: Franz Deuticke.

———. 1992. *The Incest Theme in Literature and Legend.* First published 1912, translated by George C. Richter. Baltimore: Johns Hopkins University Press.

Rattansi, P. M. 1985. "Art and Science: The Paracelsian Vision." In *Science and the Arts in the Renaissance*, edited by John W. Shirley and F. David Hoeniger, 50–57. Washington, D.C.: Folger Library.

Reed, Robert Rentoul, Jr. 1965. *The Occult on the Tudor and Stuart Stage*. Boston: Christopher Publishing House.

Reeds, Karen Meier. 1976. "Renaissance Humanism and Botany." *Annals of Science* 33: 519–42.

Rees, Graham. 1977a. "The Fate of Bacon's Cosmology in the Seventeenth Century." *Ambix* 24: 27–38.

———. 1977b. "Matter Theory: A Unifying Factor in Bacon's Natural Philosophy?" *Ambix* 24: 110–25.

———. 1996. "Bacon's Speculative Philosophy." In *The Cambridge Companion to Bacon*, edited by Markku Peltonen, 121–45. Cambridge: Cambridge University Press.

Reynolds, Myra. 1920. *The Learned Lady in England 1650–1760*. Boston: Houghton Mifflin Co.

Righter, Anne, ed. 1968. *Shakespeare, The Tempest*. New Penguin Shakespeare edition. Harmondsworth: Penguin.

Ritterbush, Phillip C. 1985. "The Organism as Symbol: an Innovation in Art." In *Science and the Arts in the Renaissance*. Edited by John W. Shirley and F. David Hoeniger, 149–67. Washington, D.C.: Folger Library.

Roberts, Jeanne Addison. 1991. *The Shakespearean Wild: Geography, Genus and Gender*. Lincoln: University of Nebraska Press.

Ronan, Colin. 1993. "There was an Elizabethan Telescope." *Bulletin of the Scientific Instrument Society* 37: 2–3.

Rondelet, Guilaume. 1558. *L'Histoire Entiere des Poissons*. In 2 parts, translated by L. Joubert, first ed. Lyon 1554. Lion.

Rondeletius, Gulielmus. 1554. *Libri de Piscibus Marinis*. In two parts: second part dated 1555 and titled *Universae aquatilium Historiae pars altera, cum veris ipsorum Imaginibus*. Lugdini.

Rosen, Edward. 1974. "Harriot's Science: the Intellectual Background." In *Thomas Harriot: Renaissance Scientist*, edited by John W. Shirley, 1–15. Oxford: Oxford University Press.

Rossi, Paolo. 1968. *Francis Bacon: From Magic to Science*. Translated by Sacha Rabinovich from the 1957 edition. London: Routledge & Kegan Paul.

———. 1996. "Bacon's Idea of Science." In *The Cambridge Companion to Bacon*, edited by Markku Peltonen, 1–24. Cambridge: Cambridge University Press.

Rufus, W. Carl. 1931. "Kepler as an Astronomer." In *Johann Kepler*, edited by History of Science Society, 1–38. Baltimore: Williams & Wilkins.

Ryan, Kiernan. 1989. *Shakespeare*. Hemel Hempstead, U.K.: Harvester Wheatsheaf.

Rye, William Benchley. 1865. *England as Seen by Foreigners in the Days of Elizabeth and King James the First*. London: John Russell Smith.

Sacks, Elizabeth. 1980. *Shakespeare's Images of Pregnancy*. London: Macmillan Press.

Salingar, Leo. 1996. "The New World in The Tempest." In *Travel and Drama in Shakespeare's Time*, edited by Jean-Pierre Maquerlot and Michèle Willems, 209–22. Cambridge: Cambridge University Press.

Salmon, Vivian. 1993. *Thomas Harriot and the English Origins of Algonkian Linguistics*. Durham, U.K.: Durham Thomas Harriot Seminar.

Sanders, Charles Richard. 1949. "William Strachey, the Virginia Colony, and Shakespeare." *The Virginia Magazine of History and Biography* 57: 115–32.

Sarasohn, Lisa T. 1984. "Science Turned Upside Down: Feminism and the Natural Philosophy of Margaret Cavendish." *Huntington Library Quarterly* 47: 289–307.

Saxl, Fritz. 1936. "Veritas Filia Temporis." In *Philosophy and History: Essays Presented to Ernst Cassirer*, edited by Raymond Klibansky and H. J. Patton, 197–222. Oxford: Clarendon Press.

Scot, Reginald. 1973. *The Discovery of Witchcraft*. First published 1584. Edited by Brinsley Nicholson. Reprint of 1886, London: E. Stock. Wakefield, Yorkshire: E. P. Publishing.

Seaman, John E. 1968. "Othello's Pearl." *Shakespeare Quarterly* 19: 81–85.

Seaver, Paul S. 1995. "Work, Discipline and the Apprentice in Early Modern London." In *Wellsprings of Achievement*, edited by Penelope Gouk, 159–79. Aldershot: Variorum.

Shakespeare, William. 1968. *The First Folio*. Facsimile of 1623 prepared by Charlton Hinman. New York: W. W. Norton.

Shapin, Steven. 1996. *The Scientific Revolution*. Chicago: University of Chicago Press.

Sherman, Sandra. 1994. "Trembling Texts: Margaret Cavendish and the Dialectic of Authorship." *English Literary Renaissance* 24: 184–210.

Shirley, John W. 1949a. "George Percy at Jamestown, 1607–1612." *The Virginia Magazine of History and Biography* 57: 227–43.

———. 1949–1951b. "The Scientific Experiments of Sir Walter Raleigh, The Wizard Earl, and the Three Magi in the Tower 1603–1617." *Ambix* 4: 52–66.

———. 1974. "Sir Walter Ralegh and Thomas Harriot." In *Thomas Harriot: Renaissance Scientist*. Edited by John W. Shirley, 16–35. Oxford: Clarendon Press.

———. 1983. *Thomas Harriot: A Biography*. Oxford: Clarendon Press.

———. 1985. "Science and Navigation in Renaissance England." In *Science and the Arts in the Renaissance*, edited by John W. Shirley and F. David Hoeniger, 74–93. Washington, D.C.: Folger Library.

Shirley, John W., and David Beers Quinn. 1969. "A Contemporary List of Hariot References." *Renaissance Quarterly* 22: 9–25.

Shumaker, Wayne. 1972. *The Occult Sciences in the Renaissance: A Study in Intellectual Patterns*. Berkeley: University of California Press.

Sidney, Philip. 1961. *Apology for Poetrie*. Edited by J. C. Collins. Oxford: Clarendon.

Simmons, J. L. 1976. "Holland's Pliny and *Troilus and Cressida*." *Shakespeare Quarterly* 27: 329–32.

Sinfield, Alan. 1992. *Faultlines: Cultural Materialism and the Politics of Dissident Reading*. Oxford: Clarendon Press.

Skura, Meredith Anne. 1989. "Discourse and the Individual: The Case of Colonialism in *The Tempest*." *Shakespeare Quarterly* 40: 42–69.

Slights, Camille Wells. 1997. "Slaves and Subjects in *Othello*." *Shakespeare Quarterly* 48: 377–90.

Smith, George Frederick Herbert. 1972. *Gemstones*. 14th edition. Revised F. C. Phillips. London: Chapman and Hall.

Smith, Hilda L. 1982. *Reason's Disciples: Seventeenth Century English Feminists*. Urbana: University of Illinois Press.

Smith, John. 1986. *Works*. Edited by Philip L. Barbour. 3 vols. Chapel Hill: University of North Carolina Press.

Smith, Logan Pearsall, ed. 1907. *The Life and Letters of Sir Henry Wotton*. 2 vols. Oxford: Oxford University Press.

Snelling, David. 1994. "Prospero on the Coast of Bohemia." *Prospero: Rivista di culture anglo-germaniche* 1: 4–16.

Sokol, B. J. 1974a. "Thomas Harriot—Sir Walter Ralegh's Tutor—on Population." *Annals of Science* 31: 205–12.

———. 1974b. "Thomas Harriot's Notes on Sir Walter Ralegh's Address from the Scaffold." *Manuscripts* 26: 198–206.

———. 1980. "Numerology in Fulke Greville's *Caelica*." *Notes and Queries* 27: 327–29.

———. 1985. "A Spenserian Idea in *The Taming of the Shrew*." *English Studies* 66: 310–16.

———. 1989. "Painted Statues, Ben Jonson and Shakespeare." *Journal of the Warburg and Courtauld Institutes* 52: 250–53.

———. 1991a. "Figures of Repetition in Sidney's *Astrophil and Stella* and in the Scenic Form of *Measure for Measure*." *Rhetorica* 9: 131–46.

———. 1991b. "Holofernes in Rabelais and Shakespeare and Some Manuscript Verses of Thomas Harriot." *Etudes Rabelaisiennes* 25: 131–35.

———. 1993. "*The Tempest*, 'All torment trouble, wonder and amazement': a Kleinian reading." In *The Undiscover'd Country*, edited by B. J. Sokol, 179–216. London: Free Association Books.

———. 1994a. *Art and Illusion in The Winter's Tale*. Manchester: Manchester University Press.

———. 1994b. "The Problem of Assessing Thomas Harriot's A briefe and true report of his Discoveries in North America." *Annals of Science* 51: 1–15.

———. 1995. "Macbeth and The Social History of Witchcraft." *Shakespeare Yearbook* 6: 245–74.

———. 1996. "Poet in the Atomic Age: Robert Frost's 'That Millikan Mote' Expanded." *Annals of Science* 53: 399–412.

———. 1998. "Prejudice and Law in *The Merchant of Venice*." In *Shakespeare Survey 51*, edited by Stanley Wells, 159–73. Cambridge: Cambridge University Press.

———. 2002. "Margaret Cavendish's Poems and Fancies and Thomas Harriot's Treatise on Infinity." In *Margaret Cavendish, A Princely Brave Woman*, edited by Stephen Clucas, 151–63. Burlington: Ashgate.

———. forthcoming 2004. "Shakespearian Sources in 'Obscure' Continental European Publications: reflections on the need for 'international' book provenance studies." In *Not of an Age, but for all Time: Shakespeare Across Lands and Ages*, edited by S. Coelsch-Foisner and G. E. Szönyi. Salsburg: University of Salsburg.

Sokol, B. J., and Mary Sokol. 1996. "*The Tempest* and Legal Justification of Plantation in Virginia." *Shakespeare Yearbook* 7: 353–80.

———. 2000. *Shakespeare's Legal Language*. London: Athlone.

———. forthcoming 2003. *Shakespeare, Law and Marriage*. Cambridge: Cambridge University Press.

Spires, Margaret. 1999. "The True Face of Philosophy as Magical Object: The Limits of Wisdom and the Constitution of the (Super)Natural in Montaigne's *Essays* 1.26 and 1.27." In *Wonders, Marvels, and Monsters in Early Modern Culture*, edited by Peter G. Platt, 205–28. Newark: University of Delaware Press.

Stevens, Wallace. 1965. *Collected Poems*. New York: Alfred A. Knopf.

Strachey, William. 1625. "A True Reportory of the Wracke and Redemption of Sir Thomas Gates, Knight." In *Purchas his Pilgrimes*, 1734–58. Part 4, book 9 chap. 6. London.

———. 1844. "Lawes Divine, Morall and Martiall, &c. For the Colony Virginea Britannia." In *Tracts and Other Papers*, edited by Peter Force, 1–68. Vol. 3 no. 2. Reprint of London, 1612. Washington, D.C.: Wm. Q. Force.

———. 1953. *The History of Travell into Virginia Britania*. Edited by Louis B. Wright and Virginia Freund, transcript of the Princeton ms. presented to the Earl of Northumberland, written 1609–12. London: Hakluyt Society.

Straube, Beverly A., and William M. Kelso. 1977. *Jamestown Rediscovery Interim Report 1996*. Jamestown, Va.: APVA.

Straube, Beverly A., William M. Kelso, and Nicholas M. Luccketti. 1994. *Jamestown Rediscovery Field Report 1994*. Jamestown, Va.: APVA.

Straube, Beverly A., and Nicholas M. Luccketti. 1996. *Jamestown Rediscovery Interim Report 1995*. Jamestown, Va.: APVA.

———. 1998. *Jamestown Rediscovery Interim Report 1997*. Jamestown, Va.: APVA.

———. 1999. *Jamestown Rediscovery Interim Report 1998*. Jamestown, Va.: APVA.

Straube, Beverly A., and Seth Mallios. 2000. *Jamestown Rediscovery Interim Report 1999*. Jamestown, Va.: APVA.

Stritmatter, Roger. 2000. "By Providence Divine: Shakespeare's Awareness of Some Geneva Marginal Notes of *I Samuel*." *Notes and Queries* 245: 97–100.

Suckling, Sir John. 1971. *Works*. Edited by Thomas Clayton. 2 vols. Oxford: Clarendon Press.

Summers, Joseph H. 1973. "The Anger of Prospero." *Michigan Quarterly Review* 12: 116–35.

———. 1984. *Dreams of Love and Power: On Shakespeare's Plays*. Oxford: Clarendon Press.

Sundelson, David. 1980. "So Rare a Wonder'd Father: Prospero's *Tempest*." In *Representing Shakespeare: New Psychoanalytic Essays*, edited by Coppélia Kahn and Murray M. Schwartz, 33–53. Baltimore: Johns Hopkins University Press.

Sylvester, Joshua. 1621. *Du Bartas His Divine Weekes and Workes*. London.

Tanner, R. C. H. 1961. "On the Role of Equality and Inequality in the History of Mathematics." *British Journal for the History of Science* 1: 159–69.

Tasso, Torquato. 1600. *Godfrey of Bulloigne, or the Recovery of Jerusalem. Done into English heroicall verse by E[dward]. Fairfax*. London.

Tayler, E. W. 1979. *Milton's Poetry: Its Development in Time*. Pittsburgh: Duquesne University Press.

———. 1990. "King Lear and Negation." *English Literary Renaissance* 20: 17–39.

Taylor, E. G. R. 1967. *The Mathematical Practitioners of Tudor and Stuart England*. London: Cambridge University Press.

Taylor, F. Sherwood. 1942. "The Origins of the Thermometer." *Annals of Science* 5: 129–56.

Taylor, Mark. 1982. *Shakespeare's Darker Purpose: A Question of Incest*. New York: AMS Press.

Tedeschi, J. 1987. "The Question of Magic and Witchcraft in Two Unpublished Inquisitorial Manuals of the Seventeenth Century." *Proceedings of the American Philosophical Society* 131: 92–111.

Teixeira, Pedro. 1610. *Viage de Pedro Teixeira*. Ambres.

———. 1902. *The Travels of Pedro Texeira, with his Kings of Harmuz, and Extracts from his Kings of Persia*. Translated by William F. Sinclair, with further notes and an Introduction by Donald Ferguson. London: Hakluyt Society.

Thomas, Keith. 1971. *Religion and the Decline of Magic*. London: Weidenfeld & Nicholson.

———. 1983. *Man and the Natural World: Changing Attitudes in England 1500–1800*. London: Allen Lane.

Thorndike, Lynn. 1941–1958. *A History of Magic and Experimental Science*. 8 vols. New York: Columbia University Press.

Tierie, G. 1932. *Cornelis Drebbel*. Amsterdam: H. J. Paris.

Tiffany, Grace. 1998. "Puritanism in Comic History: Exposing Royalty in the Henry Plays." *Shakespeare Studies* 26: 256–87.

Tilley, Morris Palmer. 1950. *A Dictionary of the Proverbs in England in the Sixteenth and Seventeenth Centuries*. Ann Arbor: University of Michigan Press.

Torrens, James. 1971. "T. S. Eliot and Shakespeare: 'This Music Crept By.'" *Bucknell Review: A Scholarly Journal of Letters, Arts and Sciences* 19, no. 1: 77–96.

Traister, Barbara Howard. 1984. *Heavenly Necromancers: The Magician in English Renaissance Drama*. Columbia: University of Missouri Press.

Traversi, D. T. 1969. *An Approach to Shakespeare*. New York: Doubleday Anchor.

A True and Sincere Declaration of the Purpose and Ends of the Plantation begun in Virginia. 1610. London.

"A True Declaration of the Estate of the Colony of Virginia." 1844. In *Tracts and Other Papers*, edited by Peter Force, 1–27. Vol. 3 no. 1. Reprint of London, 1610. Washington, D.C.: Wm. Q. Force.

Turner, Frederick. 1971. *Shakespeare and the Nature of Time*. Oxford: Clarendon Press.

Turner, Gerard L'E. 1993. "There was no Elizabethan Telescope." *Bulletin of the Scientific Instrument Society* 37: 3–5.

Tymme, Thomas. 1612. *A Dialogve Philosophicall*. London.

Van Helden, Albert. 1982. "The Telescope in the Seventeenth Century." In *The Scientific Enterprise in Early Modern Europe*, edited by Peter Dear, 133–53. Chicago: University of Chicago Press.

Vaughan, Alden T. 1988. "Shakespeare's Indian: The Americanization of Caliban." *Shakespeare Quarterly* 39: 137–53.

———. 2002. "Sir Walter Raleigh's Indian Interpreters." *William and Mary Quarterly* 59: 341–76.

Vaughan, Alden T., and Virginia Mason Vaughan. 1991. *Shakespeare's Caliban: A Cultural History*. Cambridge: Cambridge University Press.

———, eds. 1999. *William Shakespeare, The Tempest (Third Arden Edition)*. London: Thomson Learning.

Vickers, Brian. 1991. "Bacon among the literati: science and language." *Comparative Criticism* 13: 249–71.

———. 1992. "Francis Bacon and the Progress of Knowledge." *The Journal of the History of Ideas* 53: 495–518.

———. 1993. *Appropriating Shakespeare*. New Haven: Yale University Press.

Wagner, Emma Brockway. 1933. *Shakespeare's The Tempest: An Allegorical Interpretation*. Yellow Springs, Ohio: Antioch Press.

Walker, D. P. 1958. *Spiritual and Demonic Magic from Ficino to Campanella*. London: The Warburg Institute.

Waller, G. F. 1976. *The Strong Necessity of Time: The Philosophy of Time in Shakespeare and Elizabethan Literature*. The Hague: Mouton.

Waller, Marguerite. 1989. "The Empire's New Clothes: Refashioning the Renaissance." In *Seeking the Woman in Late Medieval and Renaissance Writings: Essays in Feminist Contextual Criticism*, edited by Sheila Fisher and Janet E. Halley, 160–83. Knoxville: University of Tennessee Press.

Wallis, P. J. 1960–1963. "William Crashawe, The Sheffield Puritan." *Transactions of the Hunter Archaeological Society* 8: pts. 2–5.

Webster, Charles. 1982. *From Paracelsus to Newton: Magic and the Making of Modern Science*. Cambridge: Cambridge University Press.

Webster, John. 1995. *The Works*. Edited by David Gunby, David Carnegie, and Antony Hammond. Cambridge: Cambridge University Press.

Weimann, Robert. 1974. "Shakespeare and the Study of Metaphor." *New Literary History* 6: 149–67.

Weinberg, Bernard. 1961. *A History of Literary Criticism in the Italian Renaissance*. 2 vols. Chicago: University of Chicago Press.

Wells, Robin Headlam. 1994. "Locating Texts in History." In *Shakespeare and Cultural Traditions*. Edited by Tetsuo Kishi, Roger Pringle, and Stanley Wells, 323–32. Newark: University of Delaware Press.

Wells, Stanley, and Gary Taylor, eds. 1989. *William Shakespeare: The Complete Works*. Electronic edition. Oxford: Oxford University Press.

West, Gilian. 1991. "*Hamlet*: The Pearl in the Cup." *Notes and Queries* 236: 479.

West, Robert Hunter. 1939. *The Invisible World: A Study of Pneumatology in Elizabethan Drama*. Athens: University of Georgia Press.

———. 1984. *Reginald Scot and Renaissance Writings on Witchcraft*. Boston: Twayne.

Westfall, Richard S. 1982. "Science and Patronage: Galelio and the Telescope." In *The Scientific Enterprise in Early Modern Europe*, edited by Peter Dear, 113–32. Chicago: University of Chicago Press.

Westlund, Joseph. 1989. "Idealization as a Habit of Mind in Shakespeare: *The Tempest.*" *Melanie Klein and Object Relations* 7: 71–82.

———. 1995. "Idealization and the Problematic in *The Tempest.*" In *Subjects on the World's Stage: Essays on British Literature of the Middle Ages and the Renaissance*, edited by David G. Allen and Robert A. White, 239–47. Newark: University of Delaware Press.

Westman, Robert S. 1977. "Magical Reform and Astronomical Reform: The Yates Thesis Reconsidered." In *Hermeticism and the Scientific Revolution*, edited by Robert S. Westman and J. E. McGuire, 1–91. Los Angeles: University of California Press.

———. 1982. "The Melanchthon Circle, Rheticus, and the Wittenberg Interpretation of the Copernican Theory." In *The Scientific Enterprise in Early Modern Europe*, edited by Peter Dear, 7–36. Chicago: University of Chicago Press.

Weyer, Johann. 1991. *De praestigiis daemonum.* 1583 edition. Trans. John Shea. Bingingham, N.Y.: Medieval and Renaissance Texts and Studies.

Whitrow, G. J. 1980. *The Natural Philosophy of Time.* Second edition. Oxford: Clarendon Press.

———. 1988. *Time in History: The Evolution of our General Awareness of Time and Temporal Perspective.* Oxford: Oxford University Press.

———. 1990. *The Role of Time in Life and Thought in the Age of Harriot and Today.* Durham, U.K.: Thomas Harriot Seminar.

Wilcox, Donald J. 1987. *The Measure of Times Past: Pre-Newtonian Chronologies and the Rhetoric of Relative Time.* Chicago: The University of Chicago Press.

Williams, Gordon. 1994. *A Dictionary of Sexual Language and Imagery in Shakespeare and Stuart Literature.* 3 vols. London: Athlone Press.

Williamson, Marilyn L. 1986. *The Patriarchy of Shakespeare's Comedies.* Detroit: Wayne State University Press.

Willis, Deborah. 1989. "Shakespeare's *Tempest* and the Discourse of Colonialism." *SEL: Studies in English Literature, 1500–1900* 29: 277–89.

Wind, Edgar. 1961. "Platonic Tyranny and the Renaissance Fortuna: on Ficino's Reading of Laws IV 709A–712A." In *Essays in Honor of Erwin S. Panofsky*, edited by Millard Meiss, 1:491–96. 2 vols. New York: New York University Press.

———. 1968. *Pagan Mysteries of the Renaissance.* London: Faber and Faber.

Wittkower, Rudolf. 1937–38. "Chance, Time and Virtue." *Journal of the Warburg and Courtauld Institutes* 1: 313–21.

Woodman, David. 1973. *White Magic and English Renaissance Drama.* Rutherford, N.J.: Fairleigh Dickinson University Press.

Wright, Louis B. 1940. *The First Gentlemen of Virginia: Intellectual Qualities of the Early Colonial Ruling Class.* San Marino, Calif.: The Huntington Library.

Yates, Frances. 1936. *A Study of Love's Labour's Lost.* Cambridge: Cambridge University Press.

———. 1964. *Giodorno Bruno and the Hermetic Tradition.* London: Routledge & Kegan Paul.

———. 1975. *Shakespeare's Last Plays: A New Approach.* London: Routledge & Kegan Paul.

————. 1984a. "Bacon's Magic." In *Ideas and Ideals in the North European Renaissance*, 60–66. London: Routledge & Kegan Paul.

————. 1984b. "A Great Magus." In *Ideas and Ideals in the North European Renaissance*, 49–59. London: Routledge & Kegan Paul.

————. 1984c. "Imperial Mysteries." In *Ideas and Ideals in the North European Renaissance*, 214–20. London: Routledge & Kegan Paul.

Index

Works by Shakespeare (WS) appear directly under title; works by others under authors' names.